Glendon Moriarty, PsyD

Pastoral Care of Depression
Helping Clients Heal Their Relationship with God

Pre-publication
REVIEWS,
COMMENTARIES,
EVALUATIONS . . .

"**D**r. Moriarty has penned a highly usable book for both beginning and advanced therapists who understand the connection between psychopathology and the unconsciously held vision of God that lives inside all of us. It blends a highly scholarly breadth of knowledge of the literature, excellent documentation, and a readable writing style, making it accessible to practitioners of any experience level, ranging from the psychoanalytically oriented through Rogerians and Gestaltists to cognitive psychologists.

This book is eminently practical, filled with illustrations and details of intervention techniques. Moriarty focuses on assessment of God image, how it can reinforce pathology, and what the necessary moves are to make it more available to faith and health. This book has an excellent section on self-administered assessment instruments for God image—the most comprehensive currently in the literature. It draws on resources across a wide range of psychological theories, is easily applicable to a range of pathologies, and would be usable for therapists with theologies anywhere in the Christian spectrum. Beginning therapists will find it especially useful because it offers an easily learnable protocol for integrating this crucial spiritual concern into clinical practice."

Brian W. Grant, PhD
*Lois and Dale Bright Professor
of Christian Ministries,
Christian Theological Seminary, Indianapolis*

More pre-publication
REVIEWS, COMMENTARIES, EVALUATIONS . . .

"This insightful book promises to be an outstanding resource for anyone who wants to understand how psychological factors influence a person's image of God. Dr. Moriarty skillfully combines ideas from psychodynamic and cognitive-behavioral traditions to help readers understand how depressive thinking develops. He then integrates the depression material with research and theory on God images, showing with remarkable clarity how childhood hurts and depressive thought patterns can do great damage to people's perceptions of God. In addition to a sound theoretical base, the book provides practical assessment tools and detailed suggestions about how unhealthy God images can be corrected. I found this book to be tremendously helpful in both conceptual and practical terms, and I highly recommend it to scholars and clinicians alike."

Julie Exline, PhD
Assistant Professor of Psychology,
Case Western Reserve University

"Moriarty's *Pastoral Care of Depression* brings important new insights to the complexity of how people experience God and its relevancy for the counseling setting. This is an impressive and comprehensive book which does not oversimplify difficult concepts yet remains accessible. It's essential reading for all therapists and counselors working with religious individuals."

Louis Hoffman, PhD
Dean of Faculty,
Colorado School of Professional Psychology

The Haworth Pastoral Press®
An Imprint of The Haworth Press, Inc.
New York • London • Oxford

Pastoral Care
of Depression
Helping Clients Heal
Their Relationship with God

THE HAWORTH PASTORAL PRESS®
Haworth Series in Chaplaincy
Andrew J. Weaver, Mth, PhD
Editor

Living Faithfully with Disappointment in the Church by J. LeBron McBride

Young Clergy: A Biographical-Developmental Study by Donald Capps

Ministering for Grief, Loss, and Death by Halbert Weidner

Prison Ministry: Hope Behind the Wall by Dennis W. Pierce

A Pastor's Guide to Interpersonal Communication: The Other Six Days by Blake J. Neff

Pastoral Care of Depression: Helping Clients Heal Their Relationship with God by Glendon Moriarty

Pastoral Care with Younger Adults in Long-Term Care by Reverend Jacqueline Sullivan

The Spirituality of Community Life: When We Come 'Round Right by Ronald P. McDonald

Pastoral Care From the Pulpit: Meditations of Hope and Encouragement by J. LeBron McBride

Pastoral Care of Depression
Helping Clients Heal Their Relationship with God

Glendon Moriarty, PsyD

The Haworth Pastoral Press®
An Imprint of The Haworth Press, Inc.
New York • London • Oxford

For more information on this book or to order, visit
http://www.haworthpress.com/store/product.asp?sku=5138

or call 1-800-HAWORTH (800-429-6784) in the United States and Canada
or (607) 722-5857 outside the United States and Canada

or contact orders@HaworthPress.com

Published by

The Haworth Pastoral Press®, an imprint of The Haworth Press, Inc., 10 Alice Street, Binghamton, NY 13904-1580.

PUBLISHER'S NOTE
The development, preparation, and publication of this work has been undertaken with great care. However, the Publisher, employees, editors, and agents of The Haworth Press are not responsible for any errors contained herein or for consequences that may ensue from use of materials or information contained in this work. The Haworth Press is committed to the dissemination of ideas and information according to the highest standards of intellectual freedom and the free exchange of ideas. Statements made and opinions expressed in this publication do not necessarily reflect the views of the Publisher, Directors, management, or staff of The Haworth Press, Inc., or an endorsement by them.

Cover design by Kerry E. Mack.

Library of Congress Cataloging-in-Publication Data

Moriarty, Glendon.
    Pastoral care of depression : helping clients heal their relationship with God / Glendon Moriarty.
        p. cm.
    Includes bibliographical references and index.
    ISBN-13: 978-0-7890-2382-7 (hc. : alk. paper)
    ISBN-10: 0-7890-2382-2 (hc. : alk. paper)
    ISBN-13: 978-0-7890-2383-4 (pbk. : alk. paper)
    ISBN-10: 0-7890-2383-0 (pbk. : alk. paper)
    1. Depressed persons—Pastoral counseling of. 2. Depression, Mental—Religious aspects—Christianity. I. Title.

BV4461.M67 2006
259'.425—dc22
                                                                    2005018356

To Nicole

Who has shown me God's love

ABOUT THE AUTHOR

Glendon Moriarty, PsyD, MA, is a licensed psychologist and Assistant Professor in the School of Psychology and Counseling at Regent University in Virginia Beach, Virginia, where he supervises doctoral-level trainees and teaches psychodynamic psychotherapy and the psychology of religion. He is also the founder of the God Image Institute (http://www.godimage.com), the first agency in the country dedicated to helping people change their emotional experience of God. Since 1998, he has lectured, trained, and counseled numerous people about the relationship between depression and the subjective experience of God. He is a member of the American Psychological Association, the American Psychoanalytic Association, and the Christian Association for Psychological Studies.

CONTENTS

Foreword

For the first time, Moriarty has brought together recent understandings of the way a person's image of God develops and interacts with current theories about the causes and treatment of depression. Of course, theorizing about depression and about God concepts are not new. Each topic has a notable history among psychiatric and psycho/theological thinking. But, heretofore, the two have simply coexisted. They have not been related and treated as a serious subcategory of emotional disturbance. Moriarty recognizes that not only has the psychological community recently included religion among its facets of diversity to which all clinicians must attend but that a significant number of religious persons experience depressive symptoms. This publication provides the professional community with a source of theory and treatment options that combines both considerations.

Seeking help from the divine in times of stress has long been a basic theme in religious life. As the well-known couplet about the Jewish/Christian tradition suggests, "the function of religion is to comfort the afflicted as well as afflict the comfortable." Devoted believers have, since ancient times, looked to their God for solace, comfort, support, renewal, and healing. The Psalms of lament are one example of how sufferers have turned to God when their spirits were down. Psalm 31:1-5 is illustrative of this expectation:

> In you, O Lord, have I taken refuge;
> let me never be put to shame;
> deliver me in your righteousness.
>
> Incline your ear to me;
> make haste to deliver me.
>
> Be my strong rock, a castle to keep me safe,
> for you are my crag and my stronghold;
> for the sake of your name, lead me and guide me;

The Psalms quoted in the Foreword come from *The Book of Common Prayer* (American, 1979).

> Take me out of the net that they have secretly set for me,
> for you are my tower of strength.
>
> Into your hands I commend my spirit,
> for you have redeemed me,
> O Lord, O God of truth.

A modern counselor would class the sense of desperation expressed here as *exogenous depression* and the confidence confessed as that of a person whose God image was definitely positive.

A somewhat different picture might be gleaned from Psalm 22:1-11:

> My God, my God, why have you forsaken me?
> and are so far from my cry
> and from the words of my distress?
>
> O my God, I cry in the daytime, but you do not answer;
> by night as well, but I find no rest.
>
> Yet you are the Holy One,
> enthroned upon the praises of Israel.
>
> Our forefathers put their trust in you;
> they trusted in you and were not put to shame.
>
> But as for me, I am a worm and no man,
> scorned by all and despised by the people.
>
> All who see me laugh me to scorn;
> they curl their lips and wag their heads, saying,
>
> "He trusted in the Lord; let him deliver him;
> let him rescue him, if he delights in him."
>
> Yet you are he who took me out of the womb,
> and kept me safe upon my mother's breast.
>
> I have been entrusted to you ever since I was born;
> you were my God when I was still in my mother's womb.
>
> Be not far from me, for trouble is near,
> and there is none to help.

Here we have quite a different God concept, although the depressive symptoms are quite similar. This Psalm confesses doubt that God can help, whereas the previous Psalm stated confidently that God would act to restore courage and strength. Interestingly, both Psalms end with declarations of faith: Psalm 31 declares, "My times are in your hand" (verse 15) and Psalm 22 states, "Be not far away, O Lord; you are my strength; hasten to help me" (verse 18). Both Psalms include vivid descriptions of depressive symptoms and both end on a positive note, as do most Psalms. The insights into the variations in understandings of God are very perceptive, and they illustrate the wisdom behind Moriarty's efforts to probe the way such dynamics enhance or interfere with a person's ability to access divine help.

In undergoing the most stressful moments of his life, Jesus may have been accessing verses from these Psalms. Some scholars have suggested that Jesus' agonizing cry, recorded in Matthew 27:46, "My God, my God, why have you forsaken me," was his confession of despair using the words from the beginning of Psalm 22, and that his final confession, recorded in Luke 23:46, "Father, into your hands I commend my spirit," was a statement of faith quoting from Psalm 31.

When combing psychological and religious ideation, such as subjecting God concepts to developmental and functional analysis, it is always necessary to reflect upon the validity and limits of such an endeavor. Consideration of validity and limits becomes particularly important when the investigators are themselves religious persons. From the time of William James in the early 1900s to the present, psychologists of religion have been cautioned to "bracket" the "validity question." This means that statements of certainty about the actual behavior of God are outside the boundaries of what psychologists can assert with the self-limitations of their discipline. James had it right in defining his object of study as the behavior of those who *say* they believe in God. If it be true that psychology is the study of human behavior, those statements of belief in God are just one facet of human behavior, along with feelings, thoughts, and actions. Psychologists may themselves believe a God exists and have faith that God acts in their lives, but as psychologists they can make no statements about the existence or behavior of the divine. Doing so is bracketing the validity question.

In a book such as this, which unites the study of depressive symptoms and the understandings of the nature of God, psychologists such as Moriarty are shown to be on sound ground when they study the way persons think about God and relate those beliefs to treatment programs designed to relieve their symptoms. Infusing the discussion with convictions about how and whether God acts in any manner apart from through human thoughts, words, feelings, and actions confuses the discussion in a way that evokes resistance for readers rather than appropriation of the value of books such as this.

However, this delimiting of psychological expertise should be considered a strength rather than a weakness of the argument advanced in Moriarty's volume. When and whether the divine actually acts outside of human experience to relieve depressive symptoms is impossible for psychology to assert. What can be asserted is that the functional effect of such divine action is felt and filtered through human beings who themselves live with the same limitations under which psychology is practiced. Humans must live with the effects of their faith as they experience it in their emotions and thoughts and actions. They are powerless to demonstrate, in any scientific sense, the existence or the independent action of their gods. As Saint Paul of the Christian tradition stated, "We walk by faith and not by sight" (2 Cor. 5:7).

It is important to acknowledge that most people, if not all, talk about transcendent reality, i.e., God, as metaphorical and analogical. The language that transcends the common world of the five senses must be expressed in metaphors or analogies of the world that is known and experienced. This is the nature of religious language. Of course, it can also be contended that the theories of psychology (be they about intrapsychic processes or God concepts) transcend empirical observation and have their own implicit metaphors (Browning & Cooper, 2004). Nevertheless, although it can be asserted that God has agency and acts on behalf of humans to relieve depressive symptoms, it must be remembered that talk about God is always done via metaphor and analogy—not explicit observation, and that such assumed action by the divine must always be inferred indirectly or functionally, namely, by its effect on human behavior. This is what Jesus meant when he said, more than once, to persons who were healed, "Your faith has made you whole" (Mark 5:34, Luke 8:48).

Moriarty writes to the practitioner first and to depressive persons second. This book is a valuable compendium of the current theories about the nature and cause of depression coupled with recent scholarly work by psychologists of religion about the various ways people conceptualize the divine. Carl Jung reportedly said what Moriarty's writing illustrates: people not only *have* their gods, they *make* gods. This is a truth that the research on God image and God concept shows without question.

Furthermore, that Freud was right regarding his theories on childhood has been demonstrated again and again. The dependent experience of childhood is formative—especially if that childhood is religious and includes much God talk. Children develop an understanding of God through their experience with their parents. Parents, in turn, have much to do with the kind of affirmations and support that become the buttresses against depression.

Of special importance for both therapists and clients are the numerous scales and methods Moriarty provides for treatment and insight. He does not make the mistake of many in assuming that insight by itself heals. This book offers sound ways of helping to make God images and concepts more positive and to incorporate these concepts into a treatment plan.

Human life is very vulnerable. It is true that no one is promised a rose garden and life is a hard way to go. It is the exceptional life that can maintain a positive outlook at all times and under all conditions. People are subject to depression. Much thinking nowadays talks of endogenous depression that runs in families and can be inherited. I am prone to think that most depression is never completely endogenous. External factors, such as the threats to self-esteem that come with the territory of living a life on this planet, influence depression as well. I am also convinced that joining the faithful of all ages and calling on the divine for comfort, courage, and support helps. Persons throughout the ages have been certain enough about their gods to hold the conviction that they were not alone in this life and that they had assistance from transcendent reality. This assistance works, and Moriarty's book will be a seminal resource for therapists and depressed persons who will give it a try.

H. Newton Malony, MA, MDiv, PhD
Senior Professor of Psychology
Department of Clinical Psychology
Fuller Theological Seminary

REFERENCE

Browning, D.S. & Cooper, T.D. (2004). *Religious thought and the modern psychologies* 2nd ed. Minneapolis, MN: Fortress Press.

Preface

I am glad you picked up this book. If you are reading this, you are probably interested in the mechanics of a person's relationship with God. Let me warn you, the information contained within may be disturbing to some. While reading this book, you will examine ideas that are not ordinarily open to consideration. You will take the subjective experience of God from behind its glass case, open it up, dissect it, and then put it back together again. This book is about understanding why we experience God in the ways we do.

This book focuses most on the individual with depression. Many people with depression turn to God for help. Unfortunately, this action is often not as helpful as it could be. Often these people believe in a God who loves, cares, and accepts them, but they *experience* a God who rejects them. The reason for this incongruity is that each person has two ideas of God: the God concept and the God image (Rizzuto, 1979). The best way to understand the difference between the two is to compare them. The God concept is an "intellectual, mental-dictionary definition of the word 'God'" (Lawrence, 1997, p. 214). It is shaped by religious education and exists more as an abstract concept than as an immediate emotional reality. Most individuals reared in the Christian faith have a God concept characterized by love, strength, and wisdom. Beneath the surface of the intellectual concept of God exists the God image.

The God image is the subjective emotional experience of God (Lawrence, 1997; Rizzuto, 1979). It is shaped by peoples' experience of their parents and enables them to continue these earlier relational patterns. Familiarity is comfortable, so individuals pattern future relationships after what they learned in their relationships with their parents. Their relationship with God is no different. If their parents treated them as if they were always at fault, then they will use their God image to maintain this process by making themselves feel guilty. Conversely, if their parents treated them as if they were valuable, then they will use their God image for emotional support.

People who struggle with depression usually have a God image that is critical and rejecting because they had critical and rejecting parents. They may intellectually understand that God loves them and is graceful, but they cannot emotionally accept it. In order to reach such people it is necessary to communicate with them on a deeper level so that the earlier learned relationship patterns can be understood and changed. Once the patterns are changed, people with depression gain a better view of themselves and experience God as loving, rather than rejecting.

This book has two goals. The first is to provide the reader with a strong understanding of depression and the God image. The second is to furnish the reader with the therapeutic ability to change the God image. This will not be an easy task. Frankly, the only way these goals can be met is through hard work. This is not a text that you can simply breeze through and hope to understand the main ideas. The book demands something of you. It asks you to work with it, sit with it, and struggle with it, for it is only through this process that the material will come alive.

This book should be read from the beginning to the end. If you skip ahead to sections you think are more interesting, you will deprive yourself of a better understanding. For example, in Chapter 2, I have included some exercises that will reveal your unique conception of God. If you skip the exercises and read the theory first, you will distort your answers. The result will be an inaccurate look at your God image. If, however, you work through the book and do the exercises as they are designed, then you will have a more pure understanding of your God image. You can then work through the theory and interpret your results to see what factors played into the development of your own God image.

This book is written to tap your rational mind and your emotional mind. Too often, books focus solely on theory and leave the reader with only a dry understanding. On the other hand, some books focus only on the emotional experience, providing a quick and seemingly meaningful experience but knowledge quickly fades. What is needed for true learning to occur is an integration of both.

I have been exploring the God image for the past ten years. At times it has been confusing and painful, and at other times it has been enlightening and healing. These experiences have culminated in this book. As you embark on this journey, my prayer is that you better understand yourself and your God image. My hope is that you can help those who have a hurtful relationship with their God image and transform it into a healing one.

Acknowledgments

I would like to begin by thanking the therapists and clients who will use the techniques and instruments discussed in this book. Next, I want to express my appreciation to the students I work with at Regent University, whose enthusiasm, curiosity, and interest have refreshed me time and time again. I am also grateful to Rosemarie Hughes, Bill Hathaway, and my fellow colleagues in the School of Psychology and Counseling for providing me with a supportive environment to work on this project.

Throughout the writing process a number of individuals have given me editorial feedback. I am grateful for the early thoughts by Joseph Pulley-King, AnnElise Parkhurst, George Boone, and Brandi Klepper. More recently, I have greatly benefited from the insightful comments of Louis Hoffman. His thoughts have helped me open my mind to new ideas and gain an appreciation for the God image from a variety of sociocultural perspectives. I am also indebted to Rodney Hesson for his help with the NLP and experiential techniques.

A number of authors and clinicians have graciously allowed me to reprint or summarize their work. First, I am very grateful to Robert McGee for permitting me to use the parent/God image grid that he created. Similarly, I am appreciative of Bill Gaultiere for allowing me to use the God image questionnaire. Second, I am thankful to Ana-Maria Rizzuto for her pioneering work in translating the God image through the lens of object relations theory.

Finally, I would like to thank my family for their support throughout this process. The entire Brouillet family has cheered me on and I have been especially warmed by the kind thoughts from both Wendy and Roger. In addition, I am grateful to my sister, Michelle, and grandmother Edith for their continual inquiries as this project has unfolded. I am also appreciative of the interest that Ed Shea has shown in this topic and my other endeavors. My mother, Marcy, has been a huge source of support as well. Her constant words of hope and never-ending supply of encouragement have helped me jump each hurdle along the way. My father, Michael, has also been a consistent source of strength and support. Finally, I am most grateful to my lovely wife, Nicole. Her unwavering love has given me a deeper understanding of the ideas presented in this book, and her steadfast belief in me has provided me with the confidence I needed to complete this project.

PART I:
DEPRESSION AND THE GOD IMAGE

Chapter 1

Depression and Religious Experience

WHAT IS DEPRESSION?

The diagnostic name for depression is major depressive disorder (American Psychiatric Association [APA], 2000). Technically, people either have depression or they do not. The determining factor is the number of symptoms they have. However, depression can also be viewed as existing on a continuum. People with some symptoms but not enough to meet the full diagnostic criteria still suffer from some level of subclinical depression. In fact, most people experience a degree of depression at one time or another in their life.

The *Diagnostic and Statistical Manual of Mental Disorders* (DSM-IV-TR) (APA, 2000) is the reference in which all mental disorders are cataloged. In order for depression to be diagnosed, the person must exhibit five or more of the following nine symptoms during the same two-week period.

At least one of the symptoms must be either (1) depressed mood or (2) loss of interest or pleasure in once-enjoyable activities.

1. Depressed mood most of the day, nearly every day, as indicated by either subjective report (e.g., feels sad or empty) or observation made by others (e.g., appears tearful). *Note:* In children and adolescents, can be irritable mood.
2. Markedly diminished interest or pleasure in all, or almost all, activities most of the day, nearly every day (as indicated by either subjective account or observation made by others)
3. Significant weight loss when not dieting or weight gain (e.g., a change of more than 5 percent of body weight in a month), or decrease or increase in appetite nearly every day
4. Insomnia [too little sleep] or hypersomnia [too much sleep] nearly every day.

5. Psychomotor agitation [walking, talking, and/or moving in an aggravated, fidgety, manner] or retardation [walking, talking, and/or moving slower than normal] nearly every day (observable by others, not merely subjective feelings of restlessness or being slowed down)
6. Fatigue or loss of energy nearly every day
7. Feelings of worthlessness or excessive or inappropriate guilt (which may be delusional) nearly every day (not merely self-reproach or guilt about being sick)
8. Diminished ability to think or concentrate, or indecisiveness, nearly every day (either by subjective account or as observed by others)
9. Recurrent thoughts of death (not just fear of dying), recurrent suicidal thoughts without a specific plan, or a suicide attempt or a specific plan for committing suicide (p. 356)*

Depression is a mood disorder, which means that the primary difficulty is with the mood or the way a person feels. People who struggle with depression often feel as if a black cloud follows them wherever they go. They are usually unhappy and have a hard time seeing any positive aspects of their life. Depression also causes people to feel burdened by an extreme sense of guilt. They often blame themselves for sins they have not committed. They frequently feel they have done something wrong, even though they have not, and therefore believe that they deserve to be rejected by others and God.

People who are depressed have a number of difficulties that accompany their ailment (Maxmen & Ward, 1995). One problem occurs with the breakdown of close relationships. Often their initial complaints are met with a listening ear, advice, and care. However, when these efforts fail, family and friends may become frustrated and irritated. This only makes matters worse because the depressed persons then feel doubly guilty for annoying those closest to them. In an attempt to please their family and friends they then keep their concerns to themselves, which unfortunately results in increased depression.

---

*Reprinted with permission from the *Diagnostic and Statistical Manual of Mental Disorders,* Fourth Edition, Text Revision, Copyright 2000. American Psychiatric Association.

Other complicating factors include suicidal ideation, substance abuse, and impaired judgment (Maxmen & Ward, 1995). Males complete suicide twice as often as females, but females attempt more often. Males usually use active, direct methods (e.g., firearms, hanging), whereas females use more passive, indirect methods (e.g., overdose, cutting). To escape their pain, some depressed individuals learn to cope through using substances. It is not long before they learn that they can control the feeling of despair through the amount of substances they take. Eventually, many become addicted to drugs or alcohol. Because individuals with depression feel so poorly, they often misjudge and misinterpret situations. If they are not aware of their distortions, they will make decisions that have detrimental effects on their future.

Universally, women have twice as high a rate of major depressive disorder as do men (Kaplan & Sadock, 1998). The prevalence rates for women are between 10 to 25 percent, and between 5 to 12 percent for men. This is thought to be the result of "hormonal differences, the effects of childbirth, differing psychosocial stressors for women and for men, and behavioral models of learned helplessness" (Kaplan & Sadock, 1998, p. 539). The average age of onset for men and women is age forty, and 50 percent of individuals diagnosed are between ages twenty to fifty. Individuals who are single, separated, or divorced have a higher rate of depression than do those who are married. The prevalence of depression has not been found to be related to ethnicity, education, or income (APA, 2000).

Major depressive disorder is usually precipitated by a psychosocial stressor (e.g., divorce, job loss), and can occur over days or weeks or develop over months or years (Maxmen & Ward, 1995). The span of time between early depressive episodes is usually longer than the span of time between later episodes (APA, 2000). As the episodes accrue, the chances of having another increases. People who move into partial remission of symptoms have a greater chance of having another episode than do those who move into full remission of symptoms. Studies suggest that after one year, 40 percent of those diagnosed will again warrant diagnosis of a full episode, 20 percent will no longer meet full criteria, and 40 percent will no longer have a mood disorder.

HOW DOES DEPRESSION DEVELOP?

In my opinion, there are two main schools of thought in clinical psychology. The first is the psychodynamic school, and the second is the cognitive school. Psychodynamic and cognitive theorists view the same person in different ways, but both are important and give valuable insights into his or her makeup. This section reviews these theories one at a time. The psychodynamic school predates the cognitive school, so it will be reviewed first.

Psychodynamic Theory

Psyche means "soul" and *dynamic* means "with movement." Psychodynamic theory looks at the movements of the soul. This theory has a long history that started in the late 1800s and continues to evolve and change even to this day. The breadth and depth of this field is overwhelming, so the focus of this section will be limited to the foundational points for discussion. These points are taken from four different subschools of psychodynamic theory: psychoanalysis, ego psychology, object relations, and relational psychoanalysis.

Psychoanalysis

Psychoanalysis began with Sigmund Freud, an extremely controversial figure, who has had and will continue to have a tremendous impact on human thought. His ideas have been absorbed into our culture and have had a profound influence on the way we think of ourselves and others (Gay, 1989). This chapter will focus on two of his main contributions: the different levels of consciousness and the structural theory of personality.

One of Freud's (1915) greatest discoveries was that people have three different levels of consciousness: the unconscious, the preconscious, and the conscious. The iceberg is a metaphor often used to illustrate the different levels of awareness. The unconscious corresponds to the bulk of the iceberg that falls far below the surface of the water. The preconscious parallels the part of the iceberg that lies underwater but is still visible from the surface of the water. Finally, the conscious is represented by the tip of the iceberg—it is visible, but is overall a very small and unsubstantial part of the entire substance.

The unconscious, similar to the bottom layer of the iceberg, is the most powerful part of the personality. According to Freud (1915), the unconscious contains the instinctual urges that guide and direct most of conscious life. In addition, it contains thoughts and feelings that are too threatening to consciously evaluate. These thoughts and feelings are often tied to early memories that are too devastating to directly think about. When these painful incidents occur, they are not processed or worked through but are instead quickly banished from the conscious mind and relegated to the unconscious. These contents desire to be processed and understood, so they often surface in dreams and slips of the tongue. Bradshaw (1988) likens repressing issues to trying to keep beach balls underwater. You can do it with one or two, but if you add more it gets difficult and they start to pop up.

The preconscious is not nearly as powerful as the unconscious and gains information from both the unconscious mind and the conscious mind (Brenner, 1973). Sometimes the unconscious will allow information to surface to the preconscious mind that is not too threatening or anxiety provoking. The conscious mind frequently deposits information in the preconscious mind by simply removing focused attention but maintaining awareness of the information. For example, you are currently reading this book and focusing on these words, but if you think about it, you can switch your attention to the pressure your back feels leaning against the chair you are sitting on. This information, when you first sat down, was initially in your conscious mind, but then switched to your preconscious mind as you began reading this book.

According to Freud, the conscious mind, similar to the tip of the iceberg, is the weakest and most superficial part. It gains information through the senses and sometimes the preconscious mind passes it nonthreatening information (Feist & Feist, 1998). One of the great controversies marking Freud's career was his assertion that "the ego is not the master in its own house." He suggested that we often think we are in control and deliberately leading our lives, but that this is an illusion and that unconscious factors play a much stronger role in guiding our thoughts, feelings, and behaviors. Many psychodynamic theorists now believe that Freud overstated this factor (Greenburg & Mitchell, 1983). They believe that the unconscious is powerful, but not nearly as forceful as Freud originally asserted.

Another great contribution that Freud (1923) made to psycho-dynamic thought is the structural theory of personality. He divided the personality into three distinct structures: the id, the ego, and the superego. Each structure has its own unique function and interacts with different levels of consciousness (unconscious, preconscious, and conscious).

The id is primarily unconscious and, for Freud, exists at the core of the person. It is the basest part of the self and most concerned with reducing tension and gaining release. The id is governed by the pleasure principle: it does whatever it can to decrease pain and increase pleasure. The id is the only part of the personality that is present at birth. It is easily observed in infants and is characterized by egocentricity, severe emotional displays, and the need for immediate gratification. You can almost hear infants saying, "I want what I want and I want it now!" Adults who are described as infantile and who have "refused to grow up" are very id dominated. They are often characterized as impulsive, self-centered, and unrestricted (Feist & Feist, 1998).

The ego, or I, is involved in all three levels of consciousness and is the overall organizer of the personality (Brenner, 1973). It is led by the reality principle. Unlike the id, the ego is in touch with reality and manages other aspects of the personality to get the person's needs met. The id is content to scream and cry and is not overly concerned with getting actual needs met. The ego, however, develops out of the id and realizes that crying all the time is not the best way to meet needs, so it develops new and better ways of interacting with the environment. The id acts on impulse, whereas the ego practices delayed gratification. When a person is led by his or her ego, he or she is considered to be balanced and healthy (Feist & Feist, 1998).

The superego is mostly unconscious and is the moralistic aspect of the personality. The superego internalizes the standards and expectations of one's caregivers. Parents tell their children not to do things over and over again, and wonder "Why doesn't this kid get it? Why does this kid keep doing what I say not to?" After getting in trouble numerous times, children eventually figure out that if they do what their parents tell them *not* to do, they will get punished. At this point, the external parent voices are brought inside the self. It is as if children no longer need to hear their actual parents say it; instead children can regulate their parents' voices from inside themselves. A balanced superego allows a person some indulgences but keeps the person from behaving in either an aggressive or sexually inappropriate manner. An unbalanced or overactive superego strives for perfection and leaves little room for human weakness. A person dominated by the superego is characterized by deep feelings of guilt and inadequacy (Feist & Feist, 1998).

Children, through the superego, also internalize family rules, both spoken and unspoken. For example, children who have an alcoholic father learn from the unspoken commands of the mother that they are not to mention to anybody or even themselves that their father is an alcoholic. Whenever they think of their father as an alcoholic they will experience guilt. Children in this situation *should* think and talk to others about their father's problems, but because it is an implicit family rule, they will feel as if they are doing something wrong when they think or speak about their father's weakness. In this way, the superego becomes the internal representative of the parents. Rules that are both good and bad become programmed within the personality of children. These rules, once ingrained, are challenging to modify.

Ego Psychology

Other psychologists expounded upon Freud's ideas and further developed the psychodynamic school. The next major development came with the dawn of ego psychology (Hartmann, 1958). As the name implies, these theorists emphasized the ego and minimized the id and the superego. They posited that the main drive was to become independent. The focus switched from the old psychoanalytic emphasis on instincts to the new ego psychology emphasis on autonomy.

Ego psychologists were also very interested in how a person utilized defense mechanisms. According to McWilliams (1994), a person utilizes a defense in order "to accomplish the following ends: (1) the avoidance or management of some powerful, threatening feeling, usually anxiety but sometimes grief and other disorganizing emotional experiences; and (2) the maintenance of self-esteem" (p. 97). For example, projection, one of the most well-known defenses, occurs when people project their own anger onto someone else. They then experience that other person as angry with them. If a man is angry that his boss has chosen to promote someone else instead of him, and he cannot accept his anger, then he will project his anger onto his boss. As a result, he will believe that his boss is angry with him, even though his boss is not the least bit angry. If the man were to own and process his anger he would no longer experience his boss as upset with him.

Object Relations

Another major wave to have a profound influence on psychodynamic thought was the school of object relations (Fairbairn, 1954). These theorists posit that the greatest motivating force is the need to relate to others. The need for attachment and human contact is paramount and trumps all other needs. Ironically, these theorists who are most concerned with human relatedness refer to people as objects. The name should not read *object relations* but should instead read *people relations.*

Object-relations psychologists focus on how a child's relationship with his or her caregiver is developed, experienced, and internalized. The psychologists ask questions such as, "In what ways does she treat herself as her mother treated her?" or "How did this woman's childhood relationship with her father influence her choice of husband?" The basic idea is that clients' parents or main caregivers furnish them with a relational template that they use to relate to themselves and others.

These theorists observe that people bring their primary caregivers into themselves and unconsciously play their parents' voices in their minds. They pay particular attention to the process of separation-individuation, which is the degree to which a person has separated from their parents and become their own person (Horner, 1984; Mahler, Pine, & Bergman, 1975). If separation-individuation has occurred, then people listen more to themselves and less to their internalized parents. For example, if a boy grew up with workaholic parents but decided that he did not want to be a workaholic, then he would have worked through the differences he had with his parents and thus live in a more relaxed manner. This man achieved separation-individuation because he listened to himself and not to his internalized parents. If separation-individuation has not occurred, then people listen less to themselves and more to their internalized parents. If the same man had never come to terms with the differences he had with his parents he would have become a workaholic. Unknowingly, he would feel compelled to spend his life marching to his parents' drumbeat and would never discover his own.

Relational Psychoanalysis

A fourth tradition to emerge out of psychodynamic theory and practice has come to be called relational psychoanalysis. This school, similar to object relations, replaces Freud's biological focus with an interpersonal focus. These clinicians emphasize interdependence rather than independence (Jones, 1997). That is, they hold that individuals exist within a relational matrix and know themselves and others based on the web of connections that surrounds them. This theory also provides space for the integration of postmodern and constructivist thought. The staunch emphasis on objective truth that is delivered by the analyst is substituted with a more subjective focus on the mutual understandings and dialogue that unfolds between therapist and client (Stolorow & Atwood, 1992).

Integrated Perspectives

Now that some of the main points of psychodynamic thought have been briefly surveyed, these perspectives will be integrated to see how they play out in the development of depression. The form of depression discussed here is *exogenous depression,* which means that it results from personality development and situational circumstances rather than from a biochemical imbalance. Bipolar disorder is a common example of depression that results from underlying biological causes. These more endogenous forms of depression are best treated with psychotropic medications, whereas exogenous forms of depression respond positively to therapy and a combination of medication and psychotherapy.

Adults who have a depressive character usually come from homes in which their parents were experienced as cold, preoccupied, distant, neglectful, and/or abusive. If children experience their parents in this manner, they will at first respond with fierce anger (McWilliams, 1994). Something instinctual tells children they should be taken care of, and when this does not occur they feel deep pain and a resulting rage that lets their caretakers know that the environment must be corrected.

If the environment does not change, children quickly realize that their parents are not going to give them what they need, and an unconscious defense mechanism takes over (McWilliams, 1994). Children need to feel that their parents are good and caring. If children believe their parents are bad and neglectful, then they will experience a state of overwhelming anxiety. If their parents cannot be trusted, then children will live in a constant state of mistrust, fear, and hypervigilance. This is too stressful and painful for children. In order to make sense of the situation and feel safe, children train themselves to believe that they are "bad" to justify their parents' harmful behavior. They begin to think, "I'm the problem. My parents are good people and if they don't like me there must be something wrong with me. I guess I'm getting the treatment I deserve."

Thinking this way has certain survival benefits (McWilliams, 1994). The pain is too much to bear, so children partially resolve it by training themselves to think that the problem resides within themselves. This unconscious cognitive switch enables children to trust their parents and feel as safe as possible within the confines of a less-than-ideal environment. It also allows the children to believe they have gained some level of control in a situation that is factually out of their hands. If the problem lies within themselves, and not with their parents, then they should be able to control it. Children develop the belief that all they have to do is fix themselves and become perfect; if they are successful, then they can win back their parents' love.

Unfortunately, even though children strive toward perfection, parents often fail to realize how selfishly they are behaving toward their kids. Instead, the same process is played over and over again, reinforcing children's perceptions that something is deeply wrong within themselves. As children continue to develop, these characteristics become the core of their personality. Feelings of worthlessness, rejection, and guilt will begin to feel right to them. Because these relational patterns and the resulting feelings are consistent and dependable, children will feel in control and, paradoxically, secure in their insecurity.

As they move through adolescence and into adulthood, these earlier learned patterns will manifest themselves in their intimate relationships. In fact, such individuals will unconsciously seek relationships that enable them to be back in the "No matter what I do, I just can't seem to please you" role. This role is safe; it feels comfortable, and it reinforces who they are. It does not matter if it is painful, as long as it is consistent.

When people who are depressed find a person who treats them as their parents did, they take upon themselves the impossible task of trying to please this person. The person, however, will never be pleased. It never occurs to the depressed individual that they have taken on a task that cannot be achieved. As a result, they fail to realize the futility of their efforts. When their relationships fail they think the fault lies solely with them. At this point they use the defense of anger and direct their anger back at themselves rather than rightfully directing it at the other person. In this way they punish themselves, just as their parents punished them, for not being perfect. People with depression think something must be wrong with them, otherwise the impossible-to-please person would have loved them.

In sum, the development of the depressive character includes the following steps:

1. Parents are experienced as cold, distant, neglectful, preoccupied, and/or abusive.
2. Children need to feel that their parents are good in order to feel safe. The children feel neither.
3. Children then think there must be something wrong with themselves to justify their parents' abusive or neglectful behavior.
4. This happens over and over again making it a deeply ingrained pattern.
5. Feeling worthless, inadequate, and guilty feels safe because it is consistent and controllable.
6. As adolescents and adults they find people who will treat them as their parents did.
7. Even though this is painful, it feels safe, and with each reexperiencing of the earlier relational pattern, the process becomes more ingrained.

Cognitive Theory

Psychologists in the cognitive school focus on the role that thinking plays in the development and maintenance of depression. Cognitive therapy grew out of psychoanalysis in the early 1960s. The two main progenitors of this school, Aaron Beck, who developed cognitive therapy, and Albert Ellis, who developed rational emotive behavioral therapy, were practicing analysts who grew frustrated with the inefficiency of psychoanalysis. They grew tired of listening to free associations and instead began to focus on how pessimistic thinking resulted in depression.

A plethora of cognitive theories now exist, each with its own particular accent on how thinking affects feelings and behavior. This book focuses primarily on Aaron Beck's cognitive therapy. The basic assumption underlying cognitive therapy is that thoughts affect feelings and feelings affect behavior. If people can control their thoughts, then they can control the way they feel and the way they behave.

Beck (1976) observed that people are prone to depression as a result of some negative event(s) in childhood. This could be as dramatic as losing a parent or as minor as feeling as if they never fit in. He also noted that oftentimes depression-prone adults had critical parents growing up and developed perfectionistic standards. As adults these individuals may manage relatively well but be thrown into a depressive episode as a result of a negative precipitating event. This event could be the loss of a job, failure to reach a desired goal, or separation from a spouse (DeRubeis, Tang, & Beck, 2002). The magnitude of the event is important, but what is more important is the way that the person *interprets* the event. This event reactivates, or triggers, the old thoughts the person formed in childhood and consequently propels them into depression.

Beck, Emery, Rush, & Shaw (1979) observed that once people become depressed they tend to have negative thoughts about themselves, their ongoing experience, and the future. This is referred to as the *cognitive triad* (p. 11). The first component is a negative view of self. People with depression regard themselves as defective and inadequate. The second component is a negative view of ongoing experiences. People with depression feel they are ineffective in everyday relationships and activities. The third component is a negative view of the future. When they think ahead they visualize further failure and despair.

In order to simplify the ideas, cognitive theorists break depression down into three main components. The first is automatic thoughts, the second examines cognitive errors, and the third involves schemas.

Automatic Thoughts

Automatic thoughts are defined as "thoughts or visual images individuals may be unaware of unless attention is purposely focused on them" (Beck et al., 1979, p. 187). Automatic thoughts have the following specific criterial attributes:

1. They are automatic—they occur as if by reflex, without prior reasoning.
2. They are unreasonable and dysfunctional.
3. They seem completely plausible and are uncritically accepted as valid even though they seem bizarre upon reflection.
4. They are involuntary. (Beck, et al., 1979, p. 166)

People with depression have lost control of their thoughts and are unable to stop mentally beating themselves up. They are not always aware of their thoughts, but they are aware of feeling sad. It is as if the automatic thoughts are broadcast on a different frequency than their regular thoughts. Another way to explain it is to imagine that the volume is turned down too low and the conscious mind cannot hear the message. The message still results in the feeling of depression even if it is not loud enough to be consciously registered.

Automatic thoughts reinforce themselves by causing a thinking, feeling, behaving cycle to ensue (Beck, 1976). The result is that the depressed gradually increase their depression by engaging in negative thoughts, which increase depressive feelings, which leads to pro-depressive behavior, which starts the cycle over again and leads to more depressive thoughts. For example, a man might have a hard day at work and say to himself, "I'm a loser. I can't do anything right." These negative thoughts result in him feeling inferior and depreciated. Instead of sharing his thoughts with his wife, he isolates himself and watches television. The night passes and he says to himself, "I'm such a lousy husband. I should have spent time with my wife. I can't do anything right."

Cognitive Errors

The second main component of depression is comprised of cognitive errors, which are the systematic ways people with depression misinterpret their experiences (Beck et al., 1979). Aaron Beck (1976) makes the distinction between depressive and nondepressive thinking. Individuals who are depressed make absolute judgments, whereas individuals who are not depressed make relative judgments. People who are depressed make rigid statements about themselves, whereas those who are not depressed make flexible statements about themselves. Depression leaves no room for gray and causes the person to think only in terms of black and white. DeRubeis and colleagues (2002) define eleven common thinking errors:

1. *All-or-nothing thinking:* Placing experiences in one or two opposite categories—for example, flawless or defective immaculate or filthy, saint or sinner
2. *Overgeneralizing:* Drawing sweeping inferences (e.g., "I can't control my temper") from a single instance
3. *Discounting the positives:* Deciding that if a good thing has happened, it couldn't have been very important
4. *Jumping to conclusions:* Focusing on one aspect of a situation in deciding how to understand it (e.g., "The reason I haven't received a phone call from the job I applied to is that they have decided not to offer it to me")
5. *Mind reading:* Believing one knows what another person is thinking, with very little evidence
6. *Fortune-telling:* Believing one knows what the future holds while ignoring other possibilities
7. *Magnifying/minimizing:* Evaluating the importance of a negative event, or the lack of importance of a positive event, in a distorted manner
8. *Emotional reasoning:* Believing that something must be true, because it feels like it is true
9. *Making "should" statements:* Telling oneself one should do (or should have done) something, when it is more accurate to say that one would like to do (or wishes one had done) the preferred thing
10. *Labeling:* Using a label ("bad mother," "idiot") to describe a behavior, and then imputing all the meanings the label carries
11. *Inappropriate blaming:* Using hindsight to determine what one "should have done," even if one could not have known the best thing to do at the time; ignoring mitigating factors; or ig-

noring the roles played by others in determining a negative outcome (p. 353)

Schemas

Schemas are the third and final component of the cognitive-behavioral understanding of depression (Beck et al., 1979). Schemas are underlying assumptions that determine the way people interpret their environment. On a daily basis, people are presented with an overwhelming amount of information. In order to make sense of it all, people need to be able to quickly sort through and analyze it. People naturally fix their attention upon information that matches the way they already think of themselves. Unfortunately, for people who are depressed this means that they are going to automatically gravitate toward information that affirms their harmful self-perception. They will decode, interpret, and internalize information that emphasizes the negative about themselves, their current relationships, and the future. For example, healthy people leave most interactions feeling liked by other people; depressed people leave most conversations sensing people dislike them. Healthy people hear constructive criticism, evaluate themselves, and determine that they need to change some things but that they are otherwise doing a good job. People who are depressed hear constructive criticism, evaluate themselves, and feel that they are doing a terrible job. Healthy people think positively about current situations and as a result predict a bright future. People who are depressed think negatively about current situations and expect a bleak future.

Healthy versus Depressed

Why the difference between healthy people and people who are depressed? People who are healthy utilize different schemas than do people who are depressed. They could have the exact same day, but the healthy person will go home and tell his or her spouse he or she had a great day, whereas the person with depression will say the day was horrible. The different schemas cause the depressed person to interpret *neutral* stimuli in a way that affirms his or her view of himself or herself.

In sum, individuals with depression misinterpret their world to re-affirm their inadequate sense of self. They have ingrained schemas that cause them to interpret incoming information in ways that maintain their depression. This process is enhanced through the use of cognitive errors, which enable them to systematically distort their experience. Finally, automatic thoughts increase their depression by causing them to reflexively think in a negative way about themselves, ongoing experiences, and the future.

DEPRESSION IN PEOPLE WHO ARE RELIGIOUS

People who are depressed cognitively understand their faith but do not emotionally understand their faith. They have head knowledge but not heart knowledge. Depression keeps people from experiencing the liberating truths of Christianity by distorting their emotional understanding of the faith. The gray-tinted glasses that they see other people and the world through are also the glasses that they see their faith through. Just as depression causes them to think negatively about friendships and career opportunities, it also causes them to think negatively about God. The religious behaviors used to express depression will differ with each individual. However, it is likely that they will all share the characteristics of the disorder: most notably, a sense of worthlessness, guilt, fear of rejection, and perfectionism. These issues are central to depression and have a powerful influence over the way people who are depressed experience Christianity (Meissner, 1991).

What comes to your mind when you hear the word *worthlessness?* Have you ever felt worthless before? It is an empty and gnawing emotion that leaves you feeling expendable. It makes you want to shrink into the corners and become invisible. People who are depressed feel worthless. They feel unwanted, left behind, and literally of *no* value. In their mind, they deserve to be ignored and forgotten.

How does this sense of worthlessness affect their emotional understanding of Christianity? They might parrot the beliefs of their tradition (God concept) but have no real experience of God as loving (God image). They seldom felt cherished or appreciated as a child, so they have a painfully difficult time believing that God is crazy about them. They do not feel "fearfully and wonderfully made" (Psalm 139), but instead feel as if they are a mistake or an accident. It is tremendously difficult for them to accept that they have intrinsic value and were deliberately and purposefully created.

People who are depressed also experience a remarkable amount of guilt. *Guilt* occurs when you feel you have done something wrong. It is the emotion that motivates us to do penance and make ourselves right with others and God. People who are depressed, however, have more than their fair share of guilt. This feeling does not just surface after they have done something wrong but is a constant buzz (and sometimes a roar) in the background of their thoughts.

This sense of guilt often extends past the sense that they have *done* something wrong to a more shameful feeling that they *are* something wrong. This is why they often fear rejection, or punishment, even when they know they have done nothing wrong. They are chronically waiting for the other shoe to drop. They often feel that it is just a matter of time till others find out who they "really" are (Harvey & Katz, 1985). People who are depressed have the subjective sense that they are dirty and sometimes even toxic to others. They maintain a smiling face, but desperately fear that they will soon be found out and consequently rejected.

These feelings greatly affect their personal understanding of Christianity. How can they approach a pure and holy God with such evil hidden in their hearts? They are very aware of the skeletons in their closet and experience a God that focuses solely on past mistakes. They share with this God a tendency to ignore positive or neutral memories and instead hone in on the negative memories.

Another factor that plagues people who are depressed is a deep fear of rejection. *Fear of rejection* arises from the belief that one deserves to be abandoned. In childhood, people who are depressed learned to cope with this fear by becoming experts at figuring out how their caregivers wanted them to act. This dynamic carried over to adulthood and underlies most, if not all, of their relationships. They unconsciously divine what other people want and conform themselves to others' desires. They do this so the other person can feel pleased and secure, even if it means they are miserable and insecure. This is not something the depressed persons deliberately think about, but something they automatically do. They have remarkably sensitive radar that allows them to intuitively know how and what they should do to earn others' approval.

This same dynamic gets played out in their Christianity. They smile and volunteer for multiple church duties, even though they are overwhelmed with family and work. They listen to the concerns and complaints of fellow Christians, but hardly ever voice their hurts and sorrows to others. The fear of abandonment that marks their church relationships also marks their relationship with God. They do not express frustration, sadness, or pain to God. They fear that anything less than thanks and praise would result in their rejection. Their God resembles a needy, angry parent who is interested in only the positive aspects of their life and quickly grows cold if negative issues or feelings are discussed.

A final characteristic of depression is perfectionism. *Perfectionism* is characterized by a sense of profound guilt and the belief that one has failed to meet expected standards (Blatt, Quinlan, Pilkonis, & Shea, 1995). Perfectionists tend to be very self-critical. They constantly monitor themselves and are always aware of their actions and the intents behind those actions. They are self-judgers of the worst sort and know nothing of self-mercy. They focus on goals and achievements and attempt to validate their worth by piling accomplishment on accomplishment. The only problem is that they cannot rest. As soon as they accomplish something, they are off accomplishing something else. They never quite find the point they want to reach, and they constantly push themselves harder and harder to hurry up and do so. Oftentimes they set their standards too high, fail, and consequently sink further into depression.

The God they worship is remarkably similar to the God of the Pharisees. This isn't a God they have chosen but one that has been thrust upon them by a childhood riddled with harsh statements, high expectations, and consistent rejection. The road to salvation consists of being perfect and not "screwing up." They have to stay the course, because if they do not God will abandon them. Grace cannot be understood. It is simply a different language that their upbringing does not allow them to decode. They are keenly aware of their shortcomings and have tremendous difficulty fathoming a God that searches them out, forgives them, and unconditionally loves them.

People with depression often unknowingly use religion to maintain their depression and cause harm to themselves (Meissner, 1991). The characteristics of the disorder manifest in religious ways: spiritual activities become marked by a deep sense of worthlessness, guilt, fear of rejection, and perfectionism. When they come for help, it will be your job to help peel back the religious mask to reveal the depressive dynamics at the root of their religious experience.

CASE EXAMPLES: BOB AND LILITH

Two characters will now be discussed to illustrate the dynamics of depression and religious experience. The case examples and interventions that follow are composites of real and imagined clients that represent some of the common themes that emerge in God image work. These characters will make frequent appearances throughout the book to illustrate the book's concept and give an example of possible interventions between a therapist and client. Please take some time to get to know Bob and Lilith, for they will be our traveling partners for the rest of our journey.

Bob Wright is a thirty-seven-year-old, married clergyperson who came to therapy for help with depression and feeling rejected from God. He worked at a popular church and was well thought of throughout the community. Bob indicated that he was having trouble sleeping, frequently felt sad, had a low desire to engage in pleasurable activities, and was frequently exhausted. He felt like a terrible Christian, husband, and minister. He described himself as a failure because he often let God down. He indicated that he had experienced depressive symptoms in the past, but now they were getting too difficult to manage on his own. He reported that he always cognitively understood the meaning of the cross, of grace, and of forgiveness, but that he never actually felt loved and forgiven by God. He felt like God tolerated him, but was frequently disappointed with him. In particular, he felt rejected by God when he did not perform his church duties flawlessly, had sexual thoughts, and missed devotions.

Bob has been married to his wife for seventeen years. He characterized their relationship as "okay," but indicated that his wife is frequently frustrated with him because she does not feel like he gives enough to her. Bob appeared to do much for his wife, but somehow they were both convinced that he was not a good husband. When asked what sort of things he did to justify feeling so negative about himself as a husband, he mentioned only minor annoyances and nothing that could be conceived to qualify him as a "terrible" husband.

Bob has two younger siblings. He grew up as a protective big brother and often took the brunt of his father's anger. His father abused alcohol and was very critical of Bob. He expected Bob to get straight As and be the star of his athletic teams. Bob did well in school and in sports, but nowhere near what his father would have liked. As a result, his father frequently criticized him and made him feel as if he was worthless. His father's approval was extremely important to Bob, so he tried all the harder to gain his respect. Unfortunately, his efforts were never enough.

His mother was kind to Bob but never made an effort to protect him from his father. She was what is popularly referred to as an *enabler*. She implicitly let all of her children know that their father's drinking was a secret that was never to be mentioned inside or outside the house. Bob grew up feeling as if he were to blame for his family's problems and felt especially responsible for the difficult relationship he had with his father. Bob's mother was his lifeline and his only real emotional support, so he never broached the subject of his father's drinking or any other family problems, because he did not want to jeopardize losing her love and approval.

Making friends was never difficult for Bob. He was always popular and well thought of. People talked about what a great guy he was and how they could talk to him about anything. He was warm and accepting and would do whatever he could to help a friend out. The only problem with his friendships was that they were often one-way. Bob was the strong one that everyone talked to, but he never opened up and depended on others. People would often inquire about the details of his life to which he would warmly respond, but never really open up. He was uncomfortable being vulnerable and had a difficult time trusting others with less-than-positive aspects of his life.

Bob became a Christian in late adolescence and found a safe haven in the church. He discovered a way of life that was clear and unambiguous. He felt cared for and supported by his friends and ministers in the church. This environment was refreshing and starkly different from his home life that was dominated by the overwhelming presence of his father.

He finished college and went onto seminary where he became thoroughly grounded in the Christian worldview. He intellectually understood many of the theological truths of Christianity, but had a difficult time applying them to his life. For example, he could detail different perspectives on grace and forgiveness but could not allow these concepts to personally impact his life. It was as if there was a block that kept him from allowing these concepts to sink into his life.

Not much had changed in Bob's faith since seminary. He still had the same struggles with God. He could talk poignantly about forgiveness, but never *felt* forgiven. His relationship with God was at its best when he felt tolerated by God and at its worst when he felt rejected by God. He needed to learn to feel the approval, acceptance, and love of the true God.

Lilith Payne is a forty-five-year-old married deacon who sought treatment for depressive symptoms and help with "keeping up her end of the relationship" with God. She suffers from difficulty concentrating, a sense of guilt, feeling as if she doesn't measure up, ongoing sadness, and a decreased appetite. She presented as a serious woman who dressed meticulously. Lilith indicated that her depression is weighing her down and that she "needs to be rid of it." It was negatively affecting every area of her life, including her relationship with God. I got the impression that Lilith believed in a God who helps those who help themselves and at the time was not feeling too fond of her because she was "slacking" in her religious duties. She indicated that God is usually pleased with her because she is able to live an ordered and effective life, but is getting increasingly displeased with her because she is weighed down by depression and living a disordered and ineffective life.

Lilith grew up in an upper-class family. Her father was an administrator in an electronics corporation and her mother was a homemaker. From an early age Lilith was expected to present herself as a well-mannered little woman. Lilith was an only child. Her father was frequently absent from the home, so she spent most of her time with her mother. She described her mother as austere, distant, and concerned with the finer things in life. She was interested in shaping Lilith into what she wanted her to be, rather than allowing Lilith the space to develop and become who she was created to be.

Lilith learned at an early age that she was not like the other children. She was not to participate in what her mother referred to as "lower-class" activities, but was instead to be what her mother called a "refined young lady." She recollected wanting to play with the other kids but at the same time feeling forbidden and pressured to conform to her mother's wishes. Lilith naturally fell in line with her mother's mentoring and negated the more "childish" aspects of herself in order to win the acceptance and approval of her mother.

She grew up quickly, too quickly, and earned early acceptance to an Ivy League university where she studied literature and religion. She had high standards for her suitors and after getting a little close, she always seemed to find something wrong with them. Then one day she met a stagy older man who seemed interested in her. He was very independent and had sophisticated interests. She fell for him and they married shortly thereafter.

She has been married to this man for twenty years. They do not have any children. He is similar to Lilith in that he has mature interests and an industrious lifestyle. When asked to describe the quality of their relationship, she smiled and said it was "good," but crossed her legs and seemed a bit guarded as she said this. She put a tremendous amount of pressure on herself to keep up appearances. That was exactly what was happening here. She did not feel she could be forthright about her marital struggles for fear that I would devalue her and see her as less than perfect.

Her husband was similar to her mother. He was emotionally removed and seemed to value her only when she agreed with his perspective. It seemed as if he wanted her to be dependent on him in order to exert a subtle amount of control over her. He seemed to care less for her and more about what they looked like to the outside world.

Lilith maintained a pretty isolated social life. To her, friends were people that she had to impress and keep up a façade for. She had to entertain them at dinner parties and make sure that her house was spotless. Friends were not people whom she had coffee with and let down her guard. She could not allow herself to just open up and vent. Again, the fear was that if she dropped the mask and let others in they would lose respect and criticize her.

Lilith has an active church and spiritual life. She regularly plays a role in the service and has a visible presence at most church functions. Her spiritual life is usually characterized by daily reading and meditating on scriptures as well as daily prayer. However, due to her depression, she has found herself less motivated to participate in these activities. She sought treatment with the goal of getting relief from her depressive symptoms so that she could get her life in order and consequently win God's acceptance. She did not realize that she did not have to run her life rigidly to win God's love. Lilith needed to experience God caring for *all* of her and not being solely interested in her productive and industrious parts.

Chapter 2

Discovering the God Image

WHO IS YOUR GOD?: EXERCISES IN DISCOVERY

This section contains exercises that will help you uncover the details of your God image. Please complete each of the following exercises and answer the questions honestly. Upon completion of this chapter, you will have a firm understanding of your God image and the specific factors that influenced its development.

Source: Grids and questions in this chapter used with permission from *Rapha's 12-Step Program for Overcoming Chemical Dependency* (USA: Rapha Publications, 1990 15-33) (McGee, Springle, & Joiner, 1990). This exercise is reprinted here with permission from Rapha Publications. You can find more information at www.searchlight. com. Available at this Web site are important and insightful books from Robert McGee, the author of the Christian classic *The Search for Significance.*

Exercise 1: God Image Drawings

On this piece of paper, draw a picture of you and God.

On this piece of paper, draw a picture of how you feel you and God look after you have done something wrong.

Exercise 2: Parent/God Image Grids and Relationship Evaluations

As I mentioned earlier, our relationship with our parents shapes the way we experience God. This exercise will help you get a better understanding of this "shaping" process. Check the appropriate squares as you recall how your father related to you when you were young.

When I was a child, my father was . . .

Characteristics	Always	Very often	Some-times	Hardly ever	Never	Don't know
Gentle						
Stern						
Loving						
Aloof						
Disapproving						
Distant						
Close and intimate						
Kind						
Angry						
Caring						
Demanding						
Supportive						
Interested						
Discipliner						
Gracious						
Harsh						
Wise						
Holy						

Characteristics	Always	Very often	Some-times	Hardly ever	Never	Don't know
Leader						
Provider						
Trustworthy						
Joyful						
Forgiving						
Good						
Cherishing of me						
Compassionate						
Impatient						
Unreasonable						
Strong						
Protective						
Passive						
Encouraging						
Sensitive						
Just						
Unpredictable						

Evaluation of Your Relationship with Your Father

What does this inventory tell you about your relationship with your father?

_____

_____

_____

_____

_____

If you were an objective observer of the type of relationship you have just described, how would you feel about the father?

_____

_____

_____

_____

_____

About the child?

_____

_____

_____

_____

_____

How would you respond to the father? Be specific.

_____

_____

_____

_____

_____

To the child?

_____

_____

_____

_____

_____

Now complete the same exercise, this time evaluate your relationship with your mother.

When I was a child, my mother was . . .

Characteristics	Always	Very often	Some-times	Hardly ever	Never	Don't know
Gentle						
Stern						
Loving						
Aloof						
Disapproving						
Distant						
Close and intimate						
Kind						
Angry						
Caring						
Demanding						
Supportive						
Interested						
Discipliner						
Gracious						
Harsh						
Wise						
Holy						
Leader						
Provider						
Trustworthy						

Characteristics	Always	Very often	Some-times	Hardly ever	Never	Don't know
Joyful						
Forgiving						
Good						
Cherishing of me						
Compassionate						
Impatient						
Unreasonable						
Strong						
Protective						/
Passive						
Encouraging						
Sensitive						
Just						
Unpredictable						

Evaluation of Your Relationship with Your Mother

What does this inventory tell you about your relationship with your mother?

_____

_____

_____

_____

_____

If you were an objective observer of the type of relationship you have just described, how would you feel about the mother?

_____

_____

_____

_____

_____

About the child?

_____

_____

_____

_____

How would you respond to the mother? Be specific.

_____

_____

_____

_____

To the child?

_____

_____

_____

_____

Evaluating Your Relationship with God

We can begin to see how our relationships with our parents have influenced our perception of God when we evaluate our present relationship with God. The following inventory will help you to determine some of your feelings toward God. Because it is subjective, no answers are right or wrong. To ensure that the test reveals your actual feelings, please follow the instructions carefully.

1. Answer openly and honestly. Don't respond from a theological knowledge of God, but from personal experience.
2. Don't describe what the relationship *ought* to be, or what you *hope* it will be, but what it is right now.
3. Some people feel God might be displeased if they give a negative answer. Nothing is further from the truth. God is pleased with our honesty. A foundation of transparency is required for growth to occur.
4. Turn each characteristic into a question. For example: *To what degree do I really feel that God loves me? To what degree do I really feel that God understands me?*

To what degree do I really feel God is . . .

Characteristics	Always	Very often	Some-times	Hardly ever	Never	Don't know
Gentle						
Stern						
Loving						
Aloof						
Disapproving						
Distant						
Close and intimate						
Kind						
Angry						
Caring						
Demanding						
Supportive						

Characteristics	Always	Very often	Some-times	Hardly ever	Never	Don't know
Interested						
Discipliner						
Gracious						
Harsh						
Wise						
Holy						
Leader						
Provider						
Trustworthy						
Joyful						
Forgiving						
Good						
Cherishing of me						
Compassionate						
Impatient						
Unreasonable						
Strong						
Protective						
Passive						
Encouraging						
Sensitive						
Just						
Unpredictable						

What does this exercise tell you about your relationship with God?

_____

_____

_____

_____

_____

Are there any differences between what you know (theologically) and how you feel (emotionally) about God? If so, what are they?

_____

_____

_____

_____

_____

Your Father's Influence on Your Relationship with God

Now that you have examined your current relationship with God, consider how your relationship with your earthly father has influenced your perception of God. To make a comparison, transfer all of the check marks you made for your own father on pages 28 and 29 to the shaded columns on this page. When you have completed this, transfer the check marks you made on pages 34 and 35, which relate to your relationship with God, to the white columns. To make them more obvious, use an "X" for this category.

Characteristics	Always		Very often		Some- times		Hardly ever		Never		Don't know	
Gentle												
Stern												
Loving												
Aloof												

Characteristics	Always	Very often	Some- times	Hardly ever	Never	Don't know
Disapproving						
Distant						
Close and intimate						
Kind						
Angry						
Caring						
Demanding						
Supportive						
Interested						
Discipliner						
Gracious						
Harsh						
Wise						
Holy						
Leader						
Provider						
Trustworthy						
Joyful						
Forgiving						
Good						
Cherishing of me						
Compassionate						
Impatient						
Unreasonable						
Strong						

Characteristics	Always	Very often	Some-times	Hardly ever	Never	Don't know
Protective						
Passive						
Encouraging						
Sensitive						
Just						
Unpredictable						

Which characteristics are the same for both your father and God?

_____

_____

_____

_____

_____

Which characteristics are quite different (two or more boxes from each other)?

_____

_____

_____

_____

_____

What patterns (if any) do you see?

_____

_____

_____

_____

_____

Write a summary paragraph about how your perception of God has been shaped by your relationship with your father.

_____

_____

_____

_____

_____

_____

_____

_____

_____

_____

Your Mother's Influence on Your Relationship with God

How has your mother influenced your perception of God? To get a comparison, transfer all the check marks you made for your mother on pages 31 and 32 to the shaded columns on this page. Use a check mark for each category.

When you have completed this, transfer the check marks you made on pages 34 and 35, which relate to your relationship with God, to the white columns. To make them more obvious, use an "X" for this category.

Characteristics	Always		Very often		Some- times		Hardly ever		Never		Don't know	
Gentle												
Stern												
Loving												
Aloof												

Characteristics	Always	Very often	Some-times	Hardly ever	Never	Don't know
Disapproving						
Distant						
Close and intimate						
Kind						
Angry						
Caring						
Demanding						
Supportive						
Interested						
Discipliner						
Gracious						
Harsh						
Wise						
Holy						
Leader						
Provider						
Trustworthy						
Joyful						
Forgiving						
Good						
Cherishing of me						
Compassionate						
Impatient						
Unreasonable						
Strong						

Characteristics	Always	Very often	Some- times	Hardly ever	Never	Don't know
Protective						
Passive						
Encouraging						
Sensitive						
Just						
Unpredictable						

Which characteristics are the same for both your mother and God?

_____

_____

_____

_____

_____

Which characteristics are quite different (two or more boxes away from each other)?

_____

_____

_____

_____

_____

What patterns (if any) do you see?

_____

_____

_____

_____

_____

_____

Write a summary paragraph about how your perception of God has been shaped by your relationship with your mother.

_____

_____

_____

_____

_____

_____

_____

_____

_____

WHAT IS THE GOD IMAGE?

The God image can be best understood by contrasting it with the God concept. The *God concept* is the intellectual understanding of God (Lawrence, 1997). It is based on what is taught about God in catechism or Sunday school, Bible studies, and sermons. The God concept is an objective and abstract understanding of God. Most individuals reared in the Christian faith have a God concept that is characterized by love, strength, and wisdom. The *God image,* on the other hand, is the personal, emotional, and subjective experience of God (Lawrence, 1991). People need a consistent sense of self to feel secure, so they pattern future relationships after what they learned in their relationship with their parents. Their relationship with God is no different. If a child feels he or she has to be perfect to please his or her parents, then the child will feel he or she has to be perfect to please God. Conversely, if a child feels he or she can make mistakes and be accepted by his or her parents, then the child will feel he or she can make mistakes and be accepted by God.

To further illustrate the differences between the God concept and the God image, look at the drawings you did for Exercise 1. The first is meant to tap into your God concept. The directions are vague (Draw a picture of you and God) and are designed to trigger the response that you would give in everyday life. If someone asks you, "What is God like?" you will probably say "strong, loving, holy, and wise." Your picture may not display these characteristics, but if I were to ask you to explain it to me, you would probably use similar words and show me how you expressed them through your drawing.

The next picture probably tells a different story. This is meant to trigger your God image. It taps into a different part of your religious experience and asks you to draw how you *feel* you and God look when you do something wrong. Similarities probably exist between how you experience your God image when you do something wrong and how you experienced your parents when you did something wrong.

Theologically, the picture of the God concept should be no different from the picture of the God image. Time after time, however, this exercise has consistently revealed that the pictures are usually starkly different. The first may show God smiling, whereas the second shows God frowning. Other times God is hugging the person in the first picture but in the second God has His finger pointed and is berating the person for sinning. God is not surprised when people make mistakes. God's degree of love and acceptance does not decrease when people "blow it."

Why is it that people forget these beautiful truths when they are "in sin"? Why do they draw a completely un-Christian understanding of God instead of one that is Love personified? We can better answer these questions and gain a fuller understanding of the God image by reviewing how it has theoretically evolved.

Theoretical Development of the God Image

The God image has a rich psychoanalytic history. Freud initiated the study and published multiple volumes, case examples, and papers critiquing the neurotic use of religion by humankind. This paradigm ruled psychoanalytic theory until the work of D. W. Winnicott.

Winnicott did not address the issue as extensively as Freud, but he introduced the idea of transitional space, which challenged some of the main assumptions underlying Freud's arguments. Winnicott's work was left for later theorists to expound. The most notable of these is Ana-Maria Rizzuto. Her contributions and insights are invaluable. Others have furthered her thoughts and attempted to change the theory of the God image along with the changing currents in analytic theory. These theorists will be reviewed as well.

Though some of Freud's insights may have been borrowed, he crafted them in such a way that caused the scales to fall off the eyes of humankind (Ellenberger, 1970). His general theory of religion is well known. He stated that religion is a collective neurosis in which humans engage because they are not willing to accept that the universe is an impersonable and miserable place (Freud, 1927). Rather than "rationally" and "maturely" facing this "truth," humans imagine a loving God who is interested in who they are and concerned about their well-being. To Freud, Christianity is immature wish fulfillment. It is the result of a lack of courage to stand and face the truth that this is a difficult and lonely existence.

Freud undoubtedly contended with religious issues of his own (Jones, 1991; Lewis, 1967; Meissner, 1984). He did not know that future thinkers and analysts would turn his theory back on him. Their argument is as follows: If a person projects his or her wishes onto God, what does it mean if he or she projects the wish that a God does not exist? Furthermore, what does it mean if the person spends a good part of his or her life trying to convince humanity that no such thing as a deity exists, and even worse, what if it seems as if he or she obsesses over the issue, is completely one sided, and is overly hostile? It might lead one to suspect a type of *reaction formation,* which is a defense in which a person compensates by moving far in the opposite direction of what he or she actually believes. The bulky bodybuilder who inside feels weak and the intellectual who deep down believes himself or herself to be a moron represent examples of reaction formation. Along these lines, some have suggested that Freud was deeply religious but was terrified of this impulse and compensated by going in an extreme antireligious direction. Despite his prejudice and attempt to shock humankind out of what he viewed as collective denial, he has managed to make significant contributions to the psychology of religion.

Freud's theory of how individuals develop the God image contains the germ of what would later characterize object-relations theory. It examines how a boy uses his relationship with his father to unconsciously construct his God image. Freud was very paternalistic, so he minimized the importance of the mother's relationship with her child in the formation of the God image and did not even explain how females internalized a sense of God (Rizzuto, 1979). Research has since shown that both parents play significant roles in the formation of the God image and that boys and girls internalize the God image in much the same manner (Beit-Hallahmi & Argyle, 1975; Buri & Mueller, 1993).

One of Freud's main theoretical constructs that is closely associated with formation of the God image is the Oedipus complex. The complex usually begins and ends between the ages of four and six (Brenner, 1973). It is characterized by an intense longing to have the parent of the opposite sex completely to oneself. This desire gives rise to wishes of destroying the parent of the same sex. These primal desires are too overwhelming for the child and he or she fears that the parent of the same sex will retaliate and harm him or her. This anxiety is too intense, so the child represses his or her desires for the parent of the opposite sex. However, before repressing his desires a boy feels "a jealous rage against his mother for her rejection . . . and this . . . gives rise to a wish to get rid of her (kill her) and to be loved by his father in her place" (Brenner, 1973, p. 109). The energy is then transferred to the father. The previous feelings for the father now are felt about the mother, and the boy fears that she will harm him. Hence, the intense feelings for both parents become repressed (i.e., the threatening thoughts and feelings are transferred from the conscious mind to the unconscious mind). Once this occurs, the boy realizes he cannot live out his omnipotent fantasies and the Oedipus complex is resolved (Brenner, 1973). As a result of this resolution, the parental images are introjected into the psyche, which results in the formation of the superego.

This developmental time is also pivotal for the formation of the God image. It is at this time that the image of the parents and the superego become merged with the cultural idea of God. In the unconscious these representations merge and form the God image (Rizzuto, 1979).

The previous scenario happens in the normal situation. However, if the Oedipus complex is not resolved and repression does not occur, the children then have residual conflicts. For boys, if the charge for the father is not sublimated, then it resurfaces in his relationship with God. The longing for the father gets transferred onto God and manifests in a highly emotional relationship with God. These individuals are overly concerned with their God image and are slavishly preoccupied with trying to win God's approval.

This process usually happens when a male's relationship with his father is broken or absent (Rizzuto, 1979). Freud (who focused solely on males regarding this issue) observed that the religious zeal dwindles once the father, or a father surrogate, re-establishes a relationship with the man. Much of the energy that connects the person with his God image is then channeled away from the God image and toward the father or father surrogate. As a result, the man's interest in his God image decreases as his emotional relationship with his father, or father surrogate, increases.

The Oedipus complex is no longer seen as the centerpiece of psychodynamic thought. The internalization process that it highlighted is still key, but the accompanying conjectures of deep longings and intense fears are now largely discounted. The emphasis is now on the drive to relate rather than on the instinctual urges that Freud originally posited with such certainty. Freud's thoughts pointed to the right underlying principles, but his accompanying descriptions are now seen as outdated and nonessential.

Donald Winnicott (1971), a British psychoanalyst, introduced the next idea that transformed our understanding of the God image. Unlike Freud, he focused on the intricacies of the mother-child relationship. He conceptualized infants as dependent, amorphous forms who grow out of the mirroring love of the mother. Mother-child relationships are unique in that the mother is connected to the child in a way that allows her to almost magically meet her infant's needs before they are expressed. This remarkable synchronicity enables infants to believe that they and the mother are one. This omnipotent feeling is necessary to the healthy development of infants. As infants grow they are gradually able to tolerate increasing amounts of frustration. The mother adjusts her level of need satisfaction accordingly so the babies experience optimal amounts of frustration. As the children are weaned, they begin to realize that they are separate from their mother and are able to differentiate between *me* and *not me*. It is at this time that the infants move into the intermediate realm of experience.

The intermediate realm of experience is known as *transitional space* (Winnicott, 1971). It is the space between the external and the internal worlds. The space is neither completely subjective nor completely objective, but instead incorporates aspects of the two. Winnicott (1971) states,

> It is an area that is not challenged, because no claim is made on its behalf except that it shall exist as a resting-place for the individual engaged in the perpetual human task of keeping inner and outer reality separate yet interrelated. (p. 2)

Central to this developmental stage is the discovery of a transitional object. This object can take on a variety of forms, but is usually a stuffed animal or blanket. The object symbolizes the mother. It soothes and reduces anxiety and helps infants navigate through the new experience of separating and individuating.

To illustrate this concept to my students, I bring in a sharpei (the overly wrinkly looking dog) stuffed animal, affectionately known as Beans. I pass Beans around the class and ask each of the students to get an idea as to how Beans is feeling. Beans has a neutral face; he doesn't look happy or sad. His neutrality makes it easy for my students to project whatever they are feeling onto him. After all of them have finished looking at Beans I have them volunteer how they perceived Beans was feeling. Each student offers a different response, which, of course, corresponds to his or her particular mood.

Beans is a good transitional object because he is external, outside the self—not purely subjective or imaginary, and internal—each of us is allowed to project our own feelings onto him. Doing this makes him special to each of us and allows us to experience him in whatever way we need to. This idea easily translates to the God image. Most of us agree that God exists and is external, but each of us perceives God internally in a different manner. This allows the God image to be validated by others because it exists outside the self and to be personally meaningful because it is experienced inside the self.

This theory also suggests that it is not "irrational" or "infantile," as Freud suggested, to have a personal relationship with God. We have multiple parts of ourselves, some rational, some nonrational or above reason, and some irrational. The integrating of these different aspects of ourselves allows us to fully experience faith. Winnicott (1971) celebrated humans not being purely rational beings, but instead imaginative, emotional, and creative creatures. If our only experience of this world was rational, what a dry and barren experience it would be! Meissner (1984) further explored the cultural use of transitional objects. Art, literature, theater, and music depend upon the dynamics of transitional space. In each genre the author of the work initiates an experience using a variety of symbols to draw listeners out of cold reality. Listeners perceive the symbols from within and color them with subjective meaning. At this point listeners leave the rational world and imbue the current experience with a host of characteristics, some of which are beauty, love, joy, and freedom.

Ana-Maria Rizzuto (1979), in several scholarly contributions, has furthered our understanding of how the God image is a special kind of transitional object. Her greatest contribution was in interpreting the God image theory through the lens of object-relations theory. The next section reviews her work in detail.

Another contribution came from the work of M. H. Spero and John McDargh. Traditionally, in psychodynamic theory, the divine was reduced to a stew of drives, memories, and current relationships. Spero (1990) and McDargh (1983), independent of each other, suggested that a real God could exist apart from our perceptions who is interested in interacting with and changing humankind. Spero (1990) postulated that our relationships with our caregivers provided us with a relational template through which we connect to God. Through this process, a person projects his or her parental images onto his or her God image, which then connects with the real God. The real God, along with the projected images, communicates back with the person. As a result of this communication, he or she reinternalizes a modified, healthier God image.

Even people who do not believe that God exists can agree with the argument that the God image affects the self of religious individuals and can affect their other relationships. For example, Spero (1990) argues that a woman who is angry with God but fears His retaliation might repress her anger and displace it by becoming angry at someone else. The God image then, in a very real way, has impacted her sense of self and at least one other relationship.

McDargh (1983) agrees with Spero and argues that if others can affect one's view of God, then one's view of God can affect one's view of the self and others. In his words, "developments in the individual's conscious and unconscious relationship to his or her God representations may have implications for transmuting and transforming other internalizations" (p. 262). McDargh (1983) and Spero (1990) take a bold step and argue that the God image, and the God behind the God image, influence people and their relationships.

To recap, Freud emphasized the dysfunctional resolution of the Oedipus complex in the formation of the God image. Winnicott challenged Freud's assertions by introducing the healthy, nonrational need for transitional objects and transitional space. Rizzuto furthered Winnicott's thought and transformed the theory of the God image by viewing it through the lens of object relations. Finally, Spero and McDargh indicated that behind the God image could be a God who is interested in interacting with and changing humankind.

HOW DOES THE GOD IMAGE DEVELOP?

Ana-Maria Rizzuto (1979) has dedicated much of her life to discovering how the God image develops. She traced the development of the God image through the life cycle. The following review is based on her research.

Most religious parents engage in all sorts of rituals before their children are even born. First is the naming process. This is usually imbued with a significant amount of religious meaning. The parents are thinking about who their children will be, and, more unconsciously, what they want their children to be (Rizzuto, 1979). This is symbolized by choosing a name. Children then come into the world, tagged with a meaningful name and with a script that the parents would like their children to follow. Part of the process of becoming effective parents is giving up the fantasy of what children should be and instead allowing children the freedom to become who they are.

The next religious process is the dedication ceremony. Depending upon the tradition that children are born into, it is likely that before they are even aware they have already been symbolically dedicated to God (Rizzuto, 1979). The power these rituals hold over children is difficult to measure. However, what is even more difficult to measure is the parents' implicit views of the significance of their children's birth. Were the children planned for, or were they a "mistake"? One can easily decipher if parents view their children as gifts or as something they wish they could return. These external and internal processes mark attitudes that parents have toward their children. Because these attitudes are religious and meaningful in nature, as children develop they come to view themselves as either a gift from God or a random mistake.

The mother-infant relationship will determine whether children think that others, the universe, and God can be trusted (the word *mother* here also encompasses such labels as *father* or *grandmother* or *primary caretaker* and is in no way restricted to what we traditionally think of when we hear the word *mother*) (Rizzuto, 1979). Trust is not logically debated between mother and children but is instead conveyed through the attitude the mother has toward her infants (Winnicott, 1971). If the mother loves, accepts, and meets the needs of her infants, then infants conclude that others, the universe, and God can be trusted. If mothers are too busy and neglect or abuse their children, then the children will conclude that others, the universe, and God cannot be trusted.

When the former is experienced, infants feel safe. Infants can then honor their internal drive toward individuation and slowly separate from their mother. If they do not feel safe, then they will feel that they need to remain with their mother. They will not grow and separate from the mother, but will instead feel that growth is bad and that if they separate from their mother bad things will happen.

This stage has a tremendous impact on the God image (Rizzuto, 1979). Children, later as adults, will play out this same pattern with God. If they can trust their mother, then as an adult they will experience God as mature and loving. If they cannot trust their mother, then they will later experience God as a needy parent that demands too much. They may not be aware of this, but their behavior will be characterized by a great fear that if they grow too much or become too independent, then God will be unhappy and abandon them. This same fear marked their early experience of their mother. In their childhood mind, they concluded, "Growth is bad because it separates me from Mom. If I grow too much, then Mom becomes cold and abandons me. I don't like feeling alone, so I'll stay close to Mom so I won't feel rejected."

The next stage children enter, at approximately three years old, is the transitional stage (Rizzuto, 1979; Winnicott, 1971). This is marked by the development of the imagination. In a short period of time the internal world becomes populated with a variety of creatures. Elves, witches, monsters, and superheroes are some of the more popular dwellers. These imaginary creatures are utilized in play and fantasy to help children adapt to their internal and external world. In this new-found magical world, God is officially introduced.

It does not take children long to figure out that God is not like the other creatures that populate their mind (Rizzuto, 1979). Instead, God is taken seriously. Parents speak sternly about God, visit God's house, and meet with God's representatives. These are the people who are dressed in robes, who sing songs, and who tell stories about God. With this information, children begin to shape their image of God. From the behavior of adults and environmental cues, children realize that God is apparently in charge of everything, is all-powerful, and is all knowing. Children know only two other people who fit the same description: Mom and Dad. Out of necessity, children craft their God image in the likeness of their parents. If the parent-child relationship is healthy, then the God image will be healthy. If the parent-child relationship is pathological, then the God image will be pathological.

The God image is further shaped by the curiosity of children (Rizzuto, 1979). Children question everything: "Who made the sky? Where does God live? How old is God? Does God cry?" During this period children also believe that their parents know everything that they do as well as all of their thoughts. This belief is also translated to God.

The next stage of development is the oedipal phase. As mentioned earlier, it occurs between the ages of approximately four to six, and is marked by intense feelings for the parent of the opposite sex. In a healthy family, the child is able to navigate this conflict with success. The child will slowly come to the conclusion that he or she cannot have the parent of the opposite sex all to himself or herself. This is a great loss to the child, but instead of facing this reality entirely, the child unconsciously transfers all of his (her) feelings over to his (her) father (mother). He (She) no longer longs for his (her) mother (father) because he (she) sensed he (she) could not safely win all of her (his) attention; instead, now, the child hopes to win all of his (her) father's (mother's) attention. Gradually, the child becomes aware that this is not going to occur either. The child then realizes that he or she will have to wait until he or she is older to have an adult relationship. At that point, the child will see his or her parents from a more objective stance. Also, at that time, a conscious differentiation between parents and God occurs. The child now knows that his or her parents cannot hear his or her internal dialogue, but the child still thinks God can (Rizzuto, 1979).

The child who grows up in a dysfunctional family has a much more difficult time with this conflict. Because the child's fundamental needs were never satisfied, he or she will not be able to let go of his or her desire to wholly possess another. As a result, the child will constantly seek out others in an attempt to complete himself or herself. This feeling of wholeness will never be captured, and as the child moves into adolescence he or she will lock onto his or her God image in an attempt to satisfy this deep longing. The child's relationship with God will be considered highly charged. Unfortunately, this relationship will not satisfy his or her inner needs.

Similar to most traditional psychoanalysts, Rizzuto believes that at the close of the oedipal phase the child's self and the God image are almost completely fixed. She posits that two other phases in life exist in which the God image can experience minimal amounts of change (Rizzuto, 1979). The first is puberty, when the ability to think abstractly develops. The second is early adulthood, when the person has to make a variety of internal changes to adjust to the new responsibilities of life. These adjustments will affect the way the God image has been shaped but will be minimal in comparison with the earlier experiences.

Rizzuto's thoughts are helpful in understanding how the God image develops throughout the life cycle. Her views are very traditional and emphasize that the self and the God image are more or less solidified at age six. Most dynamic theorists see these initial years as very important, but they no longer believe that the self and God image are crystallized in early childhood. The self and the God image are now seen as much more fluid, adaptable, and amendable to change.

It used to be thought that the only way to change the self and the God image was through intensive psychoanalysis (three to five times a week at the tune of $16,000 per year). This belief is still held by a few diehards, but most now hold that long-term treatment is not needed to evoke significant change in the self and the God image. In fact, some research has shown that the majority of change occurs in the first eight to twelve sessions (Kopta, Howard, Lowry, & Beutler, 1994).

Two recent studies support the shift toward thinking that the self and the God image are not fixed in childhood but can significantly change through therapy in adulthood. The first study, by Tisdale et al. (1997), focused on the effectiveness of an inpatient object-relations based program on self-esteem, level of object-relations development, and God image. The researchers found that treatment significantly improved the clients' view of themselves as well as their view of God. The second study, by Cheston, Piedmont, Eanes, & Lavin (2003) sought to test whether short-term psychotherapy (without explicit intervention to change the God image) would result in a decrease in symptoms and improvement of the God image. They found that the treatment did result in a decrease of symptoms and did improve the clients' God images. After therapy, the God image was experienced as significantly more loving and compassionate.

In sum, the God image develops along with the growing personality (Rizzuto, 1979). Many important aspects of the formation of the God image occur earlier in life, when, via the relationship with the primary caregivers, children come to a variety of conclusions about others, the universe, and God. The first conclusion is whether God can be trusted. The second is whether God wants them to grow. The third determines whether they are able to distinguish between their parents and their God image. Traditional psychoanalysts believe that the self and the God image are fixed at age six, but most psychodynamic theorists now believe, and research has shown, that the self and the God image can undergo significant change through psychotherapy.

WHAT DOES YOUR GOD IMAGE REVEAL?

Now that you have gone through the exercises and have a general understanding of the God image and how it develops, you are ready to review your responses and figure out what they mean. The God image drawings exercises will be discussed first, followed by the Parent/God image grids. Having a good intellectual and emotional understanding of how your God image developed is essential to learning how to help others discover their own God image. It is necessary that you take your time and internalize the information, so you can later use it to help others.

Take a minute and review the drawings you did for the first exercise. What differences do you notice between the first and the second drawings? How does God respond to you in the first picture? How does God respond to you in the second picture? Do you see any similarities or differences between how you experienced your parents when you did something wrong and how you currently experience God when you do something you regret? Consider your second drawing and write down your responses to the following questions:

1. How is God feeling?
2. How are you feeling?
3. On a scale of one to five (1 = close; 5 = distant), how close to or distant from God do you feel? Why?
4. If you feel distant, what do you usually do to feel close again?

Now summarize your answers in a paragraph:

_____

_____

_____

_____

_____

_____

_____

_____

_____

_____

The second exercise yields more detailed information about how your childhood experience of your caregivers affects your current experience of God. The interpretation of this exercise is more obvious than the first. The questions that were asked in this exercise should be reviewed now. Take your time and think about your responses. Pay particular attention to the characteristics that your experience of God shares with your parents.

The negative characteristics (e.g., demanding, distant) that you answered "always" and "very often" are more of a central part of your person and experience of your parents and God image than are characteristics that you answered "hardly ever" or "never." "Always" and "very often" characteristics will therefore be more difficult to change. The same is true with positive characteristics that you experienced as "hardly ever" or "never." These positive characteristics were consistently lacking in your experience of your parents and your God image, and will therefore be more difficult to let yourself feel and experience. This does not mean these characteristics cannot change; it just means that these characteristics became a stronger part of your personality throughout your development and will therefore be more difficult to change.

INTEGRATING THE MATERIAL

Now that you have reviewed the exercises, it is time to integrate the material. Relax. Meditate on how your caregivers impacted your experience of God. Do not rush. Do not hurry the process. Delve into it; saturate yourself with this material so you fully understand and internalize the concepts. Do you see how your childhood experience of your caregivers impacts the way you experience God? If you do not, *do not continue*. Go back and review it again. This part is absolutely crucial. If you do not internalize and understand these principles, then the rest of the material will not be as powerful or meaningful to you.

Once you understand the information, I highly recommend that you take additional steps to strengthen your grasp on these concepts. You know yourself best, so I recommend that you integrate this information in the same manner that you apply other material to your life. Different people find particular techniques more or less helpful. What follows is a brief list of things you can do to better internalize this information.

1. You can find someone you trust, a partner or a close friend, and explain it to them. This person should also be a good listener who is empathic and interested in understanding and helping

you. When discussing this information, stay close to your feelings and explain what was personally meaningful to you about the exercises. If you do not have someone such as this that you can talk to, then you can try the following options.

2. You can pray about it. Center yourself, open up, and express your thoughts and feelings to God; then, quiet yourself and listen.

3. You can express your thoughts out loud, record them, and then replay them to yourself. Sometimes stepping outside yourself and hearing yourself think out loud can help you see things in a clear and different manner.

4. You can draw a picture of how you feel about how your experience with childhood caregivers affects your image of God. Often, expressing yourself pictorially brings you closer to your feelings. Words sometimes act as a hindrance and obscure our true feelings. Drawing or painting crosses the verbal barrier and allows you to gain more insight into what the material is saying to you.

5. If you are kinesthetically inclined you might find that acting out your thoughts and feelings is more helpful than writing or pictorially symbolizing them.

The particular techniques you choose to further integrate this information really do not matter. What matters is that you take the time and put your thoughts together and feel your feelings so that it makes intellectual and affective sense to you. You need to have both a cognitive and an emotional understanding in order for this material to change you. If you do not integrate this material into your life you will not be able to walk anyone else through the process. It is necessary that you have a strong understanding so that you can walk others down the same path, particularly those with depression.

Chapter 3

The God Image: Self, Depression, and Christian Thought

WHAT IS THE SELF?

At first this question may seem to have a rather obvious answer, but as soon as you begin to probe beneath the surface of your response you will see that it is much more difficult to define. Social psychologists have been arguing for years over the different ingredients and processes that make up the self. They are far from a definite conclusion but have agreed on a number of aspects.

The self is defined as an interpersonal tool that enables us to maintain a sense of consistency (Baumeister, 1995). It is formed through development and is the means by which people maintain a sense of constancy with their past, their present, and their expected future. The self operates as a filtering system and hones in on important information at the expense of other information. People attend to a number of variables throughout the day, and they spend the majority of their time attending to information that is consistent with who they think they are. In this way, the self is similar to a pair of glasses that are always worn. These glasses make people aware of information, events, and relationships that are pertinent to confirming who they are.

The self is the main component of the personality that influences the other subcomponents of the person. It is the master switch—when it is affected all the other parts are affected. The self can also be thought of as a major river that branches off into many other smaller rivers. If you wanted to clean the rivers you would focus on the main river because it supplies water to the smaller rivers. Similarly, change that affects the self affects the other parts of the personality.

The self influences the way a person emotionally experiences God. Benson & Spilka (1973) discovered that individuals with high self-esteem had a positive God image, whereas those with low self-esteem had a negative God image. If people have high self-esteem, then it is likely they will feel that God loves them. If they have low self-esteem, then it is likely they will feel that God does not love them. The results of this study make intuitive sense. Think about it: How often do you find people who think they are a complete failure be also convinced that God is absolutely crazy about them? On the other hand, how often do you find people who have high self-esteem convinced that God regrets creating them? These situations are abnormal; they usually do not happen. The reason they do not happen is because people's idea of self and idea of how God feels about them are usually consistent. These ideas are similar because the self has a natural tendency toward maintaining consistency. When the self changes, the God image will change along with it.

Michael Boivin (2003) has written a fascinating article titled "Finding God in Prozac or Finding Prozac in God." He discusses the role that this antidepressant has played in changing the self and God image of religious individuals. These individuals prayed, read scriptures, and used other spiritual disciplines, but did not experience relief from depression or an increase in their experience of God's love. Similar to psychotherapy, Prozac affected the self of these individuals, resulting in a decrease of depressive symptoms and an increase in their spiritual walk with God. In writing about Prozac, Boivin (2003) states, "[it is] not that it can enhance emotional or psychological well-being where prayer did not; rather that it reveals to us more than ever just how interwoven the biochemistry of the brain is to who we are and how we relate to each other and to God" (p.161).

Another theory that supports the self and God image relationship is attachment theory, which is based on the work of John Bowlby (1969) and focuses on the way that infants bond with their caregivers. The way the mother, or primary caregiver, interacts with the infant causes that infant to develop a certain way of relating to others. If the caregiver is empathic and attends to the infant's needs, then the child develops a secure attachment style (Ainsworth, 1978). If the caregiver is cold, distant, inconsistent, or abusive, then the child will develop an insecure attachment style. These attachment styles are stable and stay with the infant throughout childhood and adolescence and into adulthood (Hazan & Shaver, 1987). For example, the attachment style a boy develops in childhood will likely be the attachment style he has as an adult. If he had an insecure attachment to his mother, then he will likely have an insecure attachment to his wife.

As one might expect, individuals with secure attachment styles typically have a positive relationship with God. Sticking with this sense of consistency one would also expect that those with an insecure attachment style would have a negative relationship with God. Interestingly, however, this is not often the case. Frequently people who have insecure relationships with parents report highly spiritual behavior and a close relationship with God. This seeming paradox is explained by compensation theory, which states that when persons experience deficits in early relationships, they attempt to compensate for these needs through a highly personal relationship with God (Kirkpatrick & Shaver, 1990). Halcrow, Hall, & Hill (2003) solve this riddle by postulating that individuals with an insecure attachment with their primary caregiver still have an insecure attachment with God but attempt to compensate for this attachment by overt religious behaviors that mimic a secure relationship with God.

We have been discussing the way that the self affects the God image and I'm sure some of you might be thinking, *What about the other way around? Can a God image that becomes more positive result in a healthier self?* I wish I could give a resounding yes to this question, but no serious research has been conducted to assess whether this is the case. Despite this lack of research, I firmly believe that changing the God image can change the self.

What we do have, however, is a rich history of God breaking through and drastically affecting the lives of many individuals. It is difficult to differentiate between the effects of the God image and the real God, but most of us believe that the real God impacts us in many ways. Few of us have heard God's voice speak to us out loud or have been knocked off a horse like Saint Paul, but many of us have had our own numinous experiences that have changed our lives in both large and small ways.

Apart from Christian history and our own personal experiences of God, a few researchers have made some key points that support the role the God image plays in affecting the self. Propst (1980) compared religious and nonreligious imagery in the treatment of mild depression in religious people. She found that religious imagery is more helpful for people who are depressed than nonreligious imagery is. An example of religious imagery would be a person imagining Christ helping him or her cope with a difficult situation. Propst, Ostrom, Watkins, Dean, & Mashburn (1992) conducted a study that showed religiously oriented cognitive therapy and pastoral counseling were superior to nonreligious cognitive therapy with religious clients.

These studies show that God often plays a role in therapy. How strong of a role? This is a question we simply cannot answer yet. Cheston et al. (2003) reflect, "if one's perception of God has a direct effect on psychological well-being, then an individual's image of God represents a factor in one's psychological stability. Disturbances in one's relationship with God may exacerbate or even create psychological symptoms" (p. 104). This area of research is still in its infancy, but I believe the research will bear out what faith has indicated all along: that our relationship with God is a contributor to our psychological health and influences the way we see ourselves and others.

In sum, the self is an interpersonal tool that enables people to maintain a sense of consistency with their past, their present, and their anticipated future. The self is a filter, or a metaphorical pair of glasses we wear, that causes us to focus on information that confirms our self-understanding and to ignore information that is contrary to our sense of identity (Baumeister, 1995). This need for consistency affects all relationships, including the relationship with God. Studies have shown that people with low self-esteem have a negative relationship with God, whereas people with high self-esteem have a positive relationship with God (Benson & Spilka, 1973). Finally, though research has not "proven" it yet, we have a rich biblical history and many personal experiences that support the assertion that God can evoke positive and sustaining change in the self.

HOW DOES THE PERSON WITH DEPRESSION EXPERIENCE GOD?

People with depression experience God in a similar manner to how they experienced their parents. A brief summary of the development of the depressive character follows. For a more in-depth view, turn back to Chapter 1.

Individuals with depression usually come from homes in which their parents were experienced as cold, distant, neglectful, preoccupied, and/or abusive. Children need to feel that their parents love and care for them in order to feel safe. When they do not feel this kindness and affection, children turn their anger inward and begin to believe that they are "damaged" or "bad" in order to justify their parents' harmful behavior (McWilliams, 1994). This redirection of anger from their parents to themselves helps them adapt. It allows them to believe that their parents are "good" and therefore all they have to do is fix themselves in order to win their parents' love. Their hope is that by becoming the perfect children, they can get their parents to love them. Unfortunately, of course, this does not happen. The children never arrive at perfection or succeed in gaining the love they deserve. Instead, they are continually blamed for their parents' problems and treated as if they are worthless. Paradoxically, feeling guilty and rejected feels safe because it is consistent and controllable.

As children continue to develop and move through adolescence and into adulthood, these patterns will be re-created in their relationships, particularly their relationship with God. Such individuals will use their God image as a means of continuing where their parents ended, maintaining the underlying feelings that result in depression. Their experience of God will share the characteristics of the disorder: a sense of worthlessness, guilt, fear of rejection, and perfectionism.

Individuals who are depressed feel that God sees them as worthless. As children, they often feel as if they were a mistake and should not have been born because their parents were overwhelmed and unable to fully care for them. As a result, they often feel as if God regrets creating them. It is not uncommon for them to feel as if they are a burden to Him. People who are depressed do not feel as if they are the children of God; instead, they feel as if they are stepchildren or orphans who deserve to be rejected. They do not feel they are part of the family, but instead feel as if they are unwanted outsiders.

The God image of those who are depressed also evokes a tremendous amount of guilt. The pathological God image is armed with the secrets of the past and uses old skeletons to make them feel rotten and repulsive. People who are depressed seldom talk about these situations and instead repress them and keep them hidden. Secrets are similar to bacteria—the more you keep them in the dark the stronger and more powerful they grow. The shame depressed people feel about their secrets infuses their God image with a powerful, unholy wrath. Often, they are most ashamed of harms perpetrated on them by more powerful others. However, in the darkness of their minds, these memories become twisted and they end up blaming themselves for experiences that they suffered at the hands of others. Their harmful God image constantly reminds them of these unconfessed secrets and uses them to make the person feel filthy and deserving of rejection.

The fear of rejection they experience from God has its roots in the rejection they felt from their caregivers. As children, it became crystal clear that they were to repress their own strivings in order to please their parents. Their parents were too insecure to realize that they could let their children be independent and still love them. As a result, individuals who are depressed transfer their parents' insecurity onto God and feel that any time they grow or become more autonomous that God is going to abandon them. In addition, this God image, just as a needy and angry parent, cannot tolerate anything but happy feelings and positive feedback. People who are depressed cannot turn to their God image for comfort or help in time of need. Their God is too preoccupied and cannot be bothered or roused from self-reverie. They are doomed to struggle and manage their pain on their own and not burden their God with negative issues or complaints of any sort.

People who are depressed implicitly feel that God expects them to be perfect. Their God image, similar to their parents, is very critical and judgmental. This God image knows nothing of mercy and instead focuses on weaknesses. It is not interested in discussing positive or even neutral qualities, but instead wants to concentrate on negative characteristics, the areas where the person comes up short. Unfortunately, not much can be done that this God image is pleased with. Even performances that were good are quickly dismissed. The person could have done nine things right, but the God image of the depressed person will magnify the one thing the person did wrong.

Individuals who are depressed attempt perfection to win God's love. They are motivated by the same threat that was used by their parents—if they are not perfect they will be abandoned and rejected. When they fail in their attempt to be perfect, they feel the intense pain of rejection that they originally experienced from their parents, only now they feel this rejection more frequently. As children, they could behave in "bad" ways and get away with it without their parents knowing. Now, however, the angry parents live within, and nothing escapes God's penetrating eyes. As a result, they will feel guilty for everything they do that is less than perfect.

In their world, the only way to defend against overwhelming feelings of guilt and rejection is to maintain a state of perfection. After a

"failure" they will redouble their efforts and keep an even more scru-
pulous eye on their behavior. As long as they are perfect, God will
love them and they will not feel separated from his acceptance. Unfortunately for them, people are not perfect. Eventually, people who
are depressed break down and end up expressing their sinful side in
one way or another. At this point, the cycle is started all over again
(see Figure 3.1).

Case Examples

This section reintroduces Bob and Lilith from Chapter 1 and discusses how each of them experience God. Their cases will be briefly
reviewed to remind you who they are. To further review their histories, please turn back to Chapter 1.

Bob is a thirty-seven-year-old clergy person who is depressed and feels like
he cannot win God's approval or acceptance. He grew up with a father who
abused alcohol and who was extremely critical and rejecting of him. His
mother was passive and failed to protect him from his father's painful insults.
Bob blamed himself for his problems with this father and thought it was his
responsibility to mend their relationship. This, despite Bob's efforts, never
happened. In his early adult years, Bob married Joan. He described their
marriage as "okay," but referred to himself as a "terrible" husband. Shortly after marrying, Bob went on to the seminary and gained a solid theological understanding of the faith.

In seminary, Bob learned of a loving and accepting God, but these beliefs
were stuck in his head and never made it to his heart. The God he cognitively
understood was different from the God he emotionally experienced. The

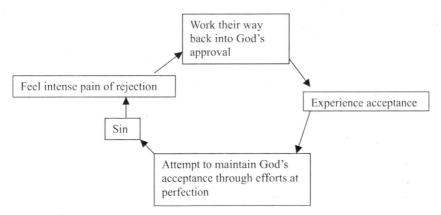

FIGURE 3.1. Religious Perfection Cycle

God he experienced seemed much more personal, real, and alive to him than the God he learned about in seminary. This God was felt and immediate, whereas the Christian God was abstract and removed. The hurtful God's edicts were automatically convincing, whereas the real God's tenets were ideas he had to deliberately think about to believe. Ironically, it seemed natural and easier to believe in this false and painful God than it was to believe in the true and healing real God.

This belief in the false God occurred effortlessly because it resembled Bob's relationship with his father. Bob often felt like he fell short and could have done better. As a result, he felt he deserved the harsh judgments and negative criticism he received from his harmful God image. He evaluated his performances and concluded that he could be a more loving husband, could be a more available pastor, and could be a better Christian. Because Bob did not do these things perfectly, in his mind, he felt justifiably disapproved of.

Bob's God image was a taskmaster that expected more from Bob than he could realistically give. As a result, Bob usually felt guilty and like he should have accomplished more. As one might guess, the idea of taking personal time was something that his brain could not compute. If he did take the morning off he would feel crippled with guilt and would not find relief until he made it into the office.

His God image also shared similarities with his relationship with his mother. Bob could not approach his God with concerns or complaints for fear that bringing up less-than-positive issues would result in emotional abandonment. Bob, as a young child, got the message that he was to keep a smiling face on despite his pain. He transferred this to his God image and, as a result, did not feel comfortable approaching God with painful issues or complaints about situations he did not understand. Instead, Bob felt it was his job to manage these burdens on his own.

Bob's God was not one of unmerited grace, but one of earned salvation. He had to perform to win a pat on the back. Bob would do his best to live a clean and holy life, but, like all of us, he would inevitably slip up. This God that tolerated him when he was close to perfect became angry and shaming whenever Bob missed the mark. At these times, he sensed God's displeasure and felt like he had to earn his way back into His good graces. Bob would repent and spend lengthy amounts of time in prayer to prove that he was sorry. He would try his hardest not to slip up again. After about two weeks of prayer and worship, Bob would feel welcomed back again by God. Unfortunately, it was only a matter of time until he did something he regretted, and would then once again find himself feeling rejected and ashamed for what he had done—disgusted with himself for failing once again.

Lilith is a forty-five-year-old woman who is depressed and feels like she is "letting God down." She presents as a serious, put-together woman with mature interests. She was raised primarily by her mother who was very concerned with keeping up appearances. As a child, Lilith was expected to be adultlike and well mannered. She conformed to her mother's wishes and disowned the playful and childlike parts of herself. She has been married for twenty years to a man who is very similar to her mother. She unknowingly describes her relationship with her husband in terms she uses to describe her relationship with her mother. Lilith characterizes their relationship as "good," but hints that her husband is subtly controlling. She serves as a deacon at a local congregation and plays a strong role in many church functions. Despite being actively involved in the church and devoutly religious, she often feels that God disapproves of her.

She understands the faith and is extremely familiar with the liturgy, but the words seem empty. She believes in propitiation but cannot seem to feel forgiven. She cognitively grasps the idea of salvation through faith but feels driven to prove her worth through works.

In many ways, her relationship with God is like her relationship with her mother. Her mother expected her to be a strong woman who always had things under control. Similarly, she feels God expects her to appear strong, even if inside she feels weak. Lilith's mother was not interested in how she felt inside and instead focused on how she looked to others. Likewise, Lilith does not feel that God is interested in her, but is instead concerned with how she is perceived by others. Lilith's mother was austere and distant. Similarly, Lilith's God is cold and removed. He is not affectionate or personal. He has expectations but no encouragement. He has demands but no directions. Her God is like the boss who leaves a list of orders and returns at the end of the day only to make sure tasks were accomplished.

Lilith seems like a pawn in the hands of her God. She is not a unique person with individual gifts and a call but is instead just another cog in the machine. She seems to be nothing more than a statistic. Her God is not interested in who she is but in what she does. This God expects her to be a human doing, rather than a human being (Bradshaw, 1988).

She attempts to stay focused on keeping her work and spiritual life ordered. However, unexpected distractions often happen and she cannot maintain her schedule. In addition, other periods occur when she gets depressed and exhausted. During these times, she cannot accomplish all that she expects of herself. She has a tremendously difficult time listening to her depressive symptoms. She ignores them until she feels like she has to rest and recover, but then she feels God's displeasure. As a result, she picks herself up and starts working just as fast as before. Her God, like a demanding boss, is not interested in her problems—he just wants the job done.

HOW IS THE GOD IMAGE RELATED
TO CHRISTIAN THOUGHT?

Humans live in an uncomfortable state of incompleteness. We intuitively know that something has gone awry, that we are supposed to be whole but are instead broken. We crave fullness but are instead wanting. We desire perfect health and love but cannot achieve it. Total wholeness is a longed-for state, but is always over the next hill or around the next corner. It is as if someone has played a cruel trick, for we have a taste for complete health but will never experience it. The sense of oneness that we long for is reminiscent of an earlier time.

Before the biblical fall of humankind, Adam and Eve existed in a state of oneness with God. They were 100 percent free, uninhibited, and innocent. After the fall, sin entered the world and they became separated from God and, consequently, self-aware. Adam and Eve no longer felt whole and were instead riddled with feeling incomplete.

White (1984) conceptualizes the imago Dei (i.e., the image of God in humankind—that which makes us uniquely human and God's children) as a deep hunger for the oneness that Adam and Eve originally experienced. Similar to these progenitors, each person begins in a state of oneness but eventually grows to be painfully aware of his or her inherent separateness. At infancy, the child is one with the caregiver and has a complete lack of self-awareness. The infant has a host of needs and is in a state of utter dependence. In a perfect world, or prior to the fall in Christian theology, none of these needs would go unmet. The person would exist in a beautiful state of wholeness. Unfortunately, parents do not meet the needs of their children in a perfect manner. As a result, children experience pain, which results in separation from the caregiver and corresponding self-awareness. All children come to learn that they are fundamentally separate from others and from God. Erich Fromm (1956) states,

> The awareness of separateness arouses anxiety; it is, indeed, the source of all anxiety . . . the deepest need of man is to overcome his separateness, to leave the prison of his aloneness . . . man—of all ages—is confronted with the solution of one and the same question: the question of how to overcome separateness, how to achieve union, how to transcend one's own individual life and find at-onement. (p. 8)

Gary Moon (1997), in his aptly titled book *Homesick for Eden*, discusses how this fundamental separation leaves us longing for God. He quotes Larry Crabb,

> Ever since God expelled Adam and Eve from the garden, we have lived in an unnatural environment—a world in which we were not designed to live. We were built to enjoy a garden without weeds, relationships without friction, fellowship without distance. But something is wrong and we know it, both within

our world and within ourselves. Deep inside we sense we're out
of the nest, always ending the day in a motel room and never at
home. (p. 11)

This longing for God calls to us and beckons us to answer it. People attempt to answer this call in a variety of ways. Faith, from this
perspective, is the manner in which people attempt to overcome their
separateness and gain completeness. Therefore, all people have faith,
because all people are compelled to try to gain wholeness (McDargh,
1983).

The way people choose to gain wholeness is intimately tied to their
personality. This is what gives meaning to their lives. Some people
profess certain theological beliefs but live in a way that suggests that
they value something other than their professed beliefs imply. This
underlying value system is what is referred to as faith—it is the
"stuff" of the personality. It is *not* the technical belief systems, the denominational tenets, or the way worship is conducted on Sunday
morning.

A person's faith is directly related to what he or she determines to
be ultimately important in life. Tillich (1958) explains,

> The dynamics of faith are the dynamics of man's ultimate con-
> cern . . . if it claims ultimacy it demands the total surrender of
> him who accepts the claim, and it promises total fulfillment
> even if all other claims have to be subjected to it or rejected in its
> name. (pp. 1-2)

All people are involved in pursuing what they determine to be of ultimate importance and, therefore, all people are involved in constructing a faith (Emmons, 1999). The dichotomy between secular and sacred is false. The executive who slaves in the office is just as involved
in his or her faith as is the seminarian who spends hours each day con-
templating the life of Christ.

That which is ultimately important in our life is our "god." We
worship it (e.g., financial security, success) in our day-to-day activities and devote ourselves to it, even if the concepts cannot be found in
any Christian creed. Due to our fallen state, we are compelled to worship to gain respite from our never-ending feeling of incompleteness.

This feeling of incompleteness motivates us to attempt to achieve
completeness. It is an innate drive toward wholeness. This feeling of

incompleteness is inescapable and popularly referred to as the "God-shaped hole in our hearts" or among intellectual types as the "existential vacuum." This great need caused Augustine to write his famous words, "Thou has made us for Thyself, O Lord, and our hearts are restless until they find rest in Thee."

People attempt to fill this void through faith. The object of their faith determines whether they are worshiping an idol or the true God. The attempt to fill what is reserved for the Divine with something that is not divine is referred to as idolatry. Jordan (1986) defines idolatry as "Anything relative that is raised to the absolute, the finite elevated to the infinite, or the transient given the status of the permanent" (p. 21). Money, fame, success, and power are some of the more obvious and popular idols that people worship. Gary Moon (1997) catalogs some of the behaviors people engage in when they worship idols. He refers to them as behavioral narcotics, which are "patterns and habits of behavior, relating, or coping which have been developed for the purpose of easing the emotional pain" (p. 42). What follows is his list of behavioral narcotics:

- *Habits of workaholism:* filling the mind so full of thoughts, dreams and activities of success that there is little room left to feel pain caused by irrational, underlying feelings of inadequacy
- *Habits of control:* constantly striving to maintain control of others, making their wills the servants of our own, and binding the hands we secretly fear will strike us
- *Habits of people pleasing:* constantly monitoring what others expect from us so that we can avoid the pain of their rejection by minimizing its likelihood; becoming in the process slaves of our servanthood
- *Habits of dependency:* always surrendering our will to the will of another (even to God) for reasons of fear and self-diagnosed inadequacy, instead of enjoying the freedom to follow the advice of love
- *Habits of perfectionism:* wearing a mask of perfection and rightness to cover inner turmoil and ambiguity
- *Habits of escape:* taking emotional vacations from pain through the use of alcohol, drugs, or self-destructive patterns of pain delaying behavior (Moon, 1997, p. 42)

Idols that are not as obvious are the ones that disguise themselves as God. Such idols are referred to as the God image: the subjective emotional experience of God that people craft from their early experience of their parents. Jordan (1986) outlines a number of key concepts that are helpful in conceptualizing the idolatrous role that the God image can play in a person's life.

- *Operational theology* is best understood in comparison with a person's "professed theology" (Jordan, 1986, p. 29). Professed theology refers to the explicit, abstract belief system that a person holds. For most Christians, this corresponds with the Nicene Creed. Operational theology, on the other hand, refers to the implicit, emotional belief system that is related to a person's early relationship with their parents. A couple of popular tenets of a depressed person's operational theology are "God gets upset when I am angry, so I should avoid expressing anger at all costs" or "God gets mad at me when I stand up for myself." Operational theology corresponds with the God image, whereas professed theology corresponds with the God concept.
- *Double idolatry* "refers to two related dimensions of psychic reality in which distorted and false perceptions of ultimate authority are directly linked with erroneous definitions and beliefs about one's self" (p. 27). The first idolatry refers to a person's relationship with their unhealthy God image, whereas the second idolatry arises out of the first and refers to the way individuals conform their life to appease their false god. For example, a person with demanding parents will internalize a perfectionistic God image (first idolatry). In order to survive, and in an attempt to redeem himself or herself, the person will live a life characterized by high expectations, self-criticalness, and rigidity (second idolatry).
- *Covenant in idolatry* refers to the contract the person has with his or her false god. The false god, via the painful relationship with the parents, spells out the terms of the relationship. The person, often unknowingly, signs on the dotted line and accepts these terms. As a result, he or she feels compelled and obligated to obey the dictates of the covenant.
- *Secular scriptures* are the "teachings, values, and beliefs transmitted by the idol [or false god]" (p. 34). The false god gives

scriptures, or directives, as to how the person is expected to live. These scriptures are often not conscious, which makes them all the more powerful. Once they are uncovered, it can be helpful to contrast them with the Scriptures of the true God. This can often be the beginning step of helping the person name and dethrone the false god.

- *Secular prayers* are the "dialog implicitly going on between the self and the idol [or false god]" (p. 34). This dialogue often occurs outside of the person's awareness. The false god speaks in a loud, demanding, and powerful manner, even though the person does not consciously "hear" it. People constantly check in with their false god with the goal of appeasing it. They let their god know what they have done in order to win a morsel of respect and love. The prayers, however, reinforce the strength of the idol, and next time the demands will be harder to meet.

Idols are ultimately unsatisfying. They temporarily dull the pain of this finite life but leave one hungering for more. Tillich (1958) states, "The inescapable consequence of idolatrous faith is 'existential disappointment'" (p. 13). Idols, similar to drugs, are temporarily satisfying, but they end up bringing bondage and restriction to life. They nullify openness and cause tunnel vision; spontaneity is squelched and rigidity is embraced. Idols enslave people to lives of despair.

How do you differentiate between an idol, or a false god, and the real God? I think a limited, but good, metaphor is a relationship with another human. Some relationships leave you feeling on guard, confused, rejected, insecure, and ignored. In general, these are thought to be unhealthy relationships. On the other hand, some relationships leave you feeling open, clear, accepted, secure, and seen. These relationships are typically viewed as healthy. Similar to the feelings you get from negative relationships, a relationship with an idol, or hurtful God image, will leave you feeling rejected and abandoned (Moon, 1997). However, the true God, similar to positive relationships, will leave you feeling accepted and loved. So, simply being aware of your emotional state after communicating with God can help you determine if it was God's voice or the voice of your internal parents.

In a perfect world the God image and the true God would be one and the same. Unfortunately, this is not the case and we often tune into negative messages from our internal critical parents and attribute them to the true God. I believe God has made parents imperfect so that we would be motivated to search out *someone* who is perfect (White, 1984). I also believe that God communicates with us through our own God image. I see the process of therapy as a means by which the God image is changed to be a better, and more accurate, receiver of God's love. The God image is similar to a filter that has to be cleaned so that we can experience God in a clear and true manner. It can also be seen as an antennae, or satellite dish, that often picks up our parents' voices and needs to be adjusted so that we can more clearly hear God's voice.

To sum up, when people enter therapy, they are searching out of their incompleteness for completeness. The therapist acts as an agent of God and helps clients better meet their needs and gain a greater experience of wholeness. The therapist and clients will work together to clean the filter, or adjust the antennae, so that clients can be more in touch with the real God. Unfortunately, therapists, just as parents, will inevitably fail. However, at that time clients will be more complete and better able to manage their pain for the transient time that they inhabit the earth.

PART II:
CHANGING THE GOD IMAGE

Chapter 4

The Therapeutic Relationship

Clients who are depressed enter therapy looking for relief from suffering. They are in a vulnerable position, sometimes ashamed or frustrated because they could not solve their problems on their own. They feel as if the darkness is slowly closing in on them and they are unable to fight it back by themselves. They have tried but have not been successful. They are wounded, in pain, and having difficulty making it on their own. They often feel lost—as if they misplaced their map and desperately need direction. It is from this darkness, pain, and confusion that clients emerge to seek help. The therapist, to the client, represents a beacon on a stormy, black night. Clients believe that the therapist can work with them to help them find light and direction.

This hope that clients bring to therapy is very powerful. It is a strong motivator that gives them the temporary ability to fight back the darkness and trust that you can help them. This initial trust provides them with the courage to believe that they can work collaboratively with you to find relief from suffering and direction in life.

This hope also often results in a necessary and natural tendency for clients to idealize you. They will believe that you have the answers, the insights, and the ability to help them grow. Research has shown that simply caring for and listening to clients at this stage often results in clients' restoration of hope and a consequent decrease in psychological symptoms (Howard, Kopta, Krause, & Orlinsky, 1986). This initial expectancy goes a long way toward helping clients believe that things can be different—that they can once again feel positive about themselves, others, and God.

This chapter focuses on ways to capitalize on these initial treatment gains by protecting and strengthening the therapeutic relationship. First, the ways that your unmet needs can hinder your work with clients will be discussed. Second, the essential characteristics of the therapeutic relationship: congruence, unconditional positive regard, and empathy will be explored. Third, and last, the different ways to develop a strong therapeutic relationship by using practical counseling skills will be outlined.

WHY CONDUCT AN HONEST EVALUATION OF YOURSELF?

The greatest tool you have in therapy is your self. You use your self to connect with and understand clients. If your self is compromised, then you run the risk of misusing the therapeutic relationship. The goal is to increase awareness of potential dangers so that these issues do not harm clients. Toward this end, this chapter will discuss common unmet needs, review problematic interpersonal patterns, and walk through an exercise to help you get in touch with the parts of yourself that influence you but operate outside of your awareness.

Unmet Needs

Humans are motivated by needs. Needs are powerful and demand to be fulfilled. Think of the last time you were driving and needed to go to the bathroom. It is difficult to think of anything other than the next rest area. You can try to think about what you are going to do when you arrive at your destination, or what book you would like to read next, but trying is about as far as you will get. As soon as you switch your attention away, it is immediately called back and urged to hurry up and stop!

Not all needs are this obvious, but many demand to be met in a more subtle and covert manner. For example, we all need to be loved and accepted. We were created to be in relationship with others. If we are not experiencing emotional closeness with our partner, then we will be motivated to find it with someone else (Harley, 2001). We might be able to temporarily focus on other things, but this need will continue to resurface until it is fulfilled. In this manner, both physical and emotional needs hijack our intentions until they are satisfied.

Many of us are extremely busy and not always mindful of making sure our needs are met. As a result, it is not uncommon for us to be distracted and have cloudy judgment. If our needs are not satisfactorily met, then the chances are increased that we will use the therapeutic relationship to meet those needs.

Our relationship with clients can be compromised by a variety of unmet needs. Sometimes therapists see clients longer than they should to fulfill financial needs. Other times, therapists have unmet personal needs that influence the way they act toward clients. For example, if a therapist is married and having a difficult time with his or her spouse, then it is likely that he or she will be experiencing tension and a little loneliness. If the therapist does not have the capacity to hold this need by not letting it interfere in the therapeutic relationship, then he or she may attempt to meet it through his or her relationship with clients. The therapist may blatantly tell clients that he or she is having a difficult time with his or her spouse, and then ask clients what he or she should do. Or, the therapist may subtly, nonverbally, communicate that he or she needs extra encouragement.

Sex is another unmet need that frequently interferes with therapy. This is one of the most common ethical violations and happens more often than therapists would like to admit. This seems shocking to many, but, once again, unmet needs cloud the judgment of the clearest mind and can cause a person to act in a manner that is harmful to clients.

Interpersonal Patterns

In addition to these common unmet needs, deeper, unique, unmet needs from our childhood may linger. These needs have been with a person for a longer time, so he or she has learned to cope with them by integrating them into his or her personality. These underlying needs manifest in the habitual ways we interact with others. We tend to repeat certain patterns of behavior over and over again in our relationships. Each of us "pulls" on those who surround us to respond to us in a certain manner (Levenson, 1995). For example, children who had to prove their worth to their parents usually grow into overachievers as adults. Overachievers need positive feedback. As a result, they often pull for it from others. They often feel insecure on the inside, so they spend much time appearing self-assured. They do this to avoid appearing insecure, for they fear that looking vulnerable would evoke reflections from others that indicate they are weak. If they were to receive this negative reflection, they would likely feel an uncomfortable amount of anxiety. As a result, they present themselves in a manner that pulls for positive feedback and wards off negative feedback.

If an overachiever becomes a therapist he or she will pull for clients to be happy and pleased with how he or she conducts therapy. Unknowingly, clients will feel compelled to talk about the positive aspects and avoid the negative aspects of treatment. This is unfortunate, because it can be healing for clients to express the aspects of a particular intervention or therapy session they do not like. This allows clients space and freedom to disagree with the therapist. If the overachieving therapist is unaware of his or her tendency to elicit only positive responses from others, then the therapist will not be able to recognize that he or she is re-creating this interpersonal pattern with clients. As a result, clients will avoid expressing their frustrations and consequently have a harder time achieving independence.

Another interpersonal pattern occurs when therapists, or clergy, pull for clients to put them on a pedestal. For example, consider a pastor who has a characteristic way of evoking too much respect from people. If you observed her relationships you might notice that people automatically defer to her. If this characterizes the kind of relationships she has outside of therapy, then this will characterize the kind of relationships she has in therapy. Clients may treat her as a guru, as if she has all the answers and can solve all their problems. This will result in her getting her needs met (e.g., being overly respected and admired), but her clients will never learn to figure out their problems for themselves. As a consequence, she will be doing them a disservice and will end up harming them more than helping them.

It is necessary to observe your relationships and become aware of any patterns you reproduce. People bring different interpersonal patterns into relationships. One does not necessarily have to create an overachieving pattern or an overly respectful pattern. Instead, a fear pattern might be created in which others are afraid to approach or disagree with you, or a help-me pattern, in which others feel compelled to help you. A number of patterns can manifest. The goal is to become aware of patterns and work through the underlying issues supporting them, so that client growth is not impeded.

Disowned Aspects of the Self

Other areas to be aware of are the parts of yourself that you disown or are uncomfortable with. This is important because you may have clients that come to you for help with issues that are similar to your own issues. If you have not worked through your issues, then it will be nearly impossible for you to help clients work through their issues. For example, a client may seek help for a condemning God image while you may also have a condemning God image. If you have not worked through this issue it will be difficult for you to help your client, because your own issues will keep getting in the way.

Through our relationship with our caregivers we learn to accept parts of ourselves and disown other parts of ourselves. Carl Jung referred to these disowned parts as the shadow, which he defines as "[t]he 'negative' side of the personality, the sum of all those unpleasant qualities we like to hide." The metaphor of the shadow is particularly fitting because these are the parts of ourselves that are not in the light (Zweig & Abrams, 1991). Disowned parts are not consciously accepted, but are instead rejected from our awareness and kept in the dark. Robert Louis Stevenson captured the essence of the shadow in his book *Dr. Jekyll and Mr. Hyde*. He developed a character to illustrate the personality split that happens in everyday life. One face is shown to ourselves and the outside world, and another face that is darker and unacceptable is kept (or attempted to be kept) hidden.

The shadow develops throughout life, but is most impacted in childhood. Children have a built-in ability to intuitively figure out what their parents like and what their parents do not like. To gain approval, children keep the parts their parents like and get rid of the parts their parents do not like. American poet Robert Bly (1988) uses metaphor to capture the dynamics of the shadow:

> When we were one or two years old we had what we might visualize as a 360-degree personality. Energy radiated out from all parts of our body and all parts of our psyche. . . . We had a ball of energy all right; but one day we noticed that our parents didn't like certain parts of the ball. . . . Behind us we have an invisible bag, and the part of us our parents don't like, we, to keep our parents' love, put in the bag. By the time we go to school our bag is quite large. . . . By the time my brother and I were twelve in Madison, Minnesota, we were known as "the nice Bly boys."

Our bags were already a mile long. . . . Then we do a lot of bag-stuffing in high school. . . . So I maintain that out of a round globe of energy the twenty-year-old ends up with a slice. (pp. 6-7)

The unwanted parts that we place in the bag are not content to stay there. It is impossible to get rid of them because they are part of who we are—part of who God created us to be. So, no matter how far we attempt to distance ourselves from them, they continually come back.

When I was growing up, a family down the street wanted to get rid of their dog. They could not tolerate the idea of putting the dog to sleep, so they drove it out of the state and dropped it off. They hoped it would find a new home and a new family. Three or four days later their dog returned. Their intentions did not matter; the dog, whether they liked it or not, was going to be part of their family.

Similar to the dog, our disowned parts return to us in a number of ways. One of the main avenues they take is through psychological symptoms. Symptoms are painful and unpleasant. We do not like them and want to be rid of them as soon as possible. Unfortunately, symptoms are not seen as helpful letters from the unconscious but as junk mail that needs to be thrown out.

Neimeyer & Raskin (2002) talk about depth-oriented brief therapy. They contend that symptoms are not problems to get rid of, but are instead signposts that guide the client on the path to wellness. Carl Jung captured the essence of this thought, when he observed that the symptom holds the key to solving the problem. I used to be a runner, but now, I somewhat hesitantly admit, I'm a speed walker. I stopped running because my knee would frequently get inflamed and cause me pain. The key word here is *frequently*. Similar to most athletes, I have the brilliant tendency to ignore pain. I felt it, but was going to run through it. My knee kept knocking on my door and saying, "Glen, listen, really, you have to stop running." Despite what I learned in anatomy and physiology courses, I decided to ignore my pain and continue running. It was not long before my knee decided to take matters into its own hands and make it nearly impossible for me to walk. It was as if my knee said, "I warned you five or six times about our problem and you decided to ignore me. Well, now I'm going to make sure you listen to me." I learned, oh did I learn, not to ignore it. The pain was not an annoyance but a signal indicating that something was wrong and needed to be corrected. It was trying to help me, but I was too stubborn to listen.

I think the same outcome occurs as did with my knee when we try to ignore psychological symptoms. It is not uncommon for people to have a headache, an unexplainable new eye twitch, or be completely exhausted for some "unknown" reason, but decide to keep pushing it. Again, in our busy world, people frequently are stressed out and have high blood pressure, but refuse to rearrange their schedule to include rest and relaxation. Their psyche, similar to my knee, is warning them. It is saying, "Hey, something is wrong here and if you do not listen, you are going to have some major problems."

We often avoid symptoms because they remind us of our shadow or the disowned aspects of ourselves. One disowned part in my shadow is a deep fear of laziness. I am paranoid that if I take a break I'm going to turn into a couch potato. I know, rationally, that this is not the case, but I still overextend myself and work too hard. I accept the productive parts of myself but disown the relaxed parts of myself. These relaxed parts call to me nicely at first. They gently tell me that life has more to offer than writing this book, preparing a paper, or doing another evaluation. They kindly remind me of great times at the beach, meaningful experiences with my wife, and fun times with friends. When this happens, I agree with the shadow and entertain the thoughts for a couple of minutes. However, because they are a symbolic part of me that I disown, I quickly repress them and turn my attention to my mental to-do list. After ignoring the shadow parts for a while, they grow frustrated and send me a bout of exhaustion or an inability to focus. Similar to my knee, they say, "You are going to take a break one way or another."

Another way the shadow attempts to get our attention is through projection (Zweig & Abrams, 1991). McWilliams (1994) defines projection as "that which is inside [that] is misunderstood as coming from outside" (p. 108). We project the parts of ourselves that are unacceptable onto others. Projection is the defense mechanism that is characterized in paranoia. People who are paranoid are very angry. They do not accept that they are angry and instead project it onto others. As a result, they experience other people as out to harm, poison, or kill them. If they accepted their anger, they would not experience people as out to get them. People who are depressed also often project their anger onto others. They automatically assume that other people, and God, are mad at them. If they integrated their anger, then they would no longer assume that people are upset with them.

We often have a hard time accepting these disowned parts because we experience them as threatening. Zweig & Abrams (1991) state:

> For this reason, we see the shadow mostly indirectly, in the distasteful traits and actions of other people *out there* where it is safer to observe it. When we react intensely to a quality in an individual or group—such as laziness or stupidity, sensuality, or spirituality—and our reaction overtakes us with great loathing or admiration, this may be our own shadow showing. We *project* by attributing this quality to the other person in an unconscious effort to banish it from ourselves, to keep ourselves from seeing it within. (p. xviii)

It is not healthy to continue to ignore your shadow. Frankly, you really do not have a choice in the matter. You can either choose to deal with it now or deal with it later. It is better to work with it on your own terms rather than to ignore it, wait until it cripples you, and then be forced to deal with it on its terms. John Bradshaw (1988) has developed an intriguing exercise to help you get in touch with your shadow. What follows is a brief summary of his exercise:

1. List the people you *really* despise and write a couple of sentences about what it is that bothers you most about them.
2. List the people again and next to their name condense your sentences into one trait that really, really, bothers you about them (e.g., Greg Smith—domineering, Jane Nielson—clingy).

The individuals and the traits you have listed represent the different parts of your shadow. These behaviors bother you in others because you do not accept them in yourself. This does not mean that you should embody them with the same intensity of those you dislike, but it does mean that you should move in that direction. If the person is to the far right of being lazy and you are on the far left, then you should consider moving more toward the middle. For example, I had a friend—I'll call him Greg—who used to dominate the group of people I associated with. He had an extremely strong personality and would voice his desires in an authoritarian and direct manner. My other friends would swallow their own suggestions and go along with what Greg recommended in order to appease him. This absolutely infuriated me. This bothered me for rational reasons, but the deeper reason was because I did not accept the aggressive side of myself. Does this mean that I should have become domineering and forced people to agree with me? Of course not. But it did mean that I needed to become more comfortable with being assertive. As soon as I integrated my interpersonal strength, Greg bothered me less and less. He no longer served as a hook for me to hang my projections on.

The shadow is similar to a creature that is stuck in a cell in the ground. We are afraid it is going to break out, so we keep piling bricks on top of the wood door that keeps it imprisoned. We compensate and hold off the disowned parts by behaving in the opposite direction (Bradshaw, 1988). So, if I am afraid of being lazy, then I become a workaholic. If I am afraid of being vulnerable, I become a macho man. This fear distorts our judgment, because in reality the shadow is nothing to be afraid of. It sends signals to us to try to get our attention, but we ignore them. All we need is the courage to take the bricks off and open the wood door to let the shadow out. If we do, we'll be pleasantly surprised to find that it is not the monster we have made it out to be, but is instead a rejected friend who has the resources we need for the rest of the journey. Jung said it best, "One does not become enlightened by imagining figures of light, but by making the darkness conscious"(quoted in Zweig & Abrams, 1991, p. xvii).

How do you go about this? How do you become aware of unmet needs, make unconscious interpersonal patterns conscious, and integrate the shadow? This book contains a number of exercises to help you do this. However, this book is just a start. The best way to become aware of your patterns and work through your issues is to begin therapy with a trained professional.

WHAT ARE THE CORE CONDITIONS
OF THE THERAPEUTIC RELATIONSHIP?

Carl Rogers (1961), the founder of client-centered therapy, conducted the pioneering work that established the importance of the core conditions, which are congruence, unconditional positive regard, and empathy. His understanding of their significance has been validated by empirical research and been accepted by most key figures in the mental health field (Feist & Feist, 1998). In fact, nearly every major theorist has integrated his views and concurs that the core conditions are essential components of the therapeutic relationship. Before turning attention to an in-depth review of the core conditions, a brief outline of Rogers's thought will be reviewed, so that you can view the core conditions in the context of his overall theory.

One of Rogers's primary assumptions is that an actualizing tendency inherent in humans leads them toward greater wholeness. That is, people naturally have a propensity toward growth and fulfillment. This actualizing tendency is not restricted to psychological growth, but results in the ongoing development of all aspects of the person.

Humans are not purely psychological, but are instead biopsycho-socialspiritual creatures (Sperry, 1999). A Christian psychology emphasizes the actualizing role that spirituality plays in an individual's life. Christians contend that humans have fallen and are then redeemed. An individual who incorporates faith into his or her life has moved past a fallen identity to a redemptive identity. The redemptive identity has more potential than the fallen identity, because it is centered on the transforming power of God. Therefore, it follows that a faith-centered person would be able to achieve a deeper, truer level of actualization than a non–faith-centered person (Carter & Narramore, 1979; Van Leeuwen, 1985).

Whether a person is religious or not, it is obvious that not everyone enjoys a life of unlimited growth and fulfillment. So, despite this internal predisposition toward wholeness, people are often obstructed or derailed in their ability to achieve ongoing health. The major roadblocks to development occur in childhood.

In an optimal environment, a child is consistently loved by his or her parents. As a result, he or she learns to love himself or herself. This initial care enables the child to develop into a self-regulated person, rather than an other-regulated person (Rogers, 1961). That is, the child will look to himself or herself to determine his or her worth, rather than look to others.

No one has perfectly accepting parents. Instead, children learn how to treat themselves through the "conditions of worth" that are placed on them by their parents (Feist & Feist, 1998, p. 464). That is, they learn that they are accepted if they behave in this manner and not in that manner. They learn to ignore their own interests and strivings in order to secure the acceptance of their significant others. As a result, they incorporate more of what others want rather than what they want. They abandon their needs and start working to satisfy another's needs.

This results in incongruence, which is the gap between the true self and the false self (Rogers, 1961). They ignore their true God-given needs and interests (the true self) and instead embody what others expect of them (the false self). The greater the disparity between the true self and false self, the greater the amount of incongruence.

Many individuals come to therapy in a state of incongruence. They have grown accustomed to forsaking their feelings to please others. One goal of therapy is to provide an environment that allows people to grow through this problem and learn to trust and follow themselves. The therapist's job is to provide the core conditions for the client to remove the roadblocks and reconvene the process of growth. Feist & Feist (1998) analogize:

> In order for a bell plant to reach its full productive potential, it must have water, sunlight and nutrient soil. Similarly, our actualization tendency is realized only under *certain conditions.* Specifically, we must be involved in a relationship with a partner who is *genuine,* or *authentic,* and who demonstrates *empathy* and *unconditional positive regard* or *acceptance* toward us. (p. 460)

Now that Rogers's overall theory has been reviewed, a more comprehensive look at the core conditions follows.

Congruence

The essence of congruence is to be who you are, to be genuine. Being congruent is the opposite of putting up a front, wearing a façade or mask, or trying to be someone you are not. Rogers (1961) said he was congruent when

> [w]hatever feeling or attitude I am experiencing would be matched by my awareness of that attitude. When this is true, then I am a unified or integrated person in that moment and hence I can be whatever I deeply *am.* (p. 282)

Another word that describes congruence is *authentic.* When a person is authentic, they are real. When a person is inauthentic, they are acting unreal or fake. Take a minute and think of a person who has struck you as inauthentic. These individuals usually come across as superficial and do not feel present or engaged in the discussion. They go through the motions but are not really listening. Other times, inauthentic people can come off as overly nice. They smile and say all the right things, but one can tell that they are not being real.

Neophyte therapists can sometimes come off as incongruent. They are so busy practicing their clinical skills that they forget who they are. This type of self-observation can be crippling. It robs them of self-trust and squelches spontaneity. To overcome this tendency to be incongruent, I encourage new therapists to trust themselves and relate to clients as if they were caring for a friend. Therapists are naturally caring people who help friends talk through issues. However, new therapists often forget these inherent tendencies and believe that they have to manufacture interest and concern when they enter the clinical setting.

Regardless of the level of experience, almost all therapists have difficulty being congruent when they have negative feelings toward clients. An implicit and dangerous assumption exists that therapists are allowed to experience only positive feelings toward clients. This is simply not true and completely unrealistic. Often a person comes for counseling after having managed to frustrate everyone else in his or her life. It is naive to think that this same person will not frustrate the therapist.

It is important for you as a therapist to be aware of your negative feelings toward clients. Therapists often think that they can hide these negative feelings behind a smile or look of concern and nice words, but the feelings often surface in unexpected ways that the therapists are not even aware of. Clients are very sensitive and are able to read therapists' nonverbal behavior and pick up on therapists' "vibes." This incongruence decreases client trust. Rogers (1961) states,

> I used to feel that if I fulfilled all the other conditions of trust-worthiness—keeping appointments, respecting the confidential nature of the interviews, etc.—and if I acted consistently the same during the interview, then this condition would be fulfilled. But experience drove home the fact that to act consistently acceptant for example, if in fact I was feeling annoyed or skeptical or some other non-acceptant feelings, I was certain in the long run to be perceived as inconsistent or untrustworthy. I

have come to realize that being trustworthy does not demand that I be rigidly consistent but that I be dependably real. (p. 50)

I learned about the importance of being congruent during my predoctoral internship. I had a psychiatrist supervisor who was very congruent; indeed, some would say too congruent. He often chose to share the feelings he had toward me, even if they were negative and I did not really want to hear them. Somewhat paradoxically though, because he did this, I felt safe with him. I knew I could trust him. He was not going to hide any criticism he had, and when he complimented me I knew he meant it.

That same year I learned a little more about congruence through relationships with troubled teens. I lived in a rougher part of town that had a number of basketball courts where these youth would regularly congregate to play. I enjoyed basketball, so I often played with them. At that same time I was seeing a client who had the same profile of the individuals that I played basketball with. That is, he could be inappropriately verbally and physically aggressive. I was doing all the "right" therapeutic practices, but this kid had no respect for me. On the court, however, I had plenty of respect. I was not in therapy with any of these young men, so I did not put any pressure on myself to be "therapeutic" with them. Instead, I was just myself—a regular guy, a little older, who wanted to play basketball. These young men enjoyed my company and would frequently open up about their struggles. These young men trusted me, whereas my client did not. I gained their trust by being congruent, whereas in the therapy office I was incongruent. I was so busy trying to be therapeutic that I failed to recognize I was being inauthentic. Eventually I became aware of the discrepancy and was able to form a real and therapeutic relationship with my client.

Unconditional Positive Regard

Stated simply, unconditional positive regard (UPR) means a nonjudgmental attitude is taken toward clients. Clients' thoughts, feelings, or behaviors are not evaluated as positive or negative. At base, they are fundamentally accepted. Feist & Feist (1998) define these terms as follows:

"Regard" means that there is a close relationship and that the therapist sees the client as an important person; "positive" indicates that the direction of the relationship is toward warm and caring feelings; and "unconditional" suggests that the positive regard is no longer dependent on specific client behaviors and does not have to be continually earned. (p. 470)

UPR is not something that happens naturally. In fact, in many ways it is the opposite of what is taught in Western culture. We are trained to be constant evaluators. This happens on both conscious and unconscious levels. This may be done consciously when we appraise a house or a car. This is often done unconsciously, without even realizing it has occured. We often, unknowingly, judge people by their appearance, occupation, ethnicity, and education. This unconscious process is subtle but very powerful.

One reason it is powerful is because it is easy. The brain likes to take shortcuts by sorting life into simple compartments. It is easier to make a snap judgment and channel life into two compartments (i.e., good and bad) than it is to sort thoughts into a variety of categories and suspend judgment. Unfortunately, we tend to gravitate toward the rapid binary system rather than embrace the open-minded multi-dimensional system.

This tendency to make quick judgments makes it difficult to practice UPR. One way to develop UPR is to practice it on yourself. Take a minute now and become aware of all the ways that you may be negatively judging yourself.

- Are your perceptions accurate?
- Does this evaluation help you?
- What would happen if you suspended this judgment and gave yourself the benefit of the doubt?
- What would happen if you listened and accepted the judged parts rather than immediately discredited them?

Your ability to validate and accept yourself influences your ability to practice UPR. Rogers (1961) states,

One way of putting this, which may seem strange to you is that if I can form a helping relationship to myself—if I can be sensitively aware of and acceptant toward my own feelings—then the likelihood is that I can form a helping relationship with another. (p. 51)

The relationship you have with yourself will define the parameters of your relationship with others.

Another factor that limits the ability to embody UPR is a lack of psychological security. It is hard to emotionally care for another person if you have little to no emotional resources for yourself. A popular metaphor is that of the emotional bank account (Covey, 1990). If your emotional balance is close to zero, then you cannot expect yourself to give emotionally to others. You have to make sure you have a healthy sum before you give to others. If you have an emotional deficit, then you might unconsciously pull resources from clients to replenish your account.

A third challenge to UPR lies in allowing yourself to really care for another person. Sometimes we have difficulty opening up and loving people we are close to. How much harder is it to care for a stranger? Therapists sometimes deal with this challenge by hiding behind their professional roles to insulate themselves from potential risks. If you open yourself and develop a real relationship with a client, then you run the risk of being hurt and maybe rejected. These fears vary with each person, but it is wise to be mindful of them so you do not unknowingly hinder your ability to practice UPR.

A final factor that inhibits UPR is our unconscious self-bias. This tendency appears to be more prominent in men and exists to a lesser degree in women (Gilligan, 1983). We naturally believe that our opinions, decisions, views, ways of living, and values are the right ones. Therefore, often without realizing it, we automatically conclude that those who differ from us are wrong. This can get played out in therapy. Rogers (1961) illustrates this by questioning himself, "Can I give the client freedom to be? Or do I feel that he should follow my advice, or remain somewhat dependent on me, or mold himself after me?" (pp. 52-53). It takes courage and maturity to validate another when he or she is different from you.

This ability to listen, care, and appreciate others, even when they are different, sometimes runs contrary to a traditional religious perspective. Often, I think well-intentioned people champion a particular view as the right way with the goal of helping others. Sometimes this takes the form of an argument or a type of moral tug-of-war. Unfortunately, as many undoubtedly know, this dogmatic way of relating is seldom helpful or effective.

Religious counselors and clergy have to trust that God, and their faith in the human relationship, speaks louder than words. People who behave self-destructively do not do so because they enjoy it. Usually they feel trapped and unable to stop what they are doing. Generally, they feel just as bad about it as you do, if not worse. They are stuck. Trying to muscle them out of sinful behavior is only going to push them farther away from you, farther away from their own good mental health, and ultimately farther away from God.

God can heal others through you if you accept them. If you do not accept them, then they will not find the healing relationship they need to explore why they think, feel, and behave in ways that are self-destructive. You create for them, via the acceptance of the problems they bring you, a sort of sanctuary in which they can fully own their harmful behavior. Once they own their behavior and stop trying to deny it, they can choose to change their behavior, so it is healthier and therefore holier.

Empathy

Empathy occurs when a therapist leaves his or her frame of reference and enters the client's frame of reference (Rogers, 1961). The therapist steps into the client's shoes and views the world through the client's eyes and imagines experiencing what the client experiences. The therapist sees, hears, and feels the client's world. Feist & Feist (1998) explain, "Empathy exists when therapists accurately sense the feelings of their clients and are able to communicate these perceptions so that the clients know that another person has entered their world of feelings without prejudice, projection, or evaluation" (p. 470). Martin (1995) gives a more informal definition: "Whatever you do that gives the client the feeling of 'exactly, that's what I was trying to say, it feels good to have someone know me so well' is evocative empathy" (p. 4).

We long to connect and be understood by others (Nichols, 1995). Think of the last time that you had something on your mind that you wanted to share. It could be a slight that happened at work, a compliment, a stressful event, or a rewarding experience. Whatever it was, it likely felt unfinished until you shared it. Our experiences require validation before they let us rest. This is particularly true when we have experienced something that is distressing. When we put our feelings into words and share them with someone we trust it is as if a weight has been lifted off our shoulders.

Unfortunately, we are not always as willing to share our experiences as we should be. We often try to explain this need to share away by telling ourselves that what we wanted to talk about wasn't that important. Think of the last time you risked sharing something with someone and they responded in an unempathic manner. They might have been distracted, preoccupied, judgmental, or uninterested. This recently occurred to me. I had just completed a project and tried to share it with a couple of friends. They acted as if they were in a hurry and wanted me to rush through it. It took me awhile to admit it, but my feelings were hurt. I should have said, "This is important to me, so if you don't have time now, then I'll show you when you do have time." Instead, regrettably, I hurriedly showed it to them and left feeling hurt.

Outside of therapy, empathic listening is typically only encountered in close relationships and is generally not expected from other relationships. However, inside of therapy empathy is always expected. Clients come to therapy to find a person who they can trust and feel understood by. Many clients do not have safe people they can talk to, so an empathic therapist is an oasis in the desert.

Being empathic is sometimes referred to as *mirroring*. That is, a good therapist will hear what a client states and then reflect it back in a clear and accurate manner. This allows clients to clearly see themselves. A mirror provides self-awareness because it reflects back to the person a true image of himself or herself. Similarly, a therapist provides self-awareness because he or she reflects back what clients are feeling. Nichols (1995) illustrates:

> When deeply felt but unexpressed feelings take shape in words that are shared and come back clarified, the result is a reassuring sense of being understood and a grateful feeling of shared humanness with one who understands. . . . Thus, in giving an account of our experience to someone who listens, we are better able to listen to ourselves. Our lives are coauthored in dialogue. (p. 10)

A mirror is a good mirror when it gives an accurate reflection, and a therapist is a good therapist when he or she gives an accurate reflection. I had a mirror once that both my wife and I loved. It had a slimming effect on whoever looked into it. We liked this mirror because it made us look trimmer and taller. The reality, however, was that we were actually a little wider and shorter. Similarly, a therapist might try to protect a person by giving only positive reflections. This slightly altered, positive image, similar to my mirror, will provide momentarily good feelings, but will ultimately fade because it is not an accurate reflection. Another type of mirror, sometimes found in fun houses, can give a less flattering perspective. It makes a person look short and fat. Similarly, a therapist can give disaffirming reflections that can result in negative and inaccurate client self-understanding.

In short, we all need to be listened to and understood by others. A therapist practices empathic listening by entering the client's world and then sharing that understanding with the client. By providing clear and accurate reflections of what the client is thinking and feeling, the client will gain greater self-awareness and self-acceptance.

Therapeutic Alliance

Empathy, congruence, and unconditional positive regard come together in the formation of the therapeutic alliance (Martin, 1995). This occurs when therapist and client have succeeded in forming a trusting relationship in which the client knows that the therapist is on their side and is going to help him or her work through his or her problems. It is as if the client says, "Okay, I have trusted you enough to let you into my world, so now let me show you what we need to improve." The two main parts of the therapeutic alliance are connection and collaboration (Teyber, 1997).

Connecting with clients may be the most powerful factor in therapy (Teyber, 1997). Psychologists have attempted to ferret out the most potent therapeutic ingredient to determine what makes people grow. Some say it is making the unconscious conscious, others say it is specific cognitive techniques, and still others say it is behavior modification. It is likely that all of these factors help, but the common denominator is the therapeutic relationship. Research has shown that the formation of the therapeutic alliance by the third session greatly impacts the outcome of therapy. Martin (1995) summarizes that "if the client felt understood, accepted and liked by the therapist, therapy was more likely to be successful. . . . Our fancy techniques may be less important than we think. . . . It really may be that *it is the connection that heals*" (p. 3).

Bonding is a word that points to what is meant by connection. Through empathic listening and reflection an attachment forms between therapist and client that enables the client to feel special to the therapist. This enables the client to open up, trust, and become vulnerable with the therapist. In addition, it gives clients the ability to invite the therapist in to help them solve their problems.

The second part of the therapeutic alliance is collaboration (Teyber, 1997). In order for therapy to be effective it has to involve active work on the part of the therapist *and* client. Many people think that this is an obvious point and that it should automatically happen. Unfortunately, even though it makes intuitive sense, it does not usually happen without conscious and deliberate planning by the therapist.

One common roadblock that inhibits collaboration is the pervasiveness of the medical model, which assumes that the physician knows what is wrong and the client does not (Teyber, 1997). The physician's role is to tell the client what to do and the client's role is to follow the physician's advice. This works well with many medical disorders, but does not work well with psychological problems. People are more psychologically complicated than this model implies. As a result, people who attempt to use this model in psychotherapy often find themselves frustrated and ineffective. Egan (2002) states, "Helpers do not 'cure' their patients. . . Helping is a two-person team effort in which helpers need to do their part and clients theirs. If either party refuses to play or plays incompetently, the entire enterprise can fail" (p. 43). Teyber (1997) outlines one way therapy differs from the medical model: "An important difference is that the clients must be active participants in their treatment planning—for example, by describing symptoms, identifying what's been helpful and what has not, and agreeing with the therapist on a particular course of treatment" (p. 35).

The ability to form a therapeutic alliance can also be influenced by the nature of the client's problems. This ability is increased when the client's problems are *ego-dystonic* (McWilliams, 1994). This means clients see their problems as a part of themselves that they want to change. They are therefore able to separate themselves from their problems and align with the therapist with the goal of resolving the problem. An example of an ego-dystonic problem is depression. Most people who are depressed come to therapy because they are in pain and want to work with the therapist to decrease that pain.

The ability to form a therapeutic alliance is decreased when the problem is *ego-syntonic* (McWilliams, 1994). This means that other people see the problem, but the client does not. The problem bothers other people, but it does not bother the client. A common ego-syntonic problem is alcoholism. Many people who struggle with alcoholism deny that they have a problem, even though their spouse has left them, they have lost their job, and they have no money. Other ego-syntonic problems occur when a person is forced to come to therapy. A not uncommon example occurs when a well-intentioned wife offers an ultimatum to coerce her unwilling husband into counseling. Because he is not there of his own volition, and because he does not believe he has a problem, he will be very difficult to work with.

People with ego-syntonic problems require long periods of rapport and trust building before they can even begin to consider that they might have a problem (McCullough-Vaillant, 1997). After considerable time, some people with ego-syntonic problems are able to separate themselves from their problems and move into an ego-dystonic state, which increases their ability to collaborate with the therapist.

To recap, integration of empathy, congruence, and unconditional positive regard results in the formation of the therapeutic alliance. When this occurs, the client feels connected to the therapist and desires to collaborate with the therapist to solve his or her problems. You the therapist and the client form an attachment, isolate the problem, and then work together to resolve the issue. From this experience the client learns three main things: (1) because you care for him or her, the client learns that he or she is valuable and consequently learns to care for himself or herself, (2) because you provided unconditional positive regard, the client will learn to honor rather than disown himself or herself to please others, and (3) because the client works with you, he or she gains confidence in his or her ability to solve problems (Teyber, 1997). Once these three tasks are accomplished, you have met the main goal of therapy and successfully worked yourself out of a job.

WHAT COUNSELING SKILLS STRENGTHEN THE THERAPEUTIC RELATIONSHIP?

Building strong therapeutic relationships is an art. Erich Fromm (1956) posits that there are two parts to any art: (1) mastery of the theory and (2) mastery of the practice. The theory has been discussed, and attention will now turn to the practice of developing strong relationships. Some people are blessed with personalities that naturally make them good therapists, just as some athletes are blessed with height and strength that enable them to naturally excel in their sport. Fortunately, unlike professional sports, being a therapist is not solely restricted to those with innate therapeutic dispositions. The art of building strong relationships can be learned by practicing counseling skills.

When I first started playing basketball I was kind of awkward. I could not get a feel for the basketball and was a terrible dribbler. Each day I would practice a different skill. Sometimes I would pass the ball back and forth between my hands and other times I would dribble the ball around cones. It was not long before I greatly improved my ball-handling skills. Gradually, maneuvering the ball became second nature to me. I could do it without even thinking about it. Counseling skills develop in a similar manner. At first, they will be awkward and a little clumsy. However, as they are practiced they will become more natural and comfortable. Eventually, with enough practice, the skills will become integrated into who you are. This section focuses on a number of skills you can utilize to help strengthen therapeutic relationships.

Reading Nonverbal Behavior

Have you ever had a conversation with someone and felt as if they were angry with you even though they denied it? Most of us have had the experience of sensing that something is wrong even if the other person does not verbally state it. We have this ability because we have two different language systems: the nonverbal and the verbal.

We naturally attend to nonverbal communication because it is our first language. We are able to express our needs and desires long before we have the ability to verbally articulate them. This nonlinguistic ability predates our linguistic ability, because the nonlanguage parts of the brain develop and function earlier than the language parts of the brain.

The ability to express and understand nonverbal language is hard-wired into our system. Children naturally respond to others based on their interpretation of nonverbal behavior. The nonverbal system stays with us throughout our development, but eventually decreases in importance because we develop a verbal communication system. In general, the nonverbal tends to be quick and closely related to emotions, whereas the verbal tends to be slower and closely related to thoughts (Goleman, 1997). The speed of the nonverbal system sometimes sacrifices accuracy. Fortunately, the nonverbal system can be trained and integrated with the verbal system to more correctly interpret clients' nonverbal behavior.

Even with training, however, reading nonverbal behavior is an inexact science (Egan, 2002). It should be understood as a therapeutic tool that helps to reveal how clients are feeling, but not as the conclusive, authoritative statement on what a client is feeling. As with all language, it is subject to therapist distortion and/or misunderstanding.

There are three main components of nonverbal behavior: presentation, body language, and paralanguage (Egan, 2002; Hill & O'Brien, 2002). Presentation consists of grooming, clothing, weight, height, and fitness. Body language involves closed or open stance, gestures, facial expressions, and eye contact. Paralanguage includes voice volume, hesitancy in responding, and sentence organization.

All facets of nonverbal language or what they mean will not be reviewed here, but some areas will be discussed to illustrate the importance of this skill. Let's look at Bob and Lilith's nonverbals to paint a clearer picture. Bob presented as overweight and slightly disheveled, which could be interpreted as him not having the time or the energy to physically care for himself. Lilith, on the other hand, was thin and stylishly dressed without a hair out of place. This could be construed as being overly concerned with appearance and very invested in what others think of her. Bob maintained an open posture but frequently looked down when discussing sensitive subjects. This could mean that he felt trusting toward me but guilty and ashamed when discussing certain topics. Lilith usually crossed her arms and legs, which could be read as being guarded or closed off. Bob would often open up and easily share his feelings, whereas Lilith would hesitate for several seconds before revealing her feelings. Bob's paralanguage suggests that he was less anxious, whereas Lilith's paralanguage indicates that she screened her responses out of fear of being judged.

Again, keep in mind that these are just potential meanings that need to be understood in context. People may cross their arms because they are guarded *or* because they are cold *or* because of any number of other reasons. Another could be overweight because of lack of self-care *or* a medical complication, and so forth. We have to guard against making snap judgments based solely on nonverbal behavior.

It is very important to be aware of client nonverbals, but is equally important to be aware of your own nonverbals. Clients pick up on our inferred communication very readily. Often they were treated poorly by their caregivers, so they learned to be incredibly good at quickly interpreting nonverbals to escape negative consequences. For this reason, they will unconsciously be attuned to you and closely monitor your behavior. Clients can interpret a yawn, a glance at the clock, or a look out the window to mean that you are bored and uninterested in them. It is therefore very important to be conscious of your nonverbals, so you can create a safe and trusting atmosphere.

Egan (2002) recommends visibly tuning into clients by following his SOLER acronym.

> **S**quarely face the patient
> **O**pen posture
> **L**ean toward the client
> **E**ye contact—an appropriate amount, not too little or too much
> **R**elax and be natural in these behaviors (p. 69-70)

Take a minute and think about how you interact with clients. What changes, if any, would you have to make to follow the SOLER model? What does your presentation, body language, and paralanguage communicate to others? Sometimes, due to our own subjectivity, we have a hard time answering these questions. It can be enlightening to talk with someone you trust about your nonverbals. You might be surprised to hear what you have been communicating.

Open-Ended Questions

Open-ended questions are used by the therapist to help clients "clarify or explore thoughts or feelings" (Hill & O'Brien, 2002, p. 110). As the name implies, these questions are used to expand or open up a client's awareness. This is the opposite of a closed question, which restricts a person to a yes-or-no answer. Think of how you would respond to the following questions:

How would you describe your relationship with God?
Do you have a good relationship with God?

The first one likely encouraged you to talk about various aspects of your relationship, whereas the second limited you to either a yes or no response. The first one results in expansion, whereas the second results in constriction.

Therapists should heed a few cautions when using open-ended questions. One, ask a limited number of questions (Egan, 2002). Clients can easily feel put off by a barrage of questions. If you feel lost, it is better to reflect and follow the client than it is to fire off more questions. Reflecting will get you out of the woods a lot quicker than asking questions will. Two, limit the amount of closed questions you ask (Hill & O'Brien, 2002). During the first couple of sessions you will ask a number of closed questions to gather information. However, once information gathering has passed, it is best to use open-ended questions. A final caution is to limit the number of "why" questions (Hill & O'Brien, 2002). This is a difficult habit to break. We frequently ask "why" questions without realizing that they often come across as critical and make clients defensive. For example, if Lilith has a hard time trusting friends, then it will *not* be helpful to ask, "Why don't you open up to your friends?" It would be more helpful to ask, "What would happen if you opened up to your friends?"

Restatement

Hill & O'Brien (2002) define restatement as "a repeating or rephrasing of the content or meaning of client's statement(s) that typically contains fewer, but similar words and usually is more concrete and clear than the client's statement" (p. 100). A restatement is used to communicate that you are following what the client is saying. Restatements tend to focus on clients' thoughts rather than feelings and help clients cognitively frame their situation.

Restatements can vary in length. They can be very short and consist of a repetition of a key word a client has stated. For example:

BOB: I keep working to prove myself to God, but I always fall short. I feel hopeless.
THERAPIST: Hopeless.

Restatements can also be midrange and consist of paraphrasing a couple of key client thoughts.

LILITH: I'm falling behind in every area of my life. I cannot afford to be depressed. People, not to mention God, expect a lot from me and I'm letting them down. I need to get through this depression and get back on track.

THERAPIST: Your depression is keeping you from meeting their expectations.

Restatements can also be longer and take the form of a summary. This usually occurs at the end of a session to recap what the client has shared.

A few technical points must be followed when using restatements. One, emphasize the main theme. Do not feel as if you have to remember everything the client said; instead, focus on just the most salient point (Hill & O'Brien, 2002). Two, do not engage in what Egan (2002) calls "tape-recorder listening" (p. 115). Try to vary your restatements rather than just parrot back what the client stated. Three, focus on the client and not on the other people in the client's life (Hill & O'Brien, 2002). For example, if Bob says, "All of these people are making demands on me," an ineffective response would be "Sounds like other people are constantly making demands on you." A more effective restatement that focuses on Bob would be, "You feel others are constantly making demands on you." You cannot change the other people involved in a client's life, but you can change the way the client perceives those other people. Therefore, you will be more effective if you focus on the client, rather than on the people in the client's life.

Reflection of Feelings

Reflection of feelings is similar to restatement but emphasizes the emotion the client is experiencing (Hill & O'Brien, 2002). The emotion could be articulated in the client's words or it could be hinted at by the client's nonverbal behavior. The goal is to bring the emotion to the surface and encourage the client to feel it in the here and now (Teyber, 1997). For example, if Lilith talks about how she *felt* rejected by God in the recent past, she should be encouraged to step into that feeling in the present to describe how it currently feels. The focus on the present intensifies the experience and makes it more tangible, whereas talking about an emotion in the past diminishes its power by distancing from it and making it less touchable.

Many clients find it difficult to identify and express their emotions. Some have grown up in situations in which they never learned to recognize how they are feeling. Children learn how they are feeling by the reflections they are given from their caregivers. A child who has a tantrum will learn that he or she is experiencing anger if his or her mother kindly says, "You feel angry right now." Eventually, through receiving parental reflections on a number of different emotions, children learn to recognize when they feel glad, sad, mad, or scared. If parental reflections are not present, children will have a much harder time identifying their emotions. The parents of these children were not the best mirrors, so the children do not know how to "see" how they are feeling. As adults they experience the physical sensations that accompany emotions but do not know how to label them as feelings. A person who is depressed might feel heavy, weighed down, and tired, but not know that she is experiencing sadness. Likewise, a person may have tense shoulders and a knot in his stomach, but not realize he is anxious.

People may also have difficulty expressing their emotions because they are afraid of what will happen if they express their feelings (McCullough-Vaillant, 1997). Emotions are very powerful and are often repressed because people fear they will become overwhelmed if they begin to express their feelings. Clients who deny their sadness fear they will be overcome with grief and spend the remainder of their life in tears. Individuals who suppress their anger fear they will become a rageaholic and physically or emotionally harm others. These fears are very real and are often successful at keeping the forbidden emotions locked out of awareness. Although very threatening to the person, these emotions are almost never as overwhelming as the person believes. Shortly after the feelings are experienced, they subside, and the person regains a sense of balance and control.

Your role as a therapist includes using the skill of reflecting emotion to help clients integrate their feelings. Through being a clear and accurate mirror you will help clients recognize their physical sensations (e.g., clenched fists) and pair them with the corresponding emotion (e.g., anger). In addition, by providing a safe and welcoming environment, you will allow clients to risk owning and expressing their repressed emotion.

A number of practical tips can be followed to increase your efficacy in this area. Egan (2002) recommends following a simple formula to help learn this skill:

> *You feel* . . . [here name the correct emotion expressed by the client] . . . *because* . . . [here indicate the correct experiences that give rise to the feelings]. (p. 98)

For example:

THERAPIST TO LILITH: "*You feel* insecure *because* you have not met what you feel God is expecting of you."

THERAPIST TO BOB: "*You feel* distant from God *because* you feel you have let Him down."

Another practical tip that helps reflect emotion is to build up your feeling-words vocabulary (Hill & O'Brien, 2002). Most therapists start off with a limited ability to identify feelings. Fortunately, this is easy to fix. First, read the list of feeling words below. Second, carry a copy of the list with you and identify how you are feeling throughout the day. Third, practice identifying how other people are feeling by using the previously outlined formula. As with any skill, the more you practice, the better you will become.

Feeling Word List

MAD:	angry, furious, enraged, disgusted, annoyed, frustrated, resentful, put out, disappointed
SCARED:	fearful, afraid, terrified, threatened, insecure, inadequate, inferior, timid, uneasy, worried, apprehensive, unsure, shy, nervous, anxious
SAD:	hopeless, sorrowful, empty, upset, down, helpless, discouraged, hurt, gloomy, useless, grieved, despairing, distraught, miserable, unhappy, dejected
GLAD:	happy, calm, cheerful, content, joyful, amused, excited, eager, warm, pleasant, tranquil, serene, peaceful
LONELY:	lost, isolated, distant, separated, dejected, left out, detached, forgotten, solitary, abandoned, secluded

ASHAMED: embarrassed, guilty, remorseful, weird, rejected, hu-
miliated, disgraced, shameful

It is important to keep a couple of things in mind when reflecting
emotion. First, focus on the main emotion. Do not attempt to capture
all of the client's feelings; just focus on the strongest one (Hill
& O'Brien, 2002). Second, try to reflect an emotion that is in the right
"family" of emotions (Egan, 2002, p. 99). The words in capital letters
listed previously represent the main families of emotions. For example, if Lilith infers that she feels insecure, then, ideally, the therapist
should verbally match that emotion by reflecting back that she feels
insecure. However, if the therapist cannot get an exact match, then he
or she should try to be in the right family of emotions. Scared is the
main family that insecure falls under, so words such as inadequate or
inferior would be close reflections because they are in the right family. If the therapist mirrored back that she was angry, then this would
be an ineffective reflection because it is in the wrong family of
emotions.

To sum up, building strong therapeutic relationships is an art. As
with any art, the more you practice the better you will become. At
first, using these skills may feel awkward, but with continued use
they will gradually become a natural part of who you are. Regular
practice of these skills will provide you with the ability to build and
strengthen therapeutic relationships.

Chapter 5

God Image Assessment

WHY IS GOD IMAGE ASSESSMENT IMPORTANT?

God image assessment is important because it enables a therapist to clarify problems with a client's relationship with God. To illustrate the importance of assessment, think about what happens when your car breaks down. If you are similar to most people, you probably take it to the local garage and explain what the main problem appears to be. The mechanic will then ask you a number of questions to narrow down the possibilities. In addition, the mechanic may take the car for a drive, look at the engine, or hook it up to a computer to pinpoint the malfunction. Once the mechanic has identified the problem, he or she can begin to take steps to fix the problem. Similarly, when you as therapist assess the God image you function as a type of psychospiritual mechanic. You first identify the problems with the client's experience of God so you can then take steps to solve these problems.

God image assessment is significant for a number of reasons. One reason is because it allows you to take a vague problem and make it a specific problem. For example, a person may state, "I feel that God is always mad at me." This is an imprecise complaint that needs to be made more precise so that it can be addressed. After conducting an assessment with this person you would be able to detail more specifically when it is that he or she feels God is mad at him or her. For example, the person may experience God as mad at him or her when he or she fails to practice regular devotions, skips church, and/or refuses to visit his or her controlling mother. God image assessment is important because it focuses a problem by naming it and making it explicit.

Another reason God image assessment is important is because it provides direction by showing the therapist where the problem lies. The therapist does not want to focus on one part of the God image if the problem lies in a different part, just as the mechanic does not want to spend time fixing the transmission if the problem lies in the alternator. For example, Lilith's God image was based almost entirely on her experience of her mother, so it would not be as helpful to focus on her relationship with her father.

A third reason is that it allows the therapist to measure the different factors that influence the God image and quantify how easy or difficult they will be to change. If a person experienced both caregivers as demanding, but only one as distant, then it will be more difficult to change the demanding part than it will be to change the distant part of a client's God image. If you want to boost the client's hope, and you know that distance from God can be easily changed, then you can use an intervention designed to decrease distance from God.

A fourth reason is that it allows you to uncover the positive aspects of the God image that can be used to increase client growth (Richards & Bergin, 1997). Many people come to therapy focused solely on problems and do not realize that they have strengths that they are overlooking. Clients' strengths are powerful because they already exist and are an integrated part of their lives. Interventions that tap into these strengths can have a powerful effect on the God image. For example, if a person feels worthless but has a strong sense of God's compassion, then you can encourage this person to meditate on His compassion to leverage himself or herself out of feeling worthless.

A fifth reason God image assessment is important is because it allows you to make relevant treatment goals. If you have a solid and detailed understanding of the client's problems you can make relevant treatment goals. For example, if a client experiences God as rejecting, then a goal would be to experience God as accepting. If a client experiences God as cold, then a goal would be to experience Him as warm. Once you set solid treatment goals you can choose interventions that will help clients reach their objectives.

The final reason assessment is important is because it allows you to measure how much a client's God image has changed. Sometimes clinicians assess clients in the beginning of therapy and then again at the end of therapy. This is referred to as pre- and posttesting and allows the therapist to see how much a client's God image has changed. Other times, therapists use testing throughout therapy to assess how certain interventions are affecting the God image. If a therapist is attempting to change a sense of God image rejection but the tests indicate that this is not occurring, then the therapist has to evaluate why the change is not happening.

God image assessment allows you to make a vague report a specific report, reveals what parts of the God image are important to focus on, and allows you to quantify how easy or difficult the different parts of the God image will be to change. It also uncovers healthy aspects of the God image that can be used to strengthen a person's relationship with God and it enables you to construct goals and delineate interventions to meet those goals. Finally, it allows you to gauge client growth by testing clients throughout the therapy process.

HOW SHOULD A GOD IMAGE ASSESSMENT INTERVIEW BE CONDUCTED?

The God image assessment interview is a semistructured protocol that focuses on the client's presenting problem, God image, personal history, and spiritual information. The interview is not a substitute for a full biopsychosocialspiritual assessment. It can be used alone or in conjunction with a more in-depth clinical interview.

A number of easy steps should be followed in conducting the God image assessment interview. If you follow these steps you will have a solid understanding of the main factors that contributed to and maintain the client's God image. This section reviews each of the steps in the interview process.

Build a Strong Relationship

The first step is to build a strong relationship with the client. This is very important because it determines the quantity and quality of what clients truthfully disclose. Think about your own comfort level when meeting a new person. If the person is inauthentic, self-preoccupied, and/or unempathic, then you will likely protect yourself by not sharing any personal information. Conversely, if the person embodies the core characteristics, then you will find yourself opening up and discussing sensitive information—sometimes disclosing more than you originally intended. Being aware of your nonverbals (e.g., SOLER) (Egan, 2002) and assuring clients of confidentiality are also essential aspects of this step.

Focus on the Chief Complaint

The second step is to focus on the presenting problem or what is sometimes referred to as the chief complaint. Some people begin therapy with the goal of changing their God image, whereas others initially present for help with what seems to be an unrelated topic (e.g., loss of a loved one, life transition) but shortly thereafter realize that their God image is interwoven with this issue and request help changing their experience of God. Regardless of how directly the client's God image is indicated in his or her problem, a number of questions can be asked to uncover the details of his or her emotional experience of God. Generally, in the first session, it is best to begin by asking clients what it is they are seeking help with. Often, clients just want to unburden themselves. They want to tell how they feel and relieve themselves of the stress they have been holding. Your job here is simply to listen and reflect. After clients have unburdened themselves, then you can begin to ask more detailed questions about their God image.

Initially, you should focus on four main areas of the presenting problem. The first is the *precipitant,* "What happens before you experience God in this manner?" The second is *duration,* "How long have you experienced God in this manner?" The third is *frequency,* "How often do you experience God in this way? How many times throughout the day? How many times throughout the week?" The final is *severity,* "On a scale of 1 to 10, with 1 being great and 10 being terrible, how would you rate your experience of God on this factor?" For example, Bob usually feels rejected by God when he is unable to complete certain ministry duties (precipitant), has experienced God's rejection in this situation since seminary (duration), feels this rejection three to four times a day when he neglects his duties (frequency), and rates it as an 8 on a scale of 1 to 10 (severity).

Acquire the Client's Personal History

The third step is to inquire about their personal history. A variety of psychosocial templates exist to draw from (see Zuckerman, 1995). In this section, I have included a sample of questions from Regent University's psychosocial and spiritual assessment, as well as other questions that I have found to be helpful.

These aspects of the client's history and current functioning will impact and be impacted by the God image. The God image does not exist in a vacuum but is instead just one component of the person's world that exists within a greater interpersonal matrix. Therefore, it is necessary to gather and analyze other relational information so that relevant inferences can be drawn about the God image.

Family History

The first area to explore is the person's family history. Virginia Satir (1972) said families are "people factories" in which individuals learn how to behave and what implicit and explicit rules to follow. Encourage clients to paint a full and colorful picture of their childhood and adolescent relationships with caregivers. This information is very important because it is the primary material that was used in the construction of the God image. A few good questions to promote exploration of this area are: How would you describe your relationship with your mother/father? What are three words you would use to describe your relationship with your mother/father? When did you feel closest to her/him? When did you feel the most distant from her/him? At that time, did you still feel connected to her/him? If not, what did you do to reestablish the connection?

Intimate Relationships

The second area to explore is the client's intimate relationship status. People often play out interpersonal patterns they learned with their parents with significant others. If a client had a rejecting parent, they will then likely find a rejecting spouse. One of the main needs of the self is consistency. Therefore, the person will feel safe and in control if he or she can maintain the same pattern learned in childhood. The current intimate relationship influences the God image because it has a powerful effect on the client's sense of self. If the person is in an unsupportive relationship with his or her partner, he or she will likely have an unsupportive relationship with his or her God image. On the contrary, if the person is in a loving relationship with his or her partner, he or she will likely have a loving relationship with his or her God image. Some helpful questions to ask include: How easy is it for you to establish love relationships? Are you married or cur-

rently in a love relationship? If they are not involved in an intimate relationship, then follow up with these questions: Do you desire to be in
this sort of a relationship? What hinders you from establishing intimate relationships? If they are in a romantic relationship then follow
up with these questions: How long have you been married or in this
relationship? How close do you feel to your partner? Can you be vulnerable and express your feelings to your partner?

Psychological History

A third area to explore is clients' psychological histories. Here you
want to inquire about other psychological issues they have experienced in the past and how, or if, they were ever resolved. Good questions to ask are: Have you ever received treatment for current or other
difficulties? Have you ever been in therapy in the past? Was the therapy helpful? What things in particular were helpful? What things
were not helpful? What did you like about your therapist? What
didn't you like about your therapist? Have you ever been diagnosed
with a mental illness? The answers to these questions will give you
hints about how your relationship with them may unfold. If clients
developed a strong therapeutic relationship in the past, they will
likely build a strong relationship with you. On the other hand, if clients had a string of unsuccessful treatment experiences, it is likely
that your work together will be more challenging. The clients' responses to what interventions were helpful and unhelpful can immediately help you narrow your treatment choices. If a previous therapist offended a client by being overly confrontational, then you will
know to be more collaborative. If a client previously responded well
to cognitive interventions, then you will know to use more of these
techniques.

Social History

A fourth area is clients' social histories. Here you are asking about
their ability to establish and maintain friendships. Psychological support is incredibly important. We are social beings and need others to
thrive. Strong friendships are essential to quality of life. The presence
or absence of these relationships indirectly affects an individual's experience of God. Some good questions to ask are: How easy is it for
you to make friends? Describe your level of trust with your friends.

Are you able to share your struggles with friends and feel supported by them?

A variety of other areas can be included in a full clinical interview. Some of these other areas include medical history, substance abuse history, educational history, occupational history, and legal history. These areas are valuable but are of secondary importance when conducting a God image assessment interview. However, the more information you have, the better your understanding of the person will be. Interested readers are referred to Martin & Moore's (1995) *Basics of Clinical Practice: A Guidebook for Trainees in the Helping Professions.*

Focus on Spiritual Information

The fourth step in the God image assessment interview process is to focus on spiritual information. Richards & Bergin (1997) view spiritual assessment as a two-tiered process: Level 1 and Level 2. Level 1 is more general and used as the spiritual part of the larger biopsychosocial*spiritual* interview. The goal of the Level 1 approach is to gain a broad understanding of what role spirituality plays in a person's life. Level 1 questions focus on religious affiliation, spiritual concerns, and metaphysical worldview. Level 2 is "indicated for clients who have a religious and spiritual worldview and lifestyle, perceive that their spiritual beliefs are relevant to their presenting problems and are willing and ready to explore spiritual issues with the therapist" (pp. 193-194). Level 2 is further divided into an "ecumenical" approach and a "denominationally specific" approach (p. 194). The *ecumenical approach* uses inclusive language and does not use terms that are specific to a particular faith tradition. This approach is used when the therapist is unfamiliar with a client's faith background. The *denominational approach* is used when the therapist is familiar with or a member of the client's denomination. Level 2 questions focus on orthodoxy of the client's beliefs, congruency between stated beliefs and lifestyle, spiritual identity, and ways that spirituality is affecting or being affected by the client's presenting problem.

Spiritual Problem-Solving Style

Richards & Bergin (1997) also recommend exploring a client's spiritual problem-solving style. Pargament et al. (1988) identified three different religious problem-solving styles, "which vary on 2 key dimensions underlying the individual's relationship with God: the locus of responsibility for the problem-solving process and the level of activity in the problem-solving process" (p. 91). The first is *deferring,* in which the person does not accept personal responsibility for solving his or her problems but instead takes a passive role by placing the responsibility onto God. The second is *self-directing,* and occurs when the person assumes responsibility for and takes an active role in solving his or her problems. The third is *collaborative,* in which the person assumes coresponsibility with God and takes an active role by cooperating with God in the resolution of his or her problems. An easy way to see this is to think of deferring as dependent, self-directing as independent, and collaborative as interdependent. Richards & Bergin (1997) suggest that once you assess a client's religious problem-solving style, you can design interventions that are tailored to his or her preferred way of coping. For example, many people who are depressed prefer the deferred coping style. To help this person increase his or her sense of competence you could encourage the person to take an active role by defining his or her problems and then empowering him or her to take specific steps to resolve the problems.

Religious Social Supports

Another spiritual area to assess is the individual's religious social supports. People who are depressed tend to be vulnerable to harmful beliefs that are promulgated by certain religious groups. In some religious settings, the staunch belief exists that problems can be resolved by simply believing or "having faith." People who are depressed may not be honest with these people if they fear they will be seen as less spiritual. They often feel ashamed of their perceived weaknesses and, as a result, do not feel spiritually or psychologically supported. Other religious groups see psychological difficulties arising from a result of being "in sin." These groups believe that people who are depressed have done something to deserve their suffering. Depressed people interact with these people and often leave feeling judged as spiritually weak or deserving of punishment. People who are depressed do not need any external criticism from "well-meaning" Christians. It is vitally important to help them see that their depression is not a result of a lack of faith or punishment for sins they committed.

Faith Crises

In addition to the previous concerns, some people become depressed as a result of a faith crisis. Rigid forms of Christianity are excellent for people who are psychologically disorganized because they bring internal and external order to their lives. One reason this faith style is so effective is because it is pervasive. The person is immersed in a structured way of thinking and develops supportive relationships based on this religious context. However, once he or she becomes stable and becomes more psychologically mature, he or she no longer requires an authoritarian faith (Baker, 1998). Unfortunately, usually his or her friendships and sense of meaning are tied to this particular form of Christianity. At that time, the person is faced with a choice of either leaving his or her main support network for a more complicated form of Christianity or staying in the network but repressing his or her internal drive toward psychospiritual growth. When you conduct a God image assessment interview it is important to assess what kind of religious community clients are involved in, and what real psychological and spiritual support they receive from being part of this fellowship.

Spiritual Disciplines

A final spiritual area to assess is the client's practice of spiritual disciplines, which include prayer, scripture reading, devotions, meditation, and worship (Richards & Bergin, 1997). Clients usually learn these activities through church services, small groups, Bible studies, or discipleship. It is likely that they will have one or two activities that they feel most comfortable using in their personal relationship with God. Inquiring about the specific way they use these disciplines and the effects they have on their personal experience of God can help you design interventions that coalesce with their natural tendencies. For example, if Lilith meditates on scripture and finds that this helps her feel God's compassion, the therapist should maximize this strength by using interventions that focus on scripture meditation.

Richards & Bergin (1997) have cataloged a number of other important areas to address (e.g., metaphysical worldview, doctrinal knowledge, religious orthodoxy, and value-lifestyle congruence). They have also reviewed a number of instruments that can be used to assess spirituality. Many of these topics and measures are beyond the focus of this book, but the interested reader is referred to their seminal book *A Spiritual Strategy for Counseling and Psychotherapy.*

Focus on the God Image

The fifth step in the God image assessment interview process involves focusing on the God image. What was learned in the presenting problem section can be built upon by gaining a comprehensive understanding of their relationship with God. The goal is to help the client paint a full and colorful picture of his or her God image. Some key questions include these: Do you have any concerns about your relationship with God? Do you believe in a personal God? How close do you feel to God currently? What was a time in your life when you felt most distant from God? What was a time in your life when you felt most close to God? In order to be fully accepted by God, what would you have to do? How important is it to know and experience God's love for you? When you do something you regret, how close, or distant, do you feel to God? If you feel distant, what do you usually do to feel close again?

HOW SHOULD THE GOD IMAGE
ASSESSMENT INSTRUMENTS BE USED?

The God image assessment instruments are psychospiritual tests that are used to measure a person's emotional experience of God. These instruments are easy to administer to promote client understanding and self-examination (Richards & Bergin, 1997). Few studies have been completed on these instruments, so they have limited scientific data. Therefore, they should not be used to make absolute statements, but only tentative inferences about a client's God image. In addition, you should conduct testing only if you have received training or are under the supervision of someone who is competent to practice in this area. This section first discusses the steps involved in the God image assessment process and then reviews the administration, scoring, and interpretation of each of the God image tests.

It is important to follow certain steps when conducting a God image assessment. The first step is to organize for the assessment. Whenever you start a new task it helps if you are prepared and have a solid understanding of what you hope to accomplish. Having a plan and a sense of direction increases your confidence and facilitates clients' trust. I cannot overstate how important this is. Think about the difference between an organized waiter and a disorganized waiter. The organized waiter helps you feel comfortable and cared for, whereas the disorganized waiter makes you feel upset and neglected. If organization is important for dinner, how important must it be when assessing a person's relationship with God?

One important aspect in organizing for an assessment is to be familiar with the God image instruments. It is necessary to have a solid understanding of what each test is measuring and be thoroughly grounded in the administration and interpretation of each of the different tests. Taking each test, scoring, and interpreting it can help you become more comfortable with this process. Another way to increase your familiarity is to administer the tests to a friend or significant other. Let them know that you are practicing and need feedback on your style and delivery.

It is also important to decide which tests you will use. Some people like to give all the tests, whereas others prefer to administer only one or two. After you familiarize yourself with the instruments you will be better able to choose the tests that best fit your style. In addition, it is important to be aware of the order in which you administer the instruments. The God image drawing is a nice complement to the interview, so many clinicians like to use it first. The God image inventory usually requires the use of a computer to administer and score, so some clinicians use it only when they know they have a computer available.

The second step is the interview, which was described in detail in the previous section. Some therapists incorporate testing in the first interview. Others conduct the initial interview and then start testing at the following session. Regardless of your preferred timing, you will want to cover all the domains listed in the previous section and then move into specific points about the testing process. The primary focus is on the reason for testing, on what you hope to accomplish by using these instruments. I tell clients something similar to the following:

> Assessment is helpful because it gives me a clear and comprehensive picture of your God image. This shortens the length of

treatment by providing insight and direction that would take much longer to develop if I did not use the instruments.

In addition, you also want to explore the client's view of testing. Some clients have unrealistic perceptions and believe that you will be able to x-ray their soul and uncover the secrets of their heart. For these people, reassure them that the main focus is on their relationship with God and *not* on illuminating the darkest corners of their mind. Be sure to give clients an opportunity to ask any questions they have. The goal is to help clients feel as comfortable as possible.

The third step is to administer and interpret the instruments. Many of the inventories involve self-reporting and do not require that you be present while the client completes them. However, you will want to be close by just in case the client is anxious or has a question. Give the client the inventories and direct him or her to a quiet and comfortable place. Make sure that the room is well lit, does not have a phone (or if it does that the ringer is shut off), is at an appropriate temperature, has relaxed seating, and is secluded to minimize distractions.

Once the client has completed the inventories, process how it was for him or her to fill out the instruments. Some good questions to ask are: Was anything unclear or confusing? What, if anything, stood out to you? Did the instruments uncover any areas that are important that we have not previously discussed? After the follow-up questions, let the client know that you will review the material and give him or her feedback at the next session.

After you receive the instruments, you are ready to start the interpretation process. Take your time when reviewing this information. Try to clear your mind of biases or presuppositions you have about the person. After you have scored them, recheck your work to verify that your results are accurate.

The fourth step is to integrate the material. This is one of the most important steps because it synthesizes the information and allows you to make inferences about the person's experience of God. First, write each test's name. Then review the results of each test and list, under each name, the main God image characteristics from that test from strongest to weakest. After you have done this for each test, look for the characteristics that are shared across tests. The more times a characteristic is listed the stronger it is, the less times the weaker it is. For example, Bob's test results look like this:

God image drawing	Parent/God image grid	God image sentence blank
1. Rejecting	1. Rejecting	1. Rejecting
2. Perfectionistic	2. Angry	2. Impatient
3. Angry	3. Disapproving	3. Angry

We can tentatively conclude that the main characteristic of his God image is that it is rejecting. We hypothesize this because it is the most significant characteristic from each of the three tests and it is consistent across the three tests. We can also conclude that Bob's God image is also characterized by anger. This is a strong characteristic because it is consistent across tests, but weaker than the rejecting characteristic because it is listed in a lower place on each test. Bob's test results do not indicate any positive characteristics, so we can hypothesize that his God image has limited emotionally supportive characteristics.

After you have ordered the test results from strongest to weakest, do the same with the information you gleaned from the interview. What were the main God image themes that emerged from the interview? List them in order of strength and then compare this list with the list you compiled from the testing results. What characteristics are supported by both the interview and the testing results? If a characteristic was present on all of the tests and the interview, then it is likely a stronger part of the client's God image. If the characteristic was present on two of three tests and the interview, then it too is likely a part of the client's God image. If the characteristic was present on one of three tests and not present in the interview, then it is probably not a part of the client's God image. The more constant a characteristic is across tests and the interview, the stronger it is. The less consistent the characteristic is, the less likely it is part of the person's God image.

Once you have identified the most salient characteristics of the person's God image, then you can begin to make inferences about the person's relationship with God. The therapist should elaborate on how the characteristic developed and is maintained relationally and cognitively. For example, Bob's God image is primarily characterized by rejection. It can be inferred that this developed through his childhood and adolescent relationship with his rejecting father. It can also be inferred that it is relationally maintained through his connec-

tion to his critical wife and is cognitively maintained through negative thinking patterns characterized by self-rejection.

The next step involves taking the information you have gathered
and using it to make treatment recommendations. After you have
listed the main problems with the person's God image, you are ready
to take practical steps to resolve these problems. First, each problem
should be translated into a goal. For example, problem: Bob feels
rejected by God; goal: Bob will feel accepted by God. After you construct the goal, the next step is to decide on specific, measurable interventions that you and the client can use to meet the goal. For example,
therapist will teach Bob to use the God image automatic thought
record; Bob will use the God image automatic thought record on a
daily basis. The specifics of the treatment planning process will be
fleshed out and become more clear and meaningful in Chapter 8.

The final step in the God image assessment process is to provide
the client test feedback. It is important to organize your feedback before communicating it to the client. I recommend writing a one-page
summary that you can give to the client that includes test results and
treatment recommendations. This should be written in layperson's
terms and should emphasize practical steps the client can take to
solve his or her problems.

Many clients are anxious when they get test feedback, so be sure to
communicate your findings and recommendations in a gentle and
caring manner. Be empathic, positive, and hopeful. Focus on their
ability to change their God image. Instilling hope will help clients
trust you and the therapy process by increasing your therapeutic alliance. Be clear about your respective roles and responsibilities as well
as about the cost, duration, and frequency of therapy sessions.

God Image Drawing

This is the same test outlined in Chapter 2 that asked you to draw
"you and God" in the first picture and then "how you feel you and
God look after you have done something wrong" in the second picture. Many therapists administer this exercise to explain the differences between the God concept and the God image by highlighting
how the first picture illustrates the intellectual understanding of God
and the second picture captures the emotional experience of God.
Once you have described the differences, you can further explore the

God image by asking clients the following questions about their second picture: How do you feel? How does God feel? How close, or distant, do you feel from God? If you feel distant, what do you usually do to feel close again?

These questions are not meant to be strictly adhered to; instead, they are meant to facilitate conversation. Help clients relax and tell you, in their own words, how they experience God. If gaps in the information occur, or if you do not understand something, ask them to clarify or explain. By the end of the conversation you should have a solid understanding of how they experience their God image when they do something wrong.

It is important to record what the client states when answering the questions and describing his or her God image. Some therapists take notes while the client is talking. The positive in this approach is that you will not forget what the client says, but the negative is that you will not be as emotionally present. Other therapists prefer to record what the client stated after the session is over. This allows you to be emotionally present but increases the chances that you will forget important aspects of the client's report. A recommended compromise involves making quick, shorthand notes that can later be referenced to jog your memory while at the same time helping you remain as emotionally connected as possible. Interpret this test by reviewing your notes and looking for recurring themes. List the themes in order of significance, the stronger at the top and the weaker at the bottom.

God Image Sentence Blank

The God image sentence blank (GISB) is a projective instrument that is used to uncover a person's emotional understanding of God. It consists of forty sentence stems that clients complete by filling in their feelings about the different aspects of their relationship with God. This is a self-report instrument that you administer simply by giving it to the client and asking him or her to fill in the blanks.

After clients complete the instrument, interpret it by looking for themes in their responses. What characteristics of their God image emerge multiple times? Do they seem worried or concerned about a particular area? Did they indicate any positive aspects of their God image? After carefully reviewing their answers, list the main characteristics of their God image from strongest to weakest.

God Image Sentence Blank

Fill in the blanks with your true feelings.
1. God is _____
2. God is most happy with me when _____
3. God is unhappy with me when _____
4. God is similar to my father _____
5. God is similar to my mother _____
6. I feel God is _____
7. God is most proud of me for _____
8. God feels distant from me when _____
9. In my life, God is most concerned about _____
10. If I could do one thing to please God, that one thing would be _____
11. When I pray I feel _____
12. When I read the scriptures I feel _____
13. The person who reminds me most of God is _____
14. The thing that reminds me most of God is _____
15. One thing I would change about my relationship with God is _____
16. God communicates to me through _____
17. God wants me to _____
18. I am worried God _____
19. God likes _____
20. God becomes distant when _____
21. I regret _____
22. The time I felt closest to God was _____
23. Sometimes God _____
24. I want God to _____
25. The main strength of my relationship with God is _____
26. The main weakness in my relationship with God is _____
27. I wish God would _____
28. God expects me _____
29. In my relationship with God, I want to increase _____
30. God always _____
31. God thinks about me when _____
32. When I was a child, God seemed _____
33. Now, God seems _____
34. Church is _____

35. I do not think God _____
36. I need God _____
37. God gets upset when _____
38. I want to understand God's _____
39. When I think of God _____
40. God feels _____

God Image/Parent Grid

This is the same instrument outlined in Chapter 2 in which you compared your experience of God with your experience of your mother and father. Robert McGee, the founder of Rapha and author of the *Search for Significance* (McGee, 1998), created this inventory to help people identify how their relationship with their parents impacted their God image. It is comprised of a number of grids and questions that ask about childhood relationships with caregivers and perceptions of God. This exercise is very powerful, because it uncovers unresolved issues by encouraging clients to take an honest look at their caregivers' strengths and weaknesses. It then shows how these characteristics impacted their God image.

The administration of this instrument is very straightforward. Similar to the other self-report instruments, simply ask clients to answer in an honest manner. Remind clients that no answer is ever wrong, and that it is important that their responses reveal how they *honestly* feel God and not how they think they *should* or *ought* to feel God. These instruments tap deep issues, so they should not be used outside of the therapeutic relationship.

After the client has filled out this exercise, review it and make note of the significant areas. These include negative characteristics on the father, mother, God image/father grid, and God image/mother grid that were marked "always" or "very often," and positive characteristics that were lacking as evidenced by "hardly ever" or "never" responses. The negative characteristics are going to be a stronger part of the client's personality because they were experienced more often in his or her significant relationships. The consistent absence of positive characteristics indicates that these will be harder for the client to learn to experience. Other significant areas to note are positive qualities that were marked "always" or "very often." These qualities can be harnessed by constructing interventions that use them to strengthen the person's relationship with God.

After reviewing the grids, focus on the client's written responses to the questions. The questions ask about the client's childhood relationship with parents and with God, and about similarities that his or her God image shares with his or her parents. These questions encourage clients to go deeper by elaborating on what they learned in the grids. Focus on the characteristics of their parents and God image that they highlight in their answers. They could have chosen any of the characteristics to discuss but instead chose to focus on a particular set of issues. Why did they choose to highlight certain issues and not others? The characteristics they focused on are likely more relevant and meaningful than the other characteristics.

GOD IMAGE QUESTIONNAIRE

William Gaultiere (Gaultiere & Gaultiere, 1989) developed the God image questionnaire (GIQ) to help clients identify their unloving God images. He has graciously allowed me to adapt and reprint the GIQ as well as the accompanying fourteen unloving God images and self-images. His Web site, www.christiansoulcare.com, has many resources to help you to experience God's love, including a free "Christian Soul Care Devotional," articles, books, and seminars.

What follows are Dr. William Gaultiere's GIQ and summaries of the fourteen unloving God images and self-images. After you administer and score the instrument, identify and then list (in order of significance) the person's main unloving God images. Next, read the summaries of the unloving God images to gain a better understanding of the person's God image.

God Image Questionnaire

The GIQ is meant to help you better understand how you see God on an emotional level. Each question asks about your *feelings* in your relationship with God. Please answer according to your feelings or experiences and not your opinions or beliefs about God. Read each question and then circle T for true and F for false.

1. At times I feel that God doesn't give His full attention to the details of my life. T F

2. When I need God it sometimes feels like He does not help me very much. T F

3. I feel like God sometimes withholds good things from me. T F

4. I feel disregarded by God at times. T F

5. I feel that God is distant from me. T F

6. At times I feel pressured to do something for God that I don't want to do. T F

7. I feel I have to do something to obtain God's favor. T F

8. To please God I feel I must measure up to His expectations. T F

9. When I confess my sin I don't always feel forgiven by God. T F

10. At times it feels unfair the way God treats me. T F

11. If I'm in a threatening situation I tend to feel unprotected by God. T F

12. I feel that my abilities are unimportant to God. T F

13. I feel unsure about whether or not God has a purpose for my future. T F

14. When I really need God I tend to feel left on my own. T F

15. I feel that I may be a bother to God if I talk to Him about a decision I need to make. T F

16. I feel that I don't get enough help with my problems from God. T F

17. At times I feel deprived of good things by God. T F

18. I feel insignificant to God. T F

19. I feel removed from God. T F

20. Sometimes I feel forced into things by God. T F

21. If I want God to do something for me then it feels like it helps my cause to do something for Him. T F

22. I feel disapproved of by God.   T   F

23. After I tell God I am sorry I still feel He may be upset   T   F
    with me.

24. I feel harshly judged by God sometimes.   T   F

25. If someone tries to take advantage of me I tend to feel   T   F
    undefended by God.

26. I feel that my abilities are doubted by God.   T   F

27. I feel unsure of whether or not God has special plans   T   F
    for my future.

28. In difficult times it feels like God isn't at my side.   T   F

Source: God Image Questionnaire © 2004 William Gaultiere, PhD. Reprinted with permission.

Scoring

To score and understand your GIQ use the following table. It has fourteen rows, one for each of the fourteen aspects of God's perfect love from 1 Corinthians 13:4-7. (The first word or term for each aspect of love is from the New International Version and the other words are my definitions.) Each aspect has two questions. "False" answers to any question on the GIQ indicate a generally and usually positive experience of God's love (or image of God) in that particular aspect.

Follow these four steps:

1. Circle each of the twenty-eight questions that you answered with "false."
2. Count one point for each "false" answer.
3. Add up the total for each row (aspect of God's love). Scores should range from 0 to 2. Scores of 2 indicate your God image strengths, areas in which you have a positive experience of that aspect of God's love. Scores of 0 indicate your God image weaknesses, areas in which you're struggling to feel God's love and need help.
4. Add up your total GIQ score for all fourteen rows combined. Scores should range from 0 to 28. Higher scores mean a closer

and more loving relationship with God, an image of God that is more positive and true to the God of the Bible.

Question Number Score	Aspect of God's love	Unloving God image
1, 15	Patient: attentive, interested	Preoccupied manager
2, 16	Kind: helpful	Statue God
3, 17	Not envious: generous, gives good gifts	Robber God
4, 18	Not boastful: esteems and shows regard	Vain Pharisee
5, 19	Not proud: close, available	Elitist aristocrat
6, 20	Not rude: gives freedom, gentle	Pushy salesman
7, 21	Not self-seeking: unconditional favor and care	Magic genie
8, 22	Not easily angered: considerate of weaknesses	Demanding drill seargeant
9, 23	No record of wrongs: forgiving, merciful	Outtogetcha police detective
10, 24	Rejoices in truth, not evil: fair, does what's right	Unjust dictator
11, 25	Protects: keeps safe, defends	Marshmallow god
12, 26	Trusts: respects, believes in abilities	Critical scrooge
13, 27	Hopeful: has good plan and purpose	Party pooper
14, 28	Perseveres: reliable, faithful	Divine disappointment

TOTAL:

Source: God Image Questionnaire © 2004 William Gaultiere, PhD. Reprinted with permission.

Unloving God Images and Self-Images

UNLOVING GOD IMAGE	UNLOVABLE SELF-IMAGE
Preoccupied managing director God: responsible to run the world and your life, but doesn't take the time or energy to be involved with you; is impatient and unavailable.	*I'm forgotten and neglected:* I'm not worth God's time and concern, the details of my life don't fit into His busy schedule; I can't disturb God with my problems.
Statue God: doesn't move to help you, but leaves you to work out things on your own; distant, impersonal, uncaring, refuses to act kindly on your behalf.	*I don't get helped:* I'm not worth God's active help and intervention in my life so I have to manage on my own; I can't get close to God, my wants and needs aren't important to Him.
Robber God: takes good things away from you, jealous of your good fortune, a "killjoy" and a "spoilsport" who ruins your good times.	*I must get all I can and hang on:* I'm not worth God's support and encouragement; I don't deserve good things; if I don't hang on to what I have, God will take it away from me.
Vain Pharisee God: brags about himself and puts you down; expects you to humiliate yourself and give him constant homage; takes credit for your successes.	*I always get put down:* I'm not worth God's esteem and praise; I should put myself down so God can be glorified; I don't deserve any credit for anything so God takes it all.
Elitist aristocrat God: considers himself un-needing of you and too good to associate with you; an elitist snob.	*I get excluded and left out:* I'm not good enough to be included in God's elite crowd; I'm not acceptable to Him; he doesn't need me for anything.
Pushy salesman God: rudely and shamefully pushes you to do things his way, violating and using you; forces himself on you, smothers you.	*I get pushed around:* I'm worthless and cheap in God's eyes; I deserve to be taken advantage of; I should be ashamed to be me; I can't say no to God; if I don't watch out God will force me to do something I don't want to do.

Magic genie God: gives you good things if you do things his way; does whatever you want him to if you follow the right formula.

I have to be in control: I'm not worth being loved by God just for me, but have to do certain things to get God to love and help me; I can get God to do whatever I want if I play His game.

Demanding drill seargeant God: always demands more and more from you and is never quite satisfied with you; gets angry and harsh with you if you don't meet His expectations; won't tolerate mistakes, weaknesses, or failures.

I must do more: I'm not worth being accepted by God unless I meet His demands; I can never do enough to earn His love and respect; I must be the best, always win, do everything right; if I mess up, I make up.

Outtogetcha police detective God: perfectionistic and legalistic; looks to catch you slip up; holds your sin against you and won't forgive you.

I have to be perfect: I'm not worth being accepted as imperfect; I have to be careful or I'll get caught making a mistake; I'm not given a second chance or forgiven.

Unjust dictator God: an unfair authority who lords his power over you; punishes you even if you're good and blesses others even if they're bad; doesn't punish those who hurt you.

I'm not treated fairly: I'm not worth fair treatment from God; I always get a raw deal; I deserve to be punished by God even when I'm good; I don't deserve for God to stand up for me when I've been wronged and treated unjustly.

Marshmallow God: weak and ineffectual; doesn't protect you or stand up for you; may overprotect you and treat you like a baby.

I'm vulnerable to harm: I'm not worthy of being protected by God; I'm dependent and helpless so I must stay away from danger.

Critical scrooge God: disbelieves in and disrespects you; won't commit to help you, but stands back and criticizes you; tells you "You won't make it," and "You can't do it."

I'm not confident: I'm not worthy of God's respect and trust; I deserve to be criticized and put down for all my failures; I'll never amount to anything; I can't do anything well.

Party pooper God: is negative, pessimistic, and hopeless about you and your life; tells you, "It won't work," and "Nothing will work for you."

I don't have hope: I'm not worth God's having a special plan and purpose for my life; my dreams and hopes aren't important to God; nothing works out the way I want it to.

Divine disappointment: is an inconsistent heartbreaker; backs away from you when you need him; breaks his promises to you.

I get let down: I'm not worth God's consistent and steadfast care; I'm afraid to trust God lest He leave me when I need Him most; I never get what God promises me.

Source: Unloving God and Self-Images © 2004 William Gaultiere, PhD. Reprinted with permission.

God Image Inventory

Richard Lawrence (1997) designed the God image inventory (GII) to measure different characteristics of a person's God image. It is comprised of 8 scales and has 156 questions. Research supports the instrument's reliability and studies are being conducted to assess its validity. It was normed on 1,580 people in the United States and should be used only with Christians.

Lawrence (1991, 1997) created the instrument to assess how the self and God image are related to a sense of belonging, goodness, and control. He divided each of these areas into two different parts. The first part is related to the self and the second part is related to the God image.

The first area is *belonging,* which is divided into two different scales: presence and challenge (Lawrence, 1997). *Presence* is related to the self and measures the degree to which a person feels God is there for him or her . It is strongly impacted by a person's childhood experience of how present or absent his or her caregivers were. The *challenge* scale measures how the childhood separation-individuation process affected the God image. Lawrence points to what this scale measures through these questions: "Does the fact that God is there for me mean that I should stay here with God, or does God's presence in my life support or even demand that I move out into and interact with the world around me? . . . [challenge is] summed up in the question 'Does God want me to grow?'" (p. 216).

The second area is *goodness,* which is divided into two separate scales: acceptance and benevolence. *Acceptance* is related to the self and is influenced by the person's childhood experience of being accepted by his or her caregivers. This scale is exemplified in the question "Am I good enough for God to love?" (p. 216). *Benevolence* is related to the God image and is affected by the client's perception of the degree of care he or she experienced from caregivers. Lawrence (1997) illustrates this scale in the question "Is God the sort of person who would want to love me?"

The third area is *control,* which is divided into influence and providence. *Influence* is related to the self and is captured in the question "How much can I control God?" (p. 216). *Providence* is related to the God image and pointed to in the question "How much can God control me?"

Administering and scoring the GII can be challenging, so I recommend using Jay Gattis's online program that allows you to administer, score, and interpret the GII, available at www.godimage.org. This program is free and easy to use. It provides you with a password that you give to clients so they can take the test from any computer that is connected to the Internet. Once a client is finished, the program scores the instrument and then sends a report detailing the client's God image to your e-mail. In order to qualify to use this service, you need to pass a brief online quiz and have an advanced degree in psychology or theology. If you prefer a paper and pencil copy, then you can send a request letter to Dr. Lawrence, St. Vincent de Paul Church, 120 North Front Street, Baltimore, MD 21202-4804.

Spiritual Assessment Inventory

Todd Hall and Keith Edwards (1996) developed the spiritual assessment inventory (SAI) to give clergy, spiritual directors, and mental health professionals a tool to assess clients' spiritual maturity, which they conceptualize as occurring on two key dimensions: "Awareness of God" and "Quality of Relationship with God" (p. 341). *Awareness* is the first scale and is based on biblical accounts of how God communicates with people and on the contemplative spiritual disciplines. The *quality* dimension is understood through the lens of object-relations theory, which views people as existing on different points along the developmental continuum. This factor is di-

vided into four different subscales: instability, disappointment, grandiosity, and realistic acceptance (Hall & Edwards, 2002).

Instability, the first subscale, represents the most immature level of
psychological development (Hall & Edwards, 1996). Individuals
who score high on the instability scale usually have borderline personality styles and tend to see the world in black-and-white terms.
That is, they have an inability to see themselves or others as both
good and bad. This dynamic spills over into their relationship with
God. Hall & Edwards (1996) state,

> They have difficulty with ambiguity in their spiritual lives. Per-
> sonal failures or disappointments based on God not fulfilling
> their expectations can lead to intense feelings of guilt or anger.
> Such people tend to have problems trusting God and viewing
> him as loving. (p. 237)

The *disappointment* subscale is closely related to the *instability*
subscale (Hall & Edwards, 2002). When this is elevated it suggests
that the person makes "excessive and unrealistic demands on God,
which lead to a great deal of disappointment and frustration with
God" (p. 353).

Grandiosity, the third quality subscale, measures narcissistic relationship styles with God and others (Hall & Edwards, 1996). People
who score high on this scale will likely be more mature than individuals who are in the instability range but less mature than people who
are in the realistic acceptance stage. Similar to the Greek myth of
Narcissus, these individuals constantly look to others and God to mirror back that they are great, special, and admirable. They often act in
an unempathic and arrogant manner and see themselves as the center
of the universe. Hall & Edwards (1996) elucidate, "Such people tend
to [be] preoccupied with their own welfare and with issues of power
and influence. They tend to be primarily concerned with God's personal protection and provision for their needs" (p. 238).

Realistic acceptance is the last quality subscale and is indicative of
the most mature level of psychological functioning (Hall & Edwards,
1996). These individuals are usually well adjusted and have an accurate understanding of themselves and others. People who have reached
this stage "are more able to experience and tolerate mixed feelings
and ambivalence in their relationships with God, and thus come to
some sense of resolution by dealing with these emotions" (p. 238).

The last scale is *impression management,* which was designed to measure how forthright a person is being in his or her responses (Hall & Edwards, 2002). Some individuals answer inauthentically, and thus inaccurately, by attempting to present themselves in an overly positive light. This scale is a recent addition to the SAI, so Hall and Edwards caution that more research is needed before using it as an indicator of a client's test-taking attitude.

Overall, the SAI is an excellent instrument. It has been used in more than thirty research studies and continues to build a strong empirical base (Hall & Edwards, 2002). The designers hope it will be increasingly used in assessment and treatment planning with religious clients. If you would like a copy of this instrument, then please contact Todd Hall at todd.hall@truth.biola.edu.

To sum up, God image assessment is a seven-step process that is used to uncover a person's God image.

1. Prepare for the testing by having a plan and being organized.
2. Conduct the God image interview.
3. Administer and interpret the instruments.
4. Review and integrate the test results with the results of the interview.
5. Make inferences about how the problematic God image characteristics developed and are maintained.
6. Design treatment goals and interventions.
7. Finally, provide test feedback that is hopeful and focuses on positive steps you can collaboratively take to change the God image from one that is harmful to one that is healing.

Chapter 6

Psychodynamic Psychotherapy

Psychodynamic psychotherapy has evolved and transformed along with the changing tides of psychodynamic theory. Psychoanalysts, who held fast to the idea that psychic energy is repressed in the id, focused on freeing this life by making the unconscious instincts conscious. Ego psychologists believed in the individual's thrust toward autonomy and emphasized challenging defense mechanisms to allow the independent self to emerge. Object relationists, who focused on the process of separation-individuation, highlighted the need to become aware of and differentiated from the internal voices of caregivers. Relational psychoanalysts emphasize "intersubjective" narratives and help clients change through new, corrective, interpersonal experiences. Each of these approaches has made important contributions to the practice of dynamic therapy while at the same time remaining faithful to the primacy of the therapeutic relationship.

The approach taken in this chapter takes key points from the previously mentioned theories and integrates them with insights from brief dynamic psychotherapy. Brief therapy concentrates the curative factors of longer-term treatment into a shorter period of time. Research has shown that brief therapy can be as effective as longer therapy in reducing symptoms (Koss & Shiang, 1993). In addition, short-term treatments save significant amounts of time and money. Time-limited dynamic psychotherapy (TLDP) is the brief therapy explained in this chapter. It was created and empirically tested by Hans Strupp and Jeffery Binder (1984). Levenson (1995) defines it as:

> TLDP is an interpersonal brief psychotherapy. Its goal is to help the patient move away from replicating dysfunctional interpersonal patterns by facilitating new experiences and understandings within the context of the therapeutic relationship. (p. 30)

Clients re-create their main interpersonal problem in the relationship with the therapist. That is, they unconsciously repeat the same
relational pattern with the therapist that causes them difficulties in
their relationships with other people. For example, I had a client once
whose main problem was that he annoyed everyone in his life. As
predicted by this model, he then unconsciously repeated the pattern
by annoying me.

Clinicians who practice dynamic therapy hold that an "interpersonal problem requires an interpersonal solution" (Levenson, 1995,
p. 30). Therefore, dynamic therapists become aware of the client's
main interpersonal problem and then interact with him or her in a way
that solves that interpersonal problem. The client who annoyed everyone also annoyed me. The other people in his life responded by
distancing themselves from him. I wanted to distance myself from
him as well, but realized that I needed to offer him a different response that would help him "see" his behavior and then change it. My
job was to hold my annoyance and then gently show him how his rude
behaviors resulted in alienating others. Instead of rejecting him,
which was my first impulse, I helped him learn a more adaptive way
of relating.

The remainder of this chapter details how this process occurs. The
first part focuses on transference, countertransference, and cyclical
maladaptive patterns. The second section illustrates and explains the
use of psychodynamic interventions. The final section discusses how
psychodynamic psychotherapy changes the client's emotional experience of God.

WHAT ARE TRANSFERENCE, COUNTERTRANSFERENCE, AND CYCLICAL MALADAPTIVE PATTERNS?

Transference

Weiner (1998) states, "Transference consists of the displacement
of feelings, attitudes or impulses experienced toward previous figures
in a person's life onto current figures to whom they do not realistically apply" (p. 196). Clients unconsciously transfer unresolved feelings and issues they have with a person from their past, usually a parent, onto the therapist. As a result, they experience the therapist as
behaving similarly to that person. For example, Bob might experi-

ence me as rejecting of him, even though I am accepting of him. His early experience of his father, who was very rejecting, will cause him to misperceive me as someone who is rejecting.

Sigmund Freud accidentally discovered transference when he first started treating patients. He was seeing a number of female patients who related to him in the same manner that they related to their parents. This initially annoyed him because he wanted to help them, but he felt as if their misperceptions were inhibiting progress. Then one day in a stroke of genius he realized that their misperceptions, or transference, might actually be helpful.

Freud hypothesized that transference allowed their main problem to immediately surface. Instead of investing a great amount of time trying to figure out what was causing their problems, he realized that they were unconsciously showing him by acting it out in the transference. Most of these problems were unresolved issues with parents. Clients projected their parents' positive and negative qualities onto Freud in order to maintain consistency with their past experience of their parents. As a result, the unresolved issues that they had with their parents reemerged in their relationship with Freud.

The therapeutic relationship then became a forum in which clients could act out and resolve the issues they had with their parents. Unconsciously, clients initially experienced Freud as their mother or father, but as they worked through these issues they came to see him more clearly. Once the issues dissipated and the transference was resolved, they realized that Freud was nothing like their parents. They perceived him less subjectively and more objectively. Their internal problems caused them to view him in a distorted fashion, but after they had worked through their issues they could see him more realistically.

Freud eventually concluded that establishing and working through the transference was the essential and curative factor in psychoanalysis. He then focused on ways to increase the transference. Freud believed that the more ambiguous he was, the more intense the transference became. He began sitting behind clients and found that this increased the transference, because they could not read and react to his facial expressions.

Humans crave clarity and abhor ambiguity, especially in relationships with other people. Early analysts deliberately structured the therapeutic relationship to increase ambiguity. They were trained to keep a blank expression so that clients could not read how they were feeling. Analysts did not do this to be cruel, but instead did this to increase the transference.

People know how to respond to another person based on the verbal and nonverbal cues that that person gives. When these cues are absent, they are forced to project onto the person to make sense of the relationship. When this occurs, they usually automatically and unconsciously respond to others as they responded to their parents.

This dynamic occurs in the therapeutic relationship and in other relationships. For example, when most people get a message that states "the boss would like to see you" they automatically assume it is because they did something wrong. As a result, they become anxious and begin to wonder what it is that they did. This situation is ambiguous because the only cue is the message. As a consequence, people are forced to structure this situation by using memories from previous experiences with caregivers. If they had a punishing mother or father, then they will likely expect that they have done something wrong. However, this is only one possible interpretation of the situation. The boss may want to congratulate them, promote them, or talk to them about a project. These other options are viable possibilities, but because they do not match the person's previous experiences they are not triggered.

I had a psychoanalytic professor in graduate school who was adept at remaining ambiguous and increasing students' transference. I am an anxious person by nature, so my angst skyrocketed when I was told that I needed to work with her on a project. I met with her on a couple of occasions and experienced the blank-slate presence (my friends and I nicknamed her "plywood," because talking to her was similar to talking to a piece of plywood). I did not know what she was thinking. I would share, but get no personal response. Predictably, I began to project my issues onto her. As a result, my anxiety and transference increased. Fortunately, I became aware of this dynamic, abstracted my issues, and was able to maintain a professional relationship.

Most psychodynamic therapists no longer recommend that you sit behind the client or maintain a blank-slate expression. Instead, most clinicians believe that the transference is sufficient without these measures. However, this does not mean that the transference does not have to be protected. Keeping real information about yourself to a minimum safeguards the transference (Weiner, 1998). The more personal information clients know about you, the less they will transfer onto you. The more that they have legitimate, reality-based feelings toward you, the less likely they will be to act out their issues with you. So, you safeguard the transference by using minimal self-disclosure and keeping the focus on the client and the treatment plan.

Depressive Transference

TLDP posits that the main interpersonal problem that clients struggle with is "learned in the past . . . maintained in the present . . . and acted out in the relationship with the therapist" (Levenson, 1995, p. 30). Many people who are depressed had parents that were neglectful, distant, and/or abusive when they were children. This caused them to feel worthless, rejected, and guilty. As they continued to develop, this pattern became a core part of their personality. They learned that they deserve to be rejected. Paradoxically, feeling worthless, rejected, and guilty, began to feel right to them (McWilliams, 1994).

People with depression maintain this earlier learned relational pattern by repeating it in current relationships (Levenson, 1995). They have an uncanny ability to communicate that they are unimportant and should be treated this way. Furthermore, they are attracted to people who will treat them as if they are unimportant. These unconscious processes, the ability to communicate that they are worthless and the ability to find people who will treat them this way, result in the maintenance of their main depressive interpersonal problem.

Individuals who are depressed will also repeat their main interpersonal problem with the therapist. They will use the same style of relating with the therapist that they use to relate to others. Levenson (1995) states that "this reenactment is an ideal situation, because it provides the therapist with the very scenario that gets the patient into difficulties in the outside world" (p. 37).

Countertransference

Two different kinds of countertransference exist. The first is very similar to transference and occurs when the therapist acts out his or her own issues and consequently misperceives clients. The second focuses on the therapist's realistic reaction to the client. This section will discuss each type of countertransference.

The first kind of countertransference arises out of unresolved feelings or issues that you have with significant others in your past. You can have positive or negative countertransference. If a client reminds you of an old friend, then you might develop companion-like feelings for this client. You could also have a client that reminds you of an old partner that you had a difficult relationship with. Negative countertransference would manifest, if you became annoyed with the person and treated him or her similarly to how you treated your old partner.

To some extent, countertransference is unavoidable. Your past will always influence your present. The problem, however, occurs when clients are misperceived in a manner that causes harm. For this reason, it is necessary to be aware of the feelings you have for your clients. Do you like them? If so, why? Do they irritate you? If so, why? If you feel as if you cannot manage your countertransference by being objective, then it is best to refer or seek supervision for the client. In addition, you should consider talking to someone about this issue so that you can overcome it. As long as the issue is unresolved, it will be a soft spot that clients could potentially touch and trigger.

The second kind of countertransference is characterized by your realistic response to the client (Levenson, 1995). That is, you are responding to the client in a manner that is not based on your projection but is instead an accurate, reality-based reaction to the client. As mentioned previously, early analysts held that you had to maintain a neutral approach to clients by taking a blank and ambiguous stance. Time-limited clinicians believe that this view is false. Contemporary theorists hold that therapists can help clients only if they are willing to become intensely and actively involved in the therapeutic relationship. Levenson (1995) states:

> The therapist cannot help reacting countertransferentially to the patient—that is, the therapist will inevitably be pushed and pulled by the patient's dysfunctional style and will respond accordingly . . . the therapist inevitably becomes "hooked" into acting out the complimentary response to the patient's inflexible, maladaptive, pattern. (p. 38)

When clients enter your office, they present you with a "microcosm" of their world (Yalom, 1995, p. 28). They relate to you as they relate to others; the reactions they evoke in you will likely be the reactions they evoke in others. TLDP posits that you cannot help but react to clients in the manner that they pull for you to react to them. This is a natural process that occurs outside of your awareness. For example, imagine a client that sulks and frustrates those around him. You will naturally feel turned off by his sulking and want to distance yourself from him. Finding yourself submerged in this client's interpersonal world is helpful because it gives you insight into how others feel toward the client. If a client says he frustrates others, then you may have an idea of what he means, but if that same client frustrates you, then you will have a visceral understanding of what he means. Once you have this deep understanding, you are in a better position to help the client. Most people in this client's life will get annoyed with him and avoid being around him. They will not be interested in explaining to him that his behavior is frustrating. As a result, he will never gain insight into his problematic behavior. Your job is to provide him with that insight.

The first step is to gain awareness and "unhook" yourself from the interpersonal problem (Levenson, 1995). In this case, you would have to unhook yourself from being frustrated and wanting to distance yourself from the client. If you cannot manage to get out of this dynamic, then you will simply offer another problematic response to the client. The frustrating sulker will have managed to annoy you and will end up feeling even worse because he managed to annoy a professional caregiver. In order to offer a different response, you have to be simultaneously inside and outside of the relationship. This is what Harry Stack Sullivan (1953) referred to as being a "participant observer." That is, you subjectively participate in the relationship and, at the same time, objectively observe it. For example, you would participate by interacting and becoming frustrated, but at the same time you would observe the relationship by being mindful of what is occurring between the two of you. Your job is to figure out how his behavior annoys you and others and then provide him with that feedback in a gentle manner.

To better understand this participating-observer concept, try this brief exercise. (1) Recognize that you are participating by reading this book. (2) Now imagine yourself looking at yourself from the upper corner of the room you are in. Be mindful of both of these experiences at the same time. Being a participant-observer involves doing this same thing in therapy. You are in the relationship by participating in it, but you are also out of it in that you are observing it.

Cyclical Maladaptive Pattern

How do you figure out what the client's main interpersonal problem is? Strupp & Binder (1984) designed the cyclical maladaptive pattern (CMP) to provide you with this information. The CMP outlines four quadrants of interpersonal information and helps you identify the individual's primary interpersonal problem. Levenson (1995) details each aspect:

1. Acts of the self—a patient's thoughts, feelings, wishes and behaviors of an interpersonal nature.
2. Expectations of others' reactions—this pertains to all statements having to do with how the patient imagines others will react to him or her in response to some interpersonal behavior.
3. Acts of others toward the self—this consists of the actual behaviors of other people, as observed and interpreted by the patient.
4. Acts of the self toward the self (introject)—this refers to the patient's behaviors or attitudes toward herself or himself—when the self is the object of the interpersonal dynamic. That is, how the person treats him or herself. (p. 49)

Levenson (1995) furthered this model by adding a fifth component, which is countertransference reactions. I add a sixth part, experience of God image.

5. Countertransference reactions—includes the way you feel in relationship with the client. How do you feel being in the room with the client? What are you pulled to do or not do? (p. 50)
6. Experience of God image—refers to the thoughts and feelings the client experiences when relating to his or her personal experience of God.

After you fill the client's information into the previous six components, you analyze the interpersonal information to determine the client's main interpersonal problem. A variety of relational problems might exist, but restrict your attention to the primary problem. If you change the one major problem, then the results will generalize and resolve the other minor interpersonal problems.

Once you have identified the main interpersonal problem, you construct the four main goals of spiritually oriented dynamic psychotherapy:

1. New experience of self and therapist (Levenson, 1995)
2. New understanding of self and therapist (Levenson, 1995)
3. New experience of self and God image
4. New understanding of self and God image

The focus on experience and understanding has its roots in Franz Alexander's (1956) corrective emotional experience. His thesis is that clients need both an emotional experience *and* intellectual insight to achieve long-term change in their interpersonal patterns.

The emphasis on experience is important for a number of reasons (Levenson, 1995). First, it allows clients to experience themselves in a different, more adaptive manner. If a client usually experiences himself or herself as weak with others, then it can be very empowering for him or her to experience himself or herself as strong with the therapist. Second, it allows clients to experience the therapist in a different, healthier way. If a client usually experiences others as rejecting, then it can be incredibly healing for him or her to experience the therapist as accepting.

The original interpersonal problems were learned through painful interactions with caregivers, so it follows that they can be unlearned through healing interactions with the therapist. The emphasis on a new understanding is also very important. A new experience is essential, but clients have to understand why that experience is significant. A new experience, without a rational understanding, results in change that quickly fades, whereas a new experience with understanding results in long-term change (Alexander, 1956). Cognitively framing the situation puts handles on the problem so that clients can more easily grasp it and guard against experiencing it again.

Bob's interpersonal information will be used to illustrate the CMP and its corresponding goals.

1. Acts of the self—"I wish I could please God" (wish); "I feel depressed" (feeling); "I think I am a poor minister" (thought)

2. Expectations of others' reactions—Bob expects to be rejected if he doesn't please others by being overly nice to them and doing what he feels they want him to do. He anticipates: "I have to meet my members' expectations or they will think I'm a slacker"; "If I fail to accomplish my spiritual duties, God will reject me."
3. Acts of others toward the self—Bob's wife is frequently domineering and tells him what to do. His congregants frequently call him for help and implicitly demand that he help them with the difficulties they are experiencing.
4. Acts of the self toward the self (introject)—Bob criticizes himself for not accomplishing enough at work. He tells himself he is inadequate because he is unable to please his wife and congregants. Bob tells himself he is worthless because he fails to be as strong of a Christian or as effective a minister as he feels he should be.
5. Countertransference reactions—Bob acts out his people-pleasing behavior with me. As a result, I feel idealized and pulled to tell him what to do.
6. Experience of God image—Bob experiences God as demanding, critical, frustrated, and rejecting. His God image expects much from Bob and makes him feel guilty when he does not accomplish everything he sets out to accomplish.

Now that we have Bob's CMP spelled out, the next step is to identify the one main interpersonal problem. Bob's main problem is that he is skilled at getting others to tell him what to do. Bob experiences a variety of other problems, but the main theme that continually emerges is that he sacrifices himself to focus his efforts on pleasing his wife, congregants, and God image. He is driven to please others because he fears that if he does not they will abandon him. As a result, he ignores his own needs and invests considerable time and energy trying to please others by doing what he feels they want him to do.

The next step is to create the spiritually oriented dynamic treatment goals. These goals are framed in response to the main interpersonal problem. The first goal is a new experience of self and a new experience of the therapist (Levenson, 1995). This goal would be met if Bob experienced himself as assertive (i.e., non–people pleasing) and the therapist as caring for him when he is not trying to please the therapist.

This will be challenging because Bob will repeat the same interpersonal pattern with me that he acts out with his wife and church members. Remember, you cannot help but naturally react to what a person pulls for. What do you think the hook with Bob would be? How would you feel pulled to respond to him? When Bob first started therapy, he interacted with me in a manner that pulled for me to tell him what to do. I found myself making strong suggestions and being overly directional. I was too forward with my recommendations and saw Bob as less strong and resourceful than he was. This is exactly what the CMP would predict. Bob's main problem is that he is skilled at getting others to tell him what to do. That is what he was doing with me. He was replicating his main interpersonal problem by working hard to please me, just as he works hard to please his wife, church members, and God image.

Once I realized I was hooked, I needed to get unhooked. I had naturally fallen into Bob's interpersonal problem and needed to get out of it to help him. Through discussing the dynamics of our relationship, Bob was eventually able to see what was occurring. He recognized that he was ignoring his own real struggles to try to figure out what I wanted so that he could please me. After this realization, Bob took risks and focused on his own needs. He allowed himself to be more assertive and confident. Bob expected me to reject him and was shocked to find out that I still cared for him. He had a new experience in which he felt valued for being himself and not for pleasing me.

The second goal is a new understanding of self and therapist (Levenson, 1995). Remember that the new experience is essential, but it needs to be complemented with a solid cognitive understanding to result in lasting change. To cement this change, Bob and I spent time talking about how his interpersonal problem developed in past relationships and is maintained in current relationships. We came to the conclusion that his tendency to get others to tell him what to do so that he could please them had its roots in his critical relationship with his father. At that time, it served as a survival mechanism to help him remain connected to his father. He had to bend and conform himself to his father's wishes in order to keep a relationship with him. A painful relationship was better than no relationship. We also concluded that his interpersonal problem is maintained through his relationship with his wife. She expects much from him but never gives him the sense that she is pleased with him. As a result, he repeats the same problem with her that he learned with his father. That is, he ignores himself and works doubly hard to please her. This problem is also maintained in his relationships with his church members. They have high expectations and he regularly sacrifices himself to take care of their wishes.

Bob realized that he did not have a choice in his childhood relationship with his father. He needed to repress himself in order to stay connected to his father. However, he did have a choice as an adult. He did not have to ignore his needs in order to please his wife and church members. Bob could take steps to care for himself. He could abstract himself from being the caretaker and give these other people the opportunity to learn to meet their own needs.

The third goal is a new experience of self and God image. Bob needed to experience himself as strong and God as caring for him when he is strong. This goal parallels the first goal in that the new experience of the self and the new experience of God is the same as the new experience of the therapist. As Bob took risks with me he was also able to take risks with God. He opened up and became real with God. As a result, he felt his relationship with God became more authentic. He was no longer acting weak and passive but was instead strong and active. This new experience of God loving him, even when he is genuine and confident, allowed him to learn to relate to God in a new, healthier manner.

The fourth goal is a new understanding of self and God image. Bob needed to understand that he projected his interpersonal problems onto his God image to maintain a sense of consistency. He experienced God as demanding and difficult to please because he experienced his father as demanding and difficult to please. Bob needed to understand that God created him to be a strong and healthy individual. God is not intimidated by Bob's strength as his earthly father was, and will not reject him for taking proper care of himself. Bob needed to comprehend that he did not have to act passive and dependent to secure God's love. Bob learned that God purposefully created him and wanted him to be strong and secure.

In order to familiarize yourself with the CMP, I strongly recommend that you fill it out with your own information. I used this tool to understand a couple of clients but gained a much better understanding when I used it to conceptualize myself. You can fill out most of it on your own, but I recommend that you ask three or four people close to you to describe their countertransferential feelings toward you. Ask them to really think about it and give you an honest response. What do you pull from others? How do you hook others? Once you do this you will have a comprehensive, objective understanding of your interpersonal behavior. Analyze your results and then distill the results into one main interpersonal problem. Then imagine what the four goals of treatment would be. What kind of new experience of self and therapist would you need? How would your experience of God change?

HOW DO PSYCHODYNAMIC INTERVENTIONS CHANGE THE SELF AND GOD IMAGE?

This section reviews a number of psychodynamic interventions that you can use to change the self and heal the God image. The first part covers the basic dynamic techniques of confrontation and interpretation. The second part focuses on time-limited interventions that emphasize here-and-now interactions between client and therapist. The third section discusses interventions that are used to identify and help clients let go of maladaptive defense mechanisms.

Basic Dynamic Techniques

Psychodynamic therapists use the basic techniques of confrontation and interpretation to help clients become more self-aware. They accomplish this by focusing on preconscious and unconscious factors that influence conscious functioning. Therapists use these techniques to help clients "see" how unconscious thoughts and feelings affect their relationships with others and God.

Therapists use confrontations to focus on thoughts or feelings that are preconscious. Weiner (1998) states, "confrontations call attention to something patients could be talking about, but are not . . . they go beyond what patients are immediately attending to, but not so far as to introduce possibilities from their unconscious" (p. 115). This technique can also be used to call attention to aspects of clients' statements that are contradictory. Clients may state they are deeply sad, while at the same time smiling. A confrontation would point out,

"You are saying that you are really sad, but you are smiling. That seems incongruent."

Psychodynamic therapists use interpretations to call attention to thoughts and feelings that are unconscious (Weiner, 1998). People repeat interpersonal patterns in their relationships, but they are often unaware of the pattern they are re-creating. If you took the time to fill out the CMP in the previous section, then you probably experienced an "aha" moment in which you became aware of and realized that you re-create interpersonal patterns. A good interpretation provides clients with this same "aha" experience. It helps them see a pattern where before they could only see chaos. It allows them to connect the dots so that a clear figure emerges from the background.

Interpretations are powerful interventions that need to be used wisely. Therapists need to keep several things in mind before delivering an interpretation (Weiner, 1998). First, the therapeutic alliance needs to be strong enough to support an interpretation. If it is not sufficiently strong, then clients will not feel safe enough to consider what is being noted. Second, interpretations should be relevant and directly pertain to an issue clients are discussing. Third, they should be simple and concise. If interpretations are convoluted, then they will not be internalized. Fourth, interpretations should be stated tentatively. They are not utterances of truth; instead, they are subjective observations offered by a fellow human being. Fifth, interpretations should address defenses before addressing the underlying conflict— the repressed, threatening thoughts and emotions.

Many short-term therapists use Karl Menninger's (1958) triangle of person to formulate interpretations (see Figure 6.1). It is a tool that helps therapists see clients' interpersonal patterns that were learned in

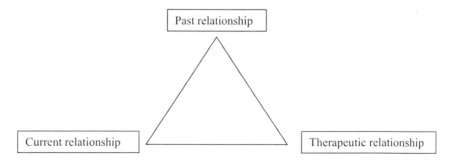

FIGURE 6.1. Triangle of Person (*Source:* Adapted from Menninger [1958].)

a past relationship, are played out in a current relationship, and are acted out in the therapeutic relationship.

Therapists offer interpretations by connecting the corners of the triangle (McCullough-Vaillant, 1997). For example, consider one of Lilith's interpersonal dynamics. Recall from her case history that her mother and husband ignored her inner feelings and instead focused on her outward appearance. An interpretation highlighting this dynamic is similar to the following:

> Lilith, I've noticed a theme in your relationships. Tell me if you think this is accurate. As a child, you learned to ignore your pain and smile to please your mother (past person). Similarly, in your relationship with your husband, I sense that you deny your difficulties to keep your husband happy (current person). Finally, in here with me, it seems you keep up a smiling front out of fear that I'd be frustrated if you were to share your real feelings (therapist).

Janis Morgan Strength (1998) expands Menninger's triangle to a square to offer interpretations addressing the person's relationship with God (see Figure 6.2). She listens for the repetition of the same theme in a person's current relationship, past relationship, therapeutic relationship, and relationship with their God image. Each piece of information represents a side of the square, which she connects before she offers an interpretation.

If the same theme is repeated in each of these relationships, then it likely represents a significant part of their personality. Direct change of the God image occurs through calling attention to this and connecting each side of the square. For example, Bob repeated a theme of letting people down and as a result he always felt overwhelmed with guilt. I would offer an interpretation to Bob to bring this to awareness:

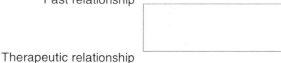

Past relationship   Current relationship

Therapeutic relationship   God image relationship

FIGURE 6.2. Square of Person (*Source:* Strength [1998]. Reprinted with permission from the *Journal of Psychology and Theology.* Copyright 1998. *Journal of Psychology and Theology.*)

It seems like you are frequently afraid that you are not doing enough to maintain your relationship with your wife (current relationship). When you recall your adolescence, you have expressed a similar regret surrounding your inability to accomplish enough to stay connected to your father (past relationship). You also consistently experience God as upset with you because you feel you let Him down when you do not achieve as much as you hope to (God image relationship). And, even today you have indicated that you think I am disappointed with you because you are not making enough progress (therapeutic relationship). There appears to be a theme that runs through each of these relationships of you feeling guilty because you do not fulfill what you feel others expect of you.

The great analyst D.W. Winnicott stated, "I make interpretations for two reasons. One, to let clients know I'm not sleeping, and two, to let them know I can be wrong." After making an interpretation, it is important to check in and see if it was received and if it was effective. If they give you more related information, then they have received it and it was effective. If they change the subject, then they have not received it and it was ineffective (Weiner, 1998).

Time-Limited Interventions

Time-limited psychotherapy provides the client with a new relationship in which they experience themselves and the therapist differently (Levenson, 1995; Strupp & Binder, 1984). Therapists facilitate this new experience by getting hooked and then unhooked. They get hooked by naturally falling into the client's interpersonal pattern and behaving in the same way everyone else does toward the client. They get unhooked by becoming aware of this problematic pattern and offering a different, healing response to the client. Therapists keep the cyclical maladaptive pattern (CMP) in mind and then act in ways that encourage the client to relate differently. This section reviews three TLDP interventions that are useful in providing the client a new experience. These interventions and others are cataloged by Stephen Butler in the *Manual for the Vanderbilt Therapeutic Strategies Scale,* which can be found in the appendix of Levenson (1995).

The first intervention is: "Therapist encourages the patient to explore feelings and thoughts about the therapist or the therapeutic relationship" (Butler, 1986, quoted in Levenson, 1995, p. 241). This intervention helps clients articulate their transference. I might say to Bob:

ME: How are you feeling toward me?

BOB: I really like you and I'm really glad to be working with you.

ME: I wonder if there is something you don't like about the therapy relationship. Is there something you are not crazy about or would like to change?

Bob allows himself to experience only positive feelings toward others. This problem has its roots in his relationship with his father who could not tolerate any form of negative feedback. Bob quickly learned that he could state only what made his father feel good about himself. This problem is maintained with his wife, who is also unable to endure negative feelings. Bob experiences negative feelings and thoughts toward others, but he quickly denies them. He would never actually express them for fear that he would be immediately rejected. Bob thinks that I will become enraged if he offers a slight criticism. When he took the leap and expressed negative feedback, he was shocked to find that I could hear and appreciate the feedback and that I was still connected to him and that our relationship was stronger because it is more honest and genuine. Providing Bob with this new experience allowed him to begin to integrate, and not deny, negative thoughts and feelings.

The second TLDP intervention is: "Therapist encourages the patient to discuss how the therapist might feel or think about the patient" (Butler, 1986, quoted in Levenson, 1995, p. 241). Clients will likely project that you feel the same way that they think others feel toward them. Consider the case of Bob again. According to the CMP, Bob expects rejection and believes he has to please me to gain my approval. My goal is to provide Bob with a new experience in which he feels accepted and cared for regardless of his performance. Visualize how this intervention played out when he was late for a session:

BOB: Sorry I'm late.

ME: How do you think I feel toward you?

BOB: You are probably very frustrated with me for being late.

ME: What makes you think I am frustrated with you?

BOB: Well, I'm late. I'm irresponsible. You cannot count on me to do things right. I feel like a real schmuck for screwing this up.

ME: What do you think I want to say to you?

BOB: Probably that you think I'm worthless . . . that you regret accepting me as a client. (Notice the transference: it sounds like he is expecting me to respond as his father would.)

ME: Have there been other people in the past or present who have told you that you are worthless for making a mistake?

BOB: Oh yeah, my father was always telling me I'm worthless and my wife doesn't say it directly, but she implies it all the time.

ME: So, you learned from your father and wife that if you make a mistake you are worthless. Similarly, you expect me to be angry with you for being late. Can you see how that is a pattern?

BOB: Yes I can. I do. I really expect you to be mad at me and reject me . . . just like my father would have. Are you mad at me?

ME: No, Bob, I'm not mad at you. I like you just as much as I did before. How does it feel to hear that?

BOB: It feels weird . . . weird, but good . . . different. I don't know if I've ever been accepted after making a mistake.

Bob expects me to reject him for being late. Notice that I did not counter this right away, but instead I allowed it to build up to get him in touch with his feelings. I then used the triangle of person to make connections to his past relationship with his father, current relationship with his wife, and transference with me. This allowed Bob to recognize the interpersonal pattern. Then I offered him a different response by telling him I still cared for him. I stayed connected to him and helped him get in touch with that feeling. This provides Bob with the new experience of feeling accepted after making a mistake.

The third intervention is: Therapist uses self-disclosure countertransference reactions to help the client see how his or her behavior affects others (Levenson, 1995). As mentioned earlier, clients evoke in you the same feelings that they evoke in others. Your job is to become aware of this and then react in a manner that is healing. Through using Bob's CMP I can predict that he would sacrifice himself to please me. I would initially be hooked into this by being very pleased with Bob, but would then realize that he was neglecting himself in order to be the perfect client. I would then give him this feedback, so that he could experience himself as being cared for even if he was not perfect.

ME: Bob, you are an excellent client. You work hard all the time, ask insightful questions, and are very committed. I find myself feeling very pleased with you, but am wondering if this might be part of the problem.

BOB: What do you mean? Problem?

ME: Well, you sacrifice yourself to make others happy and I'm wondering if you are sacrificing yourself in here to make me happy. I know you have some real hurts and issues you are struggling with, but you never bring them up. You always give a positive report, but I'm wondering if you avoid these issues out of fear that I'd be displeased with you for discussing them?

BOB: I realize that. I'm afraid that if I'm honest with how I really feel, you will grow tired of me. I want to open up about my real issues, but I'm scared you will grow frustrated with me if you knew the real me.

Addressing Defenses

Defense mechanisms help people manage anxiety by keeping threatening thoughts and feelings out of awareness. People often think and feel in ways that are incongruent with how they consciously perceive themselves. These unacceptable thoughts and feelings cause intense anxiety. In order to defend against this distress, defense mechanisms are unconsciously triggered to keep the disowned feelings from becoming conscious. Visually, the process looks similar to the following:

1. Threatening thought or feeling
2. Anxiety
3. Defense mechanism

All people, healthy and unhealthy, use defense mechanisms on a regular basis. They are a part of our personality that helps us cope with stress. Denial, for example, helps people manage overwhelming crises by minimizing the gravity of the situation (McWilliams, 1994). Without this defense, most people would immediately fall apart when confronted with an overwhelming stressor. The use of defense mechanisms becomes unhealthy when they are overly relied upon. Denial is a great tool to use to get through crises, but it is a terrible tool to use on a constant basis. Think of the woman who is married to an abusive husband who tells herself "this time he really has changed" or the man who abuses alcohol who claims to not have a drinking problem even though he has lost his wife and his job.

Defense mechanisms usually develop early in life to help children cope with situations that are out of their control. For example, anger turned toward the self, the main defense used by people who are depressed, illustrates how early learning affects later functioning (McWilliams, 1994). When children feel consistently ignored, neglected, or abused, they respond with anger. When their parents do not change and care for them more adequately, they justify their parents' behavior by thinking that something must be wrong with them and that they, therefore, deserve to be treated poorly. This gives them a sense of control, because they think if they can change themselves, then they can win back their parents' love. From that point on, whenever they experience abuse or neglect, they will direct their anger at themselves instead of at their parents, because they feel they deserve to be maltreated.

This defense was helpful in childhood, but it is not helpful in adulthood. It is now outdated because these individuals are no longer at the mercy of their parents; instead, they are adults who are responsible and capable of taking care of themselves. However, because it occurred over and over throughout their childhood, it became a central part of their character and now operates outside of their awareness. When they relate to people who demean them, they will not stand up for themselves. Instead, the anger they feel toward the demeaning person will trigger this defense and cause the anger to be redirected back to the self. They will then feel that they deserve to be treated in this manner and blame themselves for the relational problems.

In addition to anger turned toward the self, people who are religious and depressed also use undoing, projection, and somatization in a manner that causes self-harm. *Undoing* is a very common defense, which McWilliams (1994) defines as "a term that means exactly what one would think: the unconscious effort to counterbalance some affect—usually guilt or shame—with an attitude or behavior that will magically erase it." People do not know that their undoing behavior is caused by an unconscious thought or feeling about which they feel guilty. For example, a housewife who is frequently insulted by a disrespecting husband may find herself compulsively cleaning. The house may be perfectly clean to the outside eye, but to her it is filthy and must be cleaned. Her undoing process occurs in three stages:

1. The unconscious threatening thought: "I'd like to kill him for treating me this way."
2. The conscious emotion: intense guilt and anxiety
3. The defense mechanism: undoing behavior: compulsive cleaning

She does not understand that her compulsive cleaning is motivated by the intense guilt she feels for wanting to kill her husband. Cleaning is an irrational means of undoing the thought; it is an unconscious behavior employed to resolve guilt. It is the penance that atones for her sin.

The undoing defense also manifests in compulsive religious behaviors. People may pray for extended periods of time or adhere to a rigid Bible-reading schedule with the unconscious goal of resolving guilt. In some manner, these compulsive spiritual disciplines serve to undo thoughts or feelings of which they are ashamed. After a trusting relationship is established, they will begin to trust you with their forbidden impulses. Once you accept these impulses and help them integrate them, then the compulsive religious behaviors will stop. They may still participate in these activities, but they will no longer be fueled by the anxious compulsion to *have* to do them. As a result, their spiritual life will be more meaningful and psychologically healthy.

Projection is another main defense mechanism. McWilliams (1994) defines *projection* as "the process whereby what is inside is misunderstood as coming from outside." People who are depressed frequently project their anger onto others. Clients experience others as being angry with them when in fact they are the ones who are angry. They may project their anger onto you and accuse you of being angry with them. This may surprise you, particularly if you are in a pleasant mood. Inquiring as to what gave them the idea you are mad at them helps them realize that they may be misperceiving you. Exploring the projection and the underlying anger enables them to integrate it. Once the anger is integrated, the projection will dissolve, and they will no longer perceive you as angry.

Another defense mechanism discussed here is somatization. *Somatization* occurs when people convert an emotion such as anger into a bodily symptom. Instead of expressing anger, they repress it and experience it in the form of a headache, stomachache, or irritable bowel. Drawing parallels to situations in which they should have been angry but were not and instead experienced a bodily symptom will help them become aware of this process. Once aware, they can work through their anger and alleviate their bodily symptoms.

Defenses are complex behaviors that can take on a variety of forms. They are in no way limited to what are typically thought of as defense mechanisms (e.g., repression, denial, undoing, projection, etc.). At their core, defenses are any behaviors that are problematic because they cause clients to avoid functioning in a more adaptive, healthy manner (McCullough-Vaillant, 1997). For example, consider Bob and Lilith. Bob employs a number of defenses, but his main defense is his people-pleasing behaviors. Likewise, Lilith also utilizes a variety of defenses, but her main defense is her workaholic drive. Neither of these are considered defenses in the classic sense, but both operate as defenses in that they manage anxiety by keeping threatening feelings out of awareness.

Identifying the Defense

James Malan (1979) used the triangle of conflict to help therapists recognize how a defense is related to anxiety and a threatening emotion (see Figure 6.3.).

Leigh McCullough-Vaillant (1997) has furthered Malan's thought and created a number of interventions to help clients "recognize" and "relinquish" defenses (p. 20). Therapists can recognize the client's main defense by being aware of the three parts of the triangle of conflict. McCullough-Vaillant recommends asking the following three questions to gain further clarification:

1. How is the patient behaving maladaptively? (usually, a defensive behavior pattern)
2. What would be a more adaptive response? (a feeling-guided response motivated by the patient's real needs)
3. Why is the patient behaving maladaptively rather than adaptively? (probably conflict regarding the adaptive response) (p. 124)

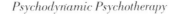

FIGURE 6.3. Triangle of Conflict (*Source:* Reprinted from D. M. Malan, *Individual psychotherapy and the science of psychodynamics,* Copyright 1979, with permission from Elsevier.)

To illustrate the clarity that asking these questions provides, consider the answers I gave for Bob. (1) Bob behaves maladaptively by people pleasing, (2) Bob would behave more adaptively by being assertive and less people pleasing, and (3) Bob behaves maladaptively because he is afraid of being assertive and feels that others would reject him, as his father did, if he were to stop pleasing them.

You can get a better understanding of these questions by asking them of yourself. In what way do you behave maladaptively? What would be a more adaptive way to respond? Why do you behave maladpatively when you know you could respond adaptively? If you take the time and answer these questions, you will gain a better understanding of yourself and the defensive process.

After you have formulated the client's triangle of conflict, you are ready to help them recognize their main defense. You can connect the different angles by saying something similar to the following:

> Bob, I've noticed that whenever you start to feel assertive (threatening feeling) you seem to get very anxious (anxiety) and then inquire about how I am doing and if there is anything you can do to help me (defense: people pleasing).

Once you have discussed this with clients, you can draw the triangle of person on a piece of paper to help them better understand their defensive process.

It is necessary for clients to get a solid understanding of how these three aspects are connected to one another. The threatening feeling begins to surface in reaction to an internal or external stimulus. The precursors of this feeling then sound the alarm by igniting the anxiety, which in turn signals the defense. Once the defense is set in motion, the threatening feeling is repressed from awareness and the person is restored to a place of psychological equilibrium. This is a difficult idea to grasp, so be sure to go over it a number of times so that they really understand it. To better understand how this works, think of Bob. He felt assertive as a child but was consequently rejected by his father. This rejection caused Bob a tremendous amount of anxiety, and Bob's assertiveness then became paired with anxiety. So, as an adult, when Bob begins to feel assertive, his anxiety increases until his defense of people pleasing is triggered to reduce his anxiety.

It is also important for clients to understand that defenses take place in the context of interpersonal relationships (McCullough-Vaillant, 1997). Think of the triangle, or square, of *persons* (Strength, 1998). Defenses are learned in the past, maintained in the present, experienced with the therapist, and acted out with the God image.

Strength (1998) recommends crafting interpretations that address how a person's defense impacts his or her God image. Many people who are depressed learn that anger is unacceptable. It is not uncommon for these people to experience suffering in life and consequently become angry with God. However, because their parents could not tolerate their anger, they project that God cannot tolerate their anger. So instead of owning their anger and expressing it to God, they repress it. As a result, they unknowingly create a disingenuous and unhealthy relationship with God. Strength recommends addressing this by connecting the different parts of the triangle of conflict. A therapist could say the following:

> It seems like you feel angry with God (threatening feeling), but this causes you distress (anxiety), so you deny (defense) this feeling, because you feel like God would be mad at you for expressing anger toward him.

Many people are afraid to express their anger toward God, because they feel as if He is a needy parent who can tolerate only positive emotions. This is tragic, because God loves us and wants us to be real, honest, and transparent with Him.

Letting Go of the Defense

After both you and the client have a thorough understanding of the defense, you are ready to help the client let go of it. This can be absolutely terrifying to the client, because the defense has been employed since childhood. Working through this issue can be one of the most difficult parts of therapy.

McCullough-Vaillant (1997) has outlined a number of steps that facilitate this relinquishing process. The first step is to point out the "negative consequences of the defenses" (p. 164). Defenses exact a strong toll by limiting a person's ability to emotionally experience life. The more emotions that we have available, the richer our lives are. The less, the narrower and more restricted it is. In addition, defenses cause the repetition of self-destructive behavior. Lilith, whose main defense is workaholism, is gradually killing herself by living a high-stress, low-pleasure life. Bob regularly harms himself by refusing to meet his basic needs in order to please others.

The second step is to help clients distinguish between the developmental "origin" of the defense and its current "maintenance" (McCullough-Vaillant, 1997, p. 168). Clients can more easily give up their defense if they recognize that it was a valid childhood response but is no longer necessary. Seeing it from a historical perspective helps them bracket it and see that it was an essential and adaptive reaction in childhood but that the threat has passed. If they understand that they no longer have to please a pathological parent, then they will be more ready to let the defense go.

The third step is to "facilitate the expression of grief over losses caused by the defensive pattern" (McCullough-Vaillant, 1997, p. 164). Defenses rob people by limiting their ability to freely relate to themselves, others, and God. What might life have been like for Bob if he wasn't compelled to please others? What would Lilith's past five years have been like if she was not a workaholic? What different experiences and relationships would they have experienced? Helping clients see how defensive behavior results in emotional and spiritual loss will motivate them to give it up.

The fourth step is to explore what the client gains from the defensive behavior (McCullough-Vaillant, 1997). As you know, people are not very motivated to give up what helps them or is in some way satisfying. Defense mechanisms are inherently rewarding in that they immediately decrease anxiety and restore the person to a sense of psychological balance. Convincing clients to give up a defense can be challenging for this very reason. However, as mentioned earlier, defenses also exact a terrible toll. The metaphorical carrot in this situation is to help clients see that letting go of their defense for more adaptive behavior will result in less anxiety in the long run and in an overall enriched emotional experience.

After walking through these steps, some clients will choose to continue to hold onto their defenses. Some clients maintain their defenses for good reason. These individuals do not let go because they have not yet developed adaptive behaviors. On the other hand, other clients have developed new, healthy, alternative behaviors, but instead choose to stubbornly hold onto their old defenses. These clients are often skilled at getting therapists to take responsibility for their change. When this happens, an exasperating psychological arm wrestling match ensues in which therapists work harder and clients dig in deeper. Rather than get into this frustrating tug-of-war, I suggest that you refuse to pick up the rope. Help them see that they can choose to continue their behavior, even if it is self-destructive, or they can choose to relinquish it (Davanloo, 1995). If they want to change, then you can help them; if they do not want to change, then you cannot help them. Therapy is a team effort that requires collaboration.

Integrating the Threatening Feeling

Once you have outlined the triangle of conflict and helped clients to identify and let go of their defenses, you are ready to help them integrate the threatening feeling (Davanloo, 1995; McCullough-Vaillant, 1997). The feeling was initially experienced in childhood without any distress but eventually became paired with anxiety. This usually occurs when children express a feeling that is unacceptable to their caregivers, who then respond by emotionally distancing, rejecting, or abandoning the child. Children quickly learn that the experience of that emotion results in intolerable pain. When such intense pain is evoked, children learn to repress or deny expression of that emotion at all costs. Soon this process becomes completely unconscious and the person experiences intense anxiety whenever the precursors of the feeling surface. As a result, the corresponding defense is triggered, which decreases the anxiety and brings the person back to a state of psychological balance.

This intervention focuses on reversing this process, so that the person can integrate and fully feel the threatening emotion *without* the corresponding anxiety. According to McCullough-Vaillant (1997) this process has two main goals: (1) break the tie between the anxiety and the threatening feeling, and (2) help the client integrate the threatening feeling back into his or her life by gradual exposure to increasing amounts of the emotion. McCullough-Vaillant (1997) calls this inability to experience the threatening emotion an "internal affect phobia" (p. 209).

She integrates behaviorism and psychoanalysis to illustrate this problem. Behaviorists designed an intervention to cure phobias, which they called graded exposure (Wolpe, 1958). As the name implies, this technique helps phobic clients manage anxiety and overcome phobias by gradually exposing them to the feared object. For example, consider a therapist who is using this intervention with a client who has a phobia of flying. First, the client would be asked to look at a picture of an airplane until the anxiety subsided. Second, the client would look at a real airplane at the airport. Third, the client would imagine himself or herself flying in the airplane. Fourth, and finally, the client would board the plane and actually fly to achieve complete exposure and overcome the phobia. The client's anxiety gradually becomes disassociated from the airplane through the process of graduated exposure.

McCullough-Vaillant's (1997) metaphor captures the essence of what occurs with clients who defensively disown their emotion. They truly are phobic of their repressed emotion; it scares them, just as an airplane, elevator, or heights scares someone else. She states, "such affective phobias require repeated imaginal exposures to the avoided inner affective response until the experience of feeling is desensitized, that is, until the affect can be experienced without [anxiety], fear, guilt, or shame" (p. 191).

How do you help clients integrate their feared emotion? McCullough-Vaillant (1997) recommends using guided imagery "in which specific scenes of interpersonal episodes and associated affects are imagined in the session" (p. 206). The goal is to help clients immerse themselves in a multisensory experience of either a memory or created fantasy in which increasing amounts of the threatening emotion are experienced and integrated.

When using guided imagery, it is important to move back and forth between the anxiety and threatening feeling points of the triangle of conflict (McCullough-Vaillant, 1997). That is, you want to be aware of the person's anxiety level while you are gradually exposing the person to his or her threatening feeling. Just as the therapist gradually exposed the client to the airplane, you want to gradually expose the client to the forbidden emotion. For example, Bob was very afraid of his own strength. I started by asking Bob to remember a time when he felt strong, and then encouraged him to go there in his mind's eye. He recalled a time when he felt strong toward his father and was consequently rejected. I asked him to recall that memory and describe it to me in as many sensory words as he could. Doing this helped him relive the memory. As I did this I also monitored his anxiety level by inquiring how he was feeling. If he began to feel overwhelmed, then I started talking to him about what was making him anxious. After the anxiety subsided, we returned to the memory with the goal of tolerating it for a while longer. As Bob's ability to tolerate his anxiety increased, I asked him to imagine himself in the situation again and to explain what he would have liked to have said to his father. Gradually increasing his exposure to this memory allowed him to integrate his disowned strength.

I also asked Bob to imagine an interpersonal scenario in which he felt strong. Again, I wanted this to be a panoramic, multisensory experience in which he could successively own more and more of his strength. The process of facilitated successive exposure to an imaginary event works the same way as it does with recalling a memory (McCullough-Vaillant, 1997). Similarly, the goal is to move back and forth between the anxiety and defense points on the triangle of conflict to regulate the client's experience. I helped Bob fully imagine himself becoming more and more assertive in a variety of interpersonal situations (with his wife, with church members, etc.). Again, just as graded exposure to a feared object (e.g., plane, snake) in real life decreases anxiety, so does graded exposure to a feared emotion in imagined scenarios decrease anxiety.

Clients can also use this technique in their prayer life to change their God image. Before using this technique with a client's God image, please see the discussion on integration and ethics in the beginning of Chapter 8. Individuals who are afraid of owning their emotion with others are also afraid of owning their emotion with God. They often fear that God will respond in the same way others have in the past. Using the graded exposure technique with God helps them integrate their disowned affect and change their personal experience of God.

The steps of using this technique with God are as follows. First, identify the threatening emotion. Next, ask clients to become aware of the God image. Then, encourage clients to experience the threatening feeling with their God image in mind. At this stage clients may get anxious or fearful. If this occurs, explore why they feel this way. Do they imagine God reacting in a certain manner? After they have explored it and the anxiety subsides, ask them to once again embrace the feeling with their God image in mind. Help them differentiate between their God image and the real God. Discuss how their God image and the real God would respond differently. After they have this awareness and the anxiety subsides, ask them to once again embrace the threatening feeling with their God image in mind. The goal is to increase the intensity of the feeling *and* the amount of time with each trial. Repeat this process over and over again until the client is able to experience the emotion without feeling anxious.

Once you have done this in therapy a number of times, you can encourage clients to do it on a daily basis for homework. Ask them to go to a quiet place in their house and practice it regularly. Experiencing the threatening emotion with God will allow them to generalize this experience to other relationships. If they learn that God accepts them when they experience a threatening feeling, then they will try feeling this way with others. Their relationship with God gives them the courage to change other relationships.

WHAT IS INTERNALIZATION AND HOW DOES IT AFFECT THE GOD IMAGE?

Internalization

Internalization is the process by which people internalize the character of other people. This is a gradual process that ends in people treating themselves as others first treated them. This occurs in a variety of relationships, but is most clear in the child-parent relationship. Adults who are depressed internalized their parents' voices in childhood in an attempt to win their parents' acceptance. These voices gradually became such a strong part of their character that as an adult they are unaware of them and instead "just feel depressed." They do not know that these voices are rooted deep in their childhood or that they replay them in order to maintain their state of depression.

Psychodynamic psychotherapy works by using this same process of internalization. The goal is for clients to internalize the character of the therapist and then learn to treat themselves as the therapist treated them (Blatt & Behrends, 1987). Through this process, the harsh internal voice of the parents becomes replaced with the empathic voice of the therapist. The therapist takes the main place in their mind and enables them to evaluate themselves with acceptance and insight. The way this happens is similar to the way it happened in their childhood development.

People with depression originally modified themselves in order to win the approval of their parents. They will remodify themselves in order to move on to the next level in therapy (Blatt & Behrends, 1987). They feel deeply connected to the therapist. This connection means a great deal to them, and they will attempt to maintain and gain more of this connection through making the changes the therapist suggests. As they change, they will begin to treat themselves as the therapist treats them.

The two primary aspects central to treatment and necessary for clients to internalize are empathy and insight (Blatt & Behrends, 1987). These need to be the two main characteristics of the way you interact with them. Both are necessary for change to occur. If you treat them only with empathy and no insight they will internalize the caring aspect of you but will never learn how to be aware of and change their dysfunctional behaviors. On the other hand, if they internalize only the interpretive, insightful side of you, and no empathy, then they will be very self-critical and will not treat themselves with the love and acceptance necessary for change to occur.

Understanding this process and acting on it can be scary. If you are questioning whether you are the right person to be taking residence in your clients' minds, you are asking yourself a good question. It is necessary to be very sensitive and very aware of the power in the therapeutic relationship. Many therapists do not like to conceptualize change in this manner because it brings to light the enormous amount of responsibility they have. You can begin to see why it is so important that you are healthy. The clients' unhealthy parents were internalized, and it resulted in depression. It is necessary that you are healthy, empathic, and insightful for clients' internalization to result in the alleviation of depression.

Internalization and the God Image

Internalization changes the God image. The self and God image are closely interconnected: as the self changes the God image also changes. People with depression, through early painful interactions with caregivers, learned to conform themselves to stay connected to their parents. As a result, they experience a rejecting God image that threatens to abandon them if they are not perfect. They unlearn these relational patterns and develop healthier patterns through internalizing the therapist. This process changes the God image.

Therapists can facilitate God image change through empathically using psychodynamic interventions. What follows is a loose construction of how the self and God image change through the internalization process (McWilliams, 1994). The steps are numbered to clarify what occurs. In reality, it is not as neat and clean as it sounds. Each step includes the main therapeutic change as well as the corresponding change in the God image.

1. *Idealization of the therapist and devaluation of the self.* Clients who are depressed often enter therapy in complete awe of the therapist (McWilliams, 1994). They believe the therapist is supercompetent and has all the answers. Conversely, they view themselves as completely helpless and worthless. This same dynamic is played out in their relationship with their God image. They view their God image as extremely powerful and view themselves as extremely weak.

2. *Projection of anger onto the therapist.* After trust is established, clients begin to project their repressed anger onto the therapist (McWilliams, 1994). The therapist is distorted to resemble clients' critical parents. Clients will reexperience the abandonment they originally experienced with their parents and will attempt to conform themselves to what they perceive as the therapist's

desires. Clients behave this way because they are terribly afraid
that the therapist will reject them if they are not perfect.

A similar process occurs in their relationship with their God
image. Their God image is very angry and demanding. The only
way they can satisfy their God image is through extreme self-
denial and through conforming to what they perceive as their
God image's desires. Unfortunately, their God image is never
pleased and they continue in their sacrificial behavior to no
avail.

3. *Therapists' interpretation of clients' perfect compliant behavior
and of clients' expression of anger.* At this stage in the therapeutic process, therapists address the clients' perfect behavior. Emphasis is placed on how they learned this behavior in their childhood relationship with their parents; it was the only choice they
had, but now it is an outdated and problematic way of behaving
(McWilliams, 1994). After addressing the defense mechanisms,
focus is placed on the underlying anger clients initially experienced but then repressed because it was too threatening.

At this point, clients may risk getting angry with the therapist
(McWilliams, 1994). At first they will be only a little angry.
They are testing the relationship to see what the consequences
will be. If therapists accept the anger, and clients realize that
nothing detrimental occurred, they will gradually express increasing amounts of anger and begin to own this aspect of themselves. At this same time, clients will let therapists know of any
hidden issues (i.e., deep dark secrets) that they have been har-
boring. They fully expect to be flat-out rejected for these past
experiences. The therapist's acceptance of these issues enables
clients to learn that they are worthy of love. As a result, they internalize the accepting characteristics of the therapist.

The corresponding change in the God image is powerful. It
becomes diffused of its wrath and persecution. The repressed
guilt and anger that once empowered it are no longer available
because the secrets have been confessed and the anger accepted
and integrated into the self. At this point, the God image will be
placed in the background of the psyche because so much of its
previous power and attraction laid in its ability to demand and
condemn.

4. *Clients' continued internalization of therapists through trans-ference and interpretation.* Clients will continue to grow through the therapeutic process. They will continually internalize the healing aspects of therapists and hence become increasingly self-aware and self-accepting (Blatt & Behrends, 1987). As this happens, clients will consistently become more confident. Correspondingly, their therapist will become deidealized (McWilliams, 1994). Nearing the end of treatment, the therapist will be perceived as a wise fellow traveler rather than a superhuman. It is at this point clients will achieve the ability to love and care for themselves, regardless of the feedback they receive from others. As a result, mature interdependence rather than immature dependence will characterize their relationships.

The corresponding change in the God image will result in its being drained of its pathological power. The qualities of the therapist will now significantly characterize clients' God images. Consequently, they will experience their God image as accepting rather than rejecting. These individuals will then experience real growth in their relationship with God. They will have a more honest relationship and a new ability to manage the ambiguity that is inherent in the faith.

Now that clients' characters have changed and the pathological God image no longer binds them they will be able to clearly see what it means to be a religious person. They will have the ability to objectively look at their beliefs and determine what it means for them to be a Christian. For the first time, their faith experience will be one that they can critically reflect upon rather than compulsively follow.

To sum up, internalization through transference and interpretation is an extremely potent technique. It changes the very structure of the self. Through therapy, clients learn to treat themselves in the same way that the therapist treats them. Anger, forbidden impulses, and deep dark secrets are no longer repressed; instead, they are carefully explored and integrated into the self. This restructuralization process allows for continuing self-acceptance and self-awareness.

Therapeutic change greatly affects the God image. Once people enter therapy, the God image gradually becomes de-energized. Clients re-create the same earlier learned relational patterns that they used with their parents and their God image with the therapist. As therapists are empathic and insightful, clients gradually internalize the character of their therapist and learn to treat themselves as their therapist treats them. This results in a corresponding change in the God image. When therapy concludes, the final result is a God image that is consistent with their healthy sense of self. The God image that was once rejecting is transformed into a God image that is accepting.

Chapter 7

Cognitive Techniques

WHAT IS COGNITIVE THERAPY?

Cognitive therapy changes the way that people think in order to change the way they feel. Thoughts are extremely powerful. To illustrate this, allow yourself to engage in this brief exercise (Beck, Emery, Rush, & Shaw, 1979). Recall something that you regret doing—something that was moderately emotionally painful. Shut your eyes and reimagine the event for approximately ten seconds, then stop. How do you feel? You likely feel a little down or sad. Now, recall a positive memory that made you feel wonderful. Again, shut your eyes and fully go there; recall the sounds, sights, and feelings. Now, even though you probably do not want to, open your eyes. How do you feel? You likely feel peaceful and grounded.

The mind is easily tricked into thinking that what we imagine is reality. That is why recalling negative and positive memories results in feelings that were originally experienced during the actual event. This exercise shows how deliberately changing the way a person thinks can change the way he or she feels.

This idea of changing thoughts to change feelings has been around for a very long time. The Apostle Paul encouraged this practice when he wrote about renewing the mind (Romans 12:2) and instructed others to think, or meditate, on true and lovely things (Phillippians 4:8). Saint Ignatius and other religious masters also used cognitive exercises to facilitate spiritual formation. However, it is the recent cognitive theorists, most notably Aaron Beck, who have simplified these concepts so that they can be practically used to help people who are suffering from mental health issues. Beck et al. (1979) define cognitive therapy as follows:

Cognitive Therapy is an active, directive, time-limited, structured approach used to treat a variety of psychiatric disorders (for example, depression, anxiety, phobias, pain problems, etc.). It is based on an underlying theoretical rationale that an individual's affect and behaviors are largely determined by the way in which he [or she] structures the world (Beck, 1976). His [or her] cognitions (verbal or pictorial "events" in his [or her] stream of consciousness) are based on attitudes or assumptions (schemas), developed from previous experiences. (p. 3)

A variety of interventions are used to change the way clients think. Behavioral techniques are used in the beginning of treatment and are particularly helpful with those who are severely depressed (Beck et al., 1979). Cognitive interventions are also used in the beginning of therapy and initially focus on changing automatic thoughts, which Beck and colleagues define as "thoughts or visual images individuals may be unaware of unless attention is purposely focused on them" (p. 166). After this, schemas are targeted, which are deeper, more ingrained thought patterns.

Therapists choose interventions based on the client's symptoms (Beck et al., 1979). The therapist and client begin by developing a list of problems that they want to address. Once they have prioritized the list, they discuss techniques that can be used to address these problems. Clients usually choose the technique that they feel most comfortable with and then experiment with it in session. The therapist walks them through the technique and makes sure that they understand how and why it is used.

After clients understand the technique, therapists often assign the practice of it for homework (DeRubeis, Tang, & Beck, 2002). Homework is a vital part of cognitive therapy. It makes therapy practical and provides clients with a greater sense of control. Clients need to understand that applying the techniques in everyday life will result in them becoming healthier more rapidly. Assignments should be clear, precise, and matched to the skill level of the clients. The therapist should review the previous week's homework assignment at the beginning of every session. This behavior encourages clients and reinforces the motivation to continue therapy.

As in other areas of cognitive therapy, the therapist wants to initially play an active and structured role early in treatment but gradually release that role so that clients can accept more responsibility

(Beck et al., 1979). Near the middle to the end stages of treatment, the therapist can assign clients the homework of becoming less depressed by next week. By not giving any explicit directions, clients are challenged to devise their own assignment. This furthers the goal of cognitive therapy by encouraging them to become their own therapists.

HOW DO COGNITIVE INTERVENTIONS AFFECT THE GOD IMAGE?

Cognitive interventions change the way people feel about themselves and God by changing the way they *think* about themselves and God. These interventions are played out in a spiritual context and alter the way a person emotionally experiences God. Therapists are in a position of power, so they have to be extra careful to not impose their beliefs and values on clients (Tan, 1994). Before using these techniques with a client's God image, please see the discussion on ethics and integration in Chapter 8. A necessary first step is to help clients articulate what they believe about God's grace, love, and forgiveness. These beliefs, based on scripture and tradition, will form the basis of how they would like to learn to experience God. Once these beliefs are spelled out, you can then work with them to change their God image so that it more closely resembles their understanding of the true God.

Some Christians may take issue with my focus on God's grace, love, compassion, and forgiveness. They may fear I am advocating for a warm and fuzzy spirituality that is absent of the suffering and hardships that are central to the cross. These individuals will read some of the imagery exercises and assert that I have gone too far in emphasizing God's healing characteristics.

I have a couple of responses to these expected, and welcomed, criticisms. One, I do not think it is possible to overemphasize God's love and forgiveness. These are essential features of the new covenant and central to our identity in Christ. Two, people who are depressed do not have a balanced understanding of Christianity. They are too aware of their sin and depravity and are not aware enough of God's mercy and grace. Three, I am not encouraging people who are depressed to lose sight of the consequences of the fall and sin, but I am asking them to open up to their understanding of the gifts of redemption and forgiveness.

So, as you read these interventions, please keep these thoughts in mind. The goal of this book is to help people who are depressed to have a more normative understanding of God—one that many of us are already blessed to have. I feel that God is always revealing God's character, but hurtful developmental occurrences cause people to miss what He is saying to and showing them. Fortunately, just as harmful experiences gave them a false perception of God, healing experiences can give them a true perception of God.

Behavioral Interventions

Helping clients change the way they behave can have a powerful effect on the way they see themselves and experience God. Many individuals who are depressed think less and less of themselves and consequently restrict more and more of their behavior (Beck et al., 1979). Their depressive thinking suffocates them and causes them to feel incompetent and unable to accomplish what they used to accomplish with ease. Therapists use behavioral interventions to help clients relearn old behaviors and develop new, healthier behaviors. The practicing of these behaviors directly affects the self and indirectly affects the God image.

One technique involves helping clients create a weekly schedule in a day planner (DeRubeis et al., 2002). It starts by having clients list tasks that they want to accomplish during the week. This can include tasks as simple as taking a shower or more complex tasks such as writing an outline for a sermon. Clients then rate the degree of pleasure and mastery on a scale of 0 to 5 for each activity. People who are depressed often think that they do not enjoy *anything* and are terrible at *everything*. When they complete this exercise it decreases all-or-nothing thinking by helping them see that they do enjoy some activities and are good at some activities. When Lilith first started treatment she felt like she had lost all of her ability to enjoy previously pleasurable activities. After completing a weekly schedule and rating the degree of pleasure she experienced, she realized that she enjoyed walking her dog and watching movies. She also felt incompetent because she told herself she was unable to effectively lead her small group. After this exercise she realized that she was better at it than she thought. Recognizing that she did enjoy activities and was competently accomplishing tasks helped her realize that she was minimizing her happiness and sense of efficacy.

Another behavioral intervention is physical exercise. A startling amount of medical and psychological research now exists that supports the beneficial effects of exercise (Superko & Tucker, 2003). Exercise releases serontonin and endorphins in the bloodstream, which results in an increased mood. Similar to medicine, however, it has to be "taken" on a regular basis to keep the chemicals in the blood stream. If a client takes medication on a random basis it will not result in decreased symptoms. Likewise, irregular exercise will not result in lasting health benefits. I started a cardio workout for one hour a day, five days a week one year ago. I now notice a huge difference in the way I feel and think about my relationships with others and God. Because exercise powerfully affects the self it also powerfully affects the way I see others and God. When I exercise I feel more hopeful and optimistic; I see things in a better light and feel closer and more connected to God. As a result, I am more able to experience His love because I am more open to it.

Automatic Thought Interventions

Do you remember when you were learning to drive a standard-transmission car? I do. I was sixteen and driving a 1986 Ford Escort. My mother and future wife were in the backseat laughing as I stalled time after time. Eventually I learned to release the clutch and shift without stalling. I was shaky for a number of months, particularly at traffic lights and stop signs, but eventually I mastered it. I now drive a stick without even thinking about it—it has become second nature to me.

Automatic thoughts are learned in much the same way that driving a standard is learned. As a child, the self-critical thoughts are conscious, awkward, and new. However, with repetition they soon become second nature. Self-defeating thoughts become automatic and occur without the person knowing that they are even happening. The same happens with driving a standard; at first it takes much deliberate thought and concentration, but the person eventually learns to shift without even realizing it. That is, the thoughts no longer consciously register—they operate outside of the person's awareness. It is in this context that Beck et al. (1979) define that "[a]utomatic thoughts are thoughts or visual images individuals may be unaware of unless attention is purposely focused upon them" (p. 187).

One reason automatic thoughts occur so effortlessly is because they follow well-worn neuronal tracks in the brain. Thoughts travel down a number of different "roads" in the brain. The "driving a standard" road does not exist at first, but with enough practice it becomes paved. Self-critical and self-harming thoughts in those who suffer from depression are paved early in childhood and only grow wider and wider because they are repeatedly practiced over and over again.

I live in the Norfolk, Virginia, area of Hampton Roads. We have one major highway that runs from downtown to the oceanfront. Imagine blocking this road and rerouting traffic. Well, this is exactly what happens in cognitive therapy. You block off the main highway, "interstate-depression," and reroute the traffic, or thoughts, down a rational, healthier, route. Initially this route is rather small and difficult to traverse, but with enough practice it becomes as wide and efficient as the depression route.

In order to accomplish this rerouting you need to work collaboratively with the client to accomplish two steps: education and transformation (Beck et al., 1979). *Education* involves teaching the client about the relationship between thoughts and feelings. *Transformation* occurs by helping the client identify and then change his or her automatic thoughts.

Education

Educating clients about automatic thoughts has to be done in a manner that is meaningful to them. As any good teacher knows, both content and delivery are important. Exercises that involve the client and are practical are highly recommended. Examples that are "sticky" (i.e., get stuck in their head) and simple are also very effective.

One way to educate clients about automatic thoughts is to lead them through the exercise that you completed in the beginning of this chapter in which you recalled a positive and a negative event. As they do this, instruct them to be mindful of any thoughts they have during the process. Asking them to do this turns up the volume on their automatic thoughts so they can be "heard." It is very likely that they will experience negative self-talk during the emotionally painful event and positive self-talk during the pleasurable event. Wright (1986) refers to this as the "inner intercom system." This exercise helps clients listen to what is being announced on their own public address system.

Transformation

The second part of changing automatic thoughts occurs through the transformation process. This is accomplished through identifying and then changing automatic thoughts. As mentioned earlier, people often have a hard time becoming aware of their automatic thoughts. Fortunately a number of tools exist that therapists can use to teach clients to help them identify them. Automatic thoughts are most available immediately after they occur, however most people do not have time to stop what they are doing and write them down (Beck et al., 1979). So most cognitive therapists ask clients to schedule fifteen minutes at the end of each day to review negative situations and negative emotions they experienced. Therapists then instruct clients to recollect what kind of thoughts they were experiencing at that time. For example, Bob recalled that he felt depressed after a board meeting and continued feeling this way for the rest of the afternoon. He recalled the situation and stated that he started feeling depressed when he realized that a couple of board members seemed uninterested when he was talking. Bob interpreted their behavior to mean that they thought he was incompetent. He told himself that he was the wrong man for the position, that they wish they would have hired someone else, and that they were frustrated with his performance. Once Bob became aware of his self-talk, he realized why he felt so depressed.

Daily practice of reviewing negative feelings and negative situations helps clients identify their automatic thoughts. Clients can then increase their awareness by carrying an index card in their pocket and checking it every time they have a harmful automatic thought (Wright, 1986). I had a client who told me that she only had two to three self-critical thoughts a day. She then started counting her thoughts on a daily basis only to find out that she was averaging twenty-five to thirty negative automatic thoughts a day!

Once clients identify their thoughts they are then ready to change them. "Collaborative empiricism" lies at the heart of this transformation process (Beck et al., 1979, p. 152). This means that the therapist and client work together to evaluate the validity of the client's thoughts.

That is, they review the automatic thoughts to see if they are accurate or inaccurate. This is accomplished through specific exercises and questions. For example, one of Bob's assumptions was that he had to please everyone by agreeing to do whatever they asked him to do. He was convinced that if he did not do this, then they would reject him. We set up an experiment in which he said no to two different requests. It turned out that the individuals still liked him and gave no sign of rejecting him. This caused Bob to reconsider the validity of this belief.

Questions are another key intervention used in the transformation process. Once a self-defeating thought is identified, therapists ask clients a number of questions to help them evaluate the accuracy of their automatic thoughts. The goal is that clients will learn to ask themselves these questions so that they can successfully change their automatic thoughts. Wright (1986) suggests the following questions:

> What evidence do you have for this thought?
> In what way might you be thinking in all or nothing terms?
> Could it be that you are confusing the facts with your perception of the facts?
> Where is the logic for this belief?
> Are you oversimplifying the situation?
> As you hear yourself thinking are you finding some words that are extreme or even exaggerated?
> What is the probability of your thought occurring?
> Are you overlooking your strengths?
> How would you approach this situation if you were not worrying about it? (pp. 89-93)

Another technique helps clients come up with and rate alternative explanations for their perceptions (Beck, 1976). Consider the previous example, Bob felt depressed because he interpreted two board members' disinterest to mean that they thought he was incompetent. Bob was sure he perceived the situation correctly. I asked him to come up with alternative explanations and specify the proportion of believability based on 100 percent. Here is a list of what he generated:

1. They think I am a failure because I am not doing as well as they expected (50 percent)
2. They had other thoughts on their mind that were distracting them (20 percent)

3. They relate to most people that way, so it does not have anything to do with me (10 percent)
4. They were uninterested, but it had to do more with the topic than it had to do with me (10 percent)
5. They were tired and wanted to go home (10 percent)

After Bob generated this list and rated the proportions of believability for each explanation, he was able to see that he had drawn a conclusion much too quickly. His depressive thinking had restricted his ability to consider the other possible explanations. Other potential reasons could exist for why the two members were distracted. Seeing and rating these alternatives helped Bob decrease his depressive thinking by helping him question the validity of his belief and allowing him to entertain other explanations. If he wanted to, Bob could further test this belief by devising a quick scale that board members could fill out. He could ask them to rate him on a number of factors. He would then have legitimate evidence as to how they feel about his performance.

Some individuals hold that their belief is valid even after working through a number of these exercises. If this occurs, then it can be freeing to ask them, "What if your perception is accurate?" (Wright, 1986). Encourage them to play out the situation so that they can project what would happen. I led Bob through this exercise and asked him the following questions: What if two of the eight board members think that you are doing a poor job? Have people thought you did a poor job in the past? What happened? Do all board members have to think you are doing a great job? When Bob answered these questions he realized that people had negatively evaluated him in the past and that he was able to hear and integrate their criticisms. Nothing bad had happened. This helped Bob see that his fears were out of proportion.

Another intervention involves having clients record their automatic thoughts (Beck et al., 1979). Clients are asked to set aside fifteen minutes each evening to record events and accompanying thoughts that led to them feeling depressed. This is completed on an automatic thought record. Clients are initially asked to complete the first three columns, which are situation, degree of emotions, and automatic thoughts. After they have mastered this, clients are asked to answer their automatic thoughts under the fourth column, which is rational response. They are then asked to rate the percentage (0 to 100 percent) of belief in the rational response. In the final column they rate the degree of belief in the original automatic thought and the subsequent degree of emotion after thinking about the rational response.

This technique can be modified to change the way a person experiences God. The therapist works with clients to uncover and then change the automatic thoughts through utilizing the God image automatic thought record—GIATR (see Exhibit 7.1). This technique is one of the most powerful and practical interventions. Clients are instructed to take fifteen minutes at the end of each day and think of specific events that caused them to feel God's disappointment. They initially fill out the first three columns: situation, feelings, and automatic thought(s). After they have mastered this, clients are asked to answer their irrational God image automatic thought under the fourth column, which is the real God response. Clients can craft the real God response by drawing on their understanding of scripture and faith. They are then asked to rate the percentage (0 to 100 percent) of belief in the real God response. In the final column, they rate the degree of belief in the automatic thought(s) and the subsequent degree of emotion after thinking about the real God response.

This technique encourages clients to dispute the irrational God image automatic thoughts by questioning whether the thoughts come from the God of Christianity or the God of their internal parents. Each time they differentiate, individuals will be made more aware and more able to change their thoughts from irrational to rational. This also helps clients own their thoughts. Instead of seeing thoughts as foreign intrusions from a punitive deity, they learn that the thoughts are self-imposed and can be self-controlled.

When introducing this technique to clients it is helpful to go over it four times. Walk them through it the first two times and then have them fill it out two more times with only minimal assistance from you. Coach them on areas that they do not seem to understand. Then assign the GIATR for homework. I usually recommend that they fill it out for five of seven days before the next appointment.

To further illustrate how this technique works, consider Bob again. Bob has a number of automatic thoughts that caused him to feel worthless and experience God as rejecting. I used this tool to help Bob identify and change these thoughts. His thoughts are recorded on

EXHIBIT 7.1. God Image Automatic Thought Record

Process	Situation #1	Situation #2	Situation #3
Situation (Actual event leading to feeling God's disappointment)	I didn't prepare adequately for that sermon. As a result, it fell flat and did not get a very good response.	I was sitting in a restaurant and had a lustful thought when I was looking at an attractive woman.	I waited at the door to meet the new family at church, but they ignored me and left in a hurry.
Feelings (Specify and rate 0 to 100)	Worthless 95	Shameful 98	Rejected 70
Automatic Thought(s) (Write irrational God image automatic thought that preceded emotions, and rate belief in irrational God image thought, 0 to 100%)	"You are a joke as a pastor. You cannot even take time to craft a decent sermon. You are an embarrassment to me." *Belief: 85%*	"What is wrong with you? You are a pastor, but a complete mess. You will never make progress in this area. You are dirty and an abomination." *Belief: 88%*	"You did a pathetic job leading the service. No wonder they did not want to talk to you. They will never come back." *Belief: 65%*
Real God Response (Drawing on your own experience of prayer and scripture, write real God response to irrational God image automatic thoughts, and rate belief in real God response, 0 to 100%)	"Bob, I do not judge you based on your performance. I love you and am proud to be your Father. You are finite and cannot always give 100 percent. Often you have to accept a less than perfect job." *Belief: 80%*	"Bob, I hear you asking for forgiveness and want you to know that I accept you and want to help you with these issues. You do not have to be ashamed or hide things from me. I love you." *Belief: 60%*	"Bob, I will never leave you or abandon you. My presence in your life is not dependent on how well the church members like you." *Belief: 40%*
Outcome (Rerate belief in irrational God image automatic thoughts, 0 to 100%, and specify and rate subsequent feelings, 0 to 100)	Belief in irrational God image response: 40% Degree of feeling worthless: 50	Belief in irrational God image response: 43% Degree of feeling shameful: 55	Belief in irrational God image response: 35% Degree of feeling rejected: 25

the Exhibit 7.1 GIATR. I have included an additional, blank GIATR for your use (see Appendix).

Cognitive Error Interventions

One morning I went into work to meet with a group of students. They were irritable, apathetic, and disgruntled. I immediately concluded that they were upset with me for my role in the project we were working on. Unknowingly I had fallen into the trap of personalization. Personalization is a cognitive error that occurs when people blame themselves for events that happen around them (Wright, 1986). After I stepped back and evaluated my thoughts, I realized that they were tired and cantankerous because we were at an 8 a.m. meeting and it was the middle of midterm week.

Personalization and other cognitive errors are frequently used by people who are depressed. Cognitive errors are the systematic or habitual ways that people misinterpret their environment (DeRubeis et al., 2002). In Chapter 1 I reviewed a list of cognitive errors. Some of the more popular are overgeneralization, polarized thinking, catastrophizing, and magnification. This section details practical steps you can take to help clients recognize and change their cognitive errors so that they have a more accurate perception of others and God.

The first step is to teach clients about cognitive errors by giving them a list of them and then reviewing each one. After this, review their GIATR and identify the cognitive errors that they use most frequently. Go over each automatic thought to identify what cognitive error they are using. Make sure they have a solid understanding of this process. Next, review a different GIATR and have them identify their cognitive errors. Make sure that they can identify them without your help. The last step is to have them memorize their main cognitive errors so that they can learn to recognize them immediately after they occur. Once they know the ways they are distorting their thoughts, they can more readily change these harmful patterns.

Cognitive errors also influence the way that clients experience their God image. The way they evaluate themselves will also be the way that they experience God evaluating them. For example, if they typically minimize their positive aspects and maximize their negative aspects, then they will also experience God as highlighting their negatives and ignoring their positives.

What follows is a list of the main cognitive errors experienced by people with a harmful God image. First, the error is defined. Second, the error is framed in the manner in which it is usually experienced from the God image. Third, practical ways to challenge and change the errors are discussed.

Filtering occurs when a person "filters" out the positive and looks only at the negative (McKay, Davis, & Fanning, 1998). I have a water filter that strains out lead and other chemicals from my drinking water. Imagine a reverse filter that took all the good parts of the water out and left only the chemicals. People with depression have a psychological filter that works in this very way. It strains out all the positives in their life and only lets the negatives through.

Filtering influences the way individuals experience God. It causes them to experience God as emphasizing their weaknesses and ignoring their strengths. This God is not interested in neutral or positive characteristics; instead this God focuses solely on mistakes and failures. A filtering God image focuses on the consequences of the fall and ignores the benefits of redemption.

Bob and I reviewed his GIATR and realized that filtering influenced the way he experienced God. Bob had a lot of positive characteristics and a number of tasks that he did well. His God image, however, emphasized his negative characteristics and tasks that he did not do as well. His God image was similar to an unfair boss. Bob could perfectly accomplish nine tasks, but if the tenth was not strongly executed then the focus would be solely on that one area.

One way to challenge a filtering God image is to "shift the focus" (McKay et al., 1998, p. 38). If the God image is telling the client that he or she is worthless by overly focusing on a weakness, then have the client shift the focus to a strength. Have him or her take the negative out from under the microscope and replace it with a positive. Shifting the focus to a different area allows the client to get out of his or her mental rut and empowers the client to experience God differently. For example, Bob came in one Monday and was really beating himself up for what he perceived as a poor sermon. He experienced his God image as questioning his competence and calling. He then shifted the focus by emphasizing what went well on that Sunday. As it turned out, almost all of the other aspects of the service went well. Bob then focused on these other areas and later prayed about them. As a result, he felt that God accepted him and was no longer focusing on that one sermon delivery.

Overgeneralization is another cognitive error that occurs when sweeping conclusions are made on one piece of evidence (Wright, 1986). I live in an old house. We added a sixteen-foot dormer on the third floor to make more room. I was already anxious about the structure of the house, but became even more so after the addition was added. I focused on the creaks in the wood floor and cracks in the plaster. Most of the creaks and cracks were already there, but I had not noticed them before. I then started *overgeneralizing* about the structure of the house. I focused on these areas and thought they were conclusive evidence that the basic structure of the house was compromised.

Absolute words characterize overgeneralization (McKay et al., 1998). Notice that I previously said "conclusive evidence"—this is an absolute statement that leaves no room for alternative interpretations. Words such as always, never, all, completely, and every mark this cognitive error (e.g., "I applied to one position and was rejected. I'll *never* get hired."). Overgeneralization is also marked by words that are used when exaggerating (e.g., huge, major, terrible, completely).

Overgeneralization can also influence the way an individual experiences God. They may hear God say things such as, "I cannot expect *anything* from you," "You *completely* screwed it up now," "You are a *huge* mess," "You cannot do *anything* right." For example, when Bob experienced a lustful thought he heard his God image say, "You are a *complete* mess. You will *never* make progress in this area."

A number of interventions can be used to challenge overgeneralizations. For the purposes of illustration, let's look at how these interventions played out with Bob's God image. One technique is quantifying (McKay et al., 1998). This occurs when a person looks at an overgeneralization and breaks it down into percentages. Bob's God image said he was a *complete* mess because he had one lustful thought. Bob then challenged this by looking at the different areas of his sexual-thought life. He realized that he had lustful thoughts about 20 percent of the time and had healthy sexual thoughts 80 percent of the time. He also realized that he was often able to change his lustful thoughts so that they were more appropriate. This helped him recognize that he is not a *complete* mess in this area but is actually doing well with an issue that most men struggle with.

Another technique involves looking for evidence to support the overgeneralization (McKay et al., 1998). What evidence proves that Bob will never make progress in this area? A brief look at Bob's past showed that he had made substantial progress regarding lustful thoughts. In fact, if a jury were to review his history, they would think his God image was way off for asserting that Bob will never make progress. In light of his past behavior, it is very likely that Bob will continue to make progress. He will surely have some setbacks and make mistakes, but he will certainly continue to grow. Once Bob gained objectivity by reflecting on his past successes he was able to gain perspective and realistically evaluate this aspect of his life.

A final technique is to refuse to allow the client or the client's God image to use negative labels (McKay et al., 1998). Often, people who are depressed experience their God image as insulting and demeaning. This name-calling sneaks under the radar because it is often the same language that was used by their caretakers. Unless attention is purposefully focused on the negative labels, they are just accepted and never questioned. Recall from Bob's GIATR that his God image called him a "mess," "dirty," and an "abomination." These harsh and harmful words are clearly not from God. The aim is to help clients identify and then change these thoughts so that they will learn to experience others and God in a healthier manner. Changing these absolute negative labels to more tempered judgments helps clients gain perspective and experience God in a more truthful manner.

Catastrophizing is a third cognitive error that is at the heart of worrying and occurs when one small, harmless issue snowballs into a large, threatening issue (Wright, 1986). "I was late for work" turns into "I'm going to get fired." "I got a C on this paper" evolves into "I'm going to fail this class and flunk out of school." In short, something small becomes a catastrophe.

Catastrophizing can also influence a person's experience of God. They will sense that God thinks that the person's life is out of his or her control and is only going to get worse. The God image will minimize the person's sense of efficacy (i.e., his or her ability to address and resolve problems) and maximize his or her self-doubt. For example, Bob was struggling in his relationship with his wife. Because Bob catastrophized, he felt that God thought that his marital problems were going to spiral out of his control and that it would just be a matter of time before he and his wife were divorced. His God image communicated that Bob was unable to solve this problem and that it would not be long until everyone knew how incompetent he really was. If he couldn't manage his family, how could he shepherd his congregation?

The main way to counter catastrophic thinking is to ask, "What are the odds?" (McKay et al., 1998, p. 40). What are the chances that Bob's God image is right? Would an outside observer believe that Bob and his wife will divorce? Helping him look at the odds enabled him to get out from seeing the situation as a certain, eventual catastrophe. He then looked at the difficult times that he and his wife had in the past and what role he had played in resolving those difficulties. In addition, he looked at the role that God played. Upon reflection, he felt that God had really helped them. He then gained a more realistic perception of his own abilities and of God's true nature. He saw that he had taken effective steps in the past, and with God's help had overcome previous difficulties. No reason could be given to believe that these same efforts would not result in the resolution of their current marital problems.

Schema Interventions

Schemas are the core beliefs that maintain a person's depression. Most depressive schemas, or underlying depressive assumptions, are unknown to clients because they are too "deep" (Beck et al., 1979); they are too close to the self to be immediately observed. The therapist learns of the client's schemas through looking for themes in his or her automatic thoughts. Certain groups of automatic thoughts will fit together and from them a certain theme will emerge. That is, they will share an underlying common denominator. Most schemas are vague and are marked by global words such as dumb, stupid, ugly, or worthless. They are also sometimes stated in "if-then propositions, 'If I am not competent, then I'm a failure'" (DeRubeis et al., 2002, p. 76). The following are some of the more popular schemas recorded by Beck (1976):

1. In order to be happy, I have to be successful in whatever I undertake.
2. To be happy, I must be accepted (liked, admired) by all people at all times.
3. If I'm not on top, I'm a flop.

4. It's wonderful to be popular, famous, and wealthy; it's terrible to be unpopular and mediocre.
5. If I make a mistake, it means I'm inept.
6. My value as a person depends on what others think of me.
7. I can't live without love. If my spouse doesn't love me, I'm worthless.
8. If somebody disagrees with me, it means he or she doesn't like me.
9. If I don't take advantage of every opportunity to advance myself, I will regret it later.

Schemas also influence the way clients experience God. The core beliefs they hold are often reflected in their God image. For example, Bob felt he had to be stellar in every area of ministry to be acceptable. His God image paralleled this pattern of thinking by expecting him to perform perfectly in every area of ministry. When Bob inevitably failed, he rejected himself and consequently also felt rejected by his God image.

Fortunately, therapists can work with clients to change their God image by challenging these underlying assumptions. One way to change a harmful God image schema is to have clients identify and then renegotiate their personal contracts with God (Beck et al., 1979). In this exercise, clients are asked what they must do to win God's approval. Usually their response will be vague, open-ended, and unrealistic. They may say, "be perfect," or "always do what God wants me to do." Once the contract is identified, it is helpful to look at it and see if it is valid or even feasible to fulfill. Next, the therapist can explore when the contract was originally made. Usually the contract was drawn up in childhood and unconsciously entered into with caregivers. As individuals grow into adolescence and adulthood the origin of the contract is forgotten and it gets mistakenly translated to God. Clients have to then re-view the contract that they are compulsively following and evaluate it with adult eyes. Once they get this distance they will be able to see that the contract is unrealistic and something they have falsely attributed to God. They can then write a new contract that is realistic and based on their adult understanding of Christianity. The new contract should be clear, specific, and rational, and include room for failures, missteps, and continued growth.

Another way to alter God image schemas is through listening for the "shoulds" in clients' conversations about God (Beck et al., 1979).

These words plague individuals with depression and are markers for the implicit rules that characterize their relationship with God. People who are depressed are often very driven. They set their expectations too high, inevitably fall short, and then harshly criticize themselves for failing. This same dynamic gets played out with their God image. They experience God as expecting too much from them. They strive to meet these unrealistic demands, but inevitably fail and feel judged and rejected by God.

Fortunately, clients can change their "shoulds," so that they do not feel themselves to be a constant failure. The first step is to have clients define the "shoulds" that they place on themselves and the "shoulds" that come from their God image. The demands they place on themselves will start with "I should . . . ," whereas the demands from their God image will begin with "You should . . . " Often these "shoulds" parallel each other. Bob, for example, often thought "I should please everyone," and also experienced his God image as communicating "You should please everyone." Some of the more common God image "shoulds" include: You should be perfect; You should not have any sexual thoughts; You should accomplish everything; You should never complain; You should always be happy; You should be completely generous; You should be perfectly hospitable; You should never be angry; You should never offend others; You should never be tired or take time out for yourself.

Once the God image "should" is identified, it can be changed. One way to challenge it is to have clients consciously choose to disobey their God image (Beck et al., 1979). For example, Bob's God image communicated that he should always be happy. Bob thought about this "should" and evaluated whether or not it was realistic and whether or not it was congruent with his Christian beliefs. He concluded that it was not realistic and not supported by his faith (e.g., Christ was not always happy and experienced anger, sadness, and frustration). Bob then disobeyed the "should" by allowing himself to experience other contrary emotions. To his surprise, nothing bad happened. Instead, he felt grounded and closer to others and God because he did not feel he had to keep up a front or be superficial.

Sometimes clients will disobey their God image and consequently become overwhelmed with guilt. At this point it is necessary to reaffirm the differences between their God image and the real God. If they consistently identify and change their guilt-causing thoughts then they can transform their God image experience from one that is guilt provoking to one that is empowering.

Another way to challenge a God image "should" is to have the client list three exceptions to it (McKay et al., 1998). For example, Lilith's God image demanded that she "should always be strong." To counter this, she listed the following three exceptions: (1) I should not be strong when I am being open and vulnerable, (2) I need not be strong when I am tired, and (3) I do not need to be strong when I am leaning on others for support. Listing these exceptions helped Lilith recognize that her God image "shoulds" were not as absolute as she originally thought. The real God was much more flexible than her rigid God image was.

Some peoples' God image schemas will persist even after renegotiating the contracts and challenging the "shoulds." One basic technique that can help surmount this resistance is to have clients list the advantages and disadvantages of experiencing their God image as they do (Beck et al., 1979). If they realize more disadvantages exist than advantages, they will be more inclined to let the schema go and change how they think.

Imagery Techniques

Imagery is a technique that uses the imagination to form healing mental pictures. This intervention is commonly used in sports psychology and health psychology. In sports psychology, athletes are trained to visualize themselves successfully completing their task (e.g., shooting a basketball or swinging a golf club) to increase their performance. In health psychology, patients use visualization to treat hypertension and other medical disorders. For example, patients often imagine their arteries expanding and their limbs getting heavy to increase relaxation and decrease blood pressure. The mind cannot tell the difference between fantasy and reality, so imagining an event results in evoking the same emotions that would occur if the event actually occurred.

Imagery is most powerful when it stimulates multiple senses and paints a detailed picture. Most individuals have strong visual, auditory, and kinesthetic sensory modalities, so effective imagery will capitalize on these strengths by using words that elicit pictures, sounds, and textures. To better illustrate this, imagine the following scene:

> You are in a forest, lying down in a circle of very tall trees. Underneath you is a cushion of soft, dry moss. The air is strongly scented with laurel and pine, and the atmosphere feels deep, still, and serene. You drink in the warmth of the sun as it streams through the branches, dappling the carpet of moss. A warm wind rises. The tall trees around you sway and bend, and the leaves rustle rhythmically with each gust. Each time the breeze swells, every muscle in your body becomes more and more relaxed. Two songbirds warble in the distance. A chipmunk chatters above. A sense of ease, peace, and joy spreads head to toe. (McKay et al., 1997, p. 64)

This is a good imagery scene because it uses words that tap what people see (a circle of trees that bend in the wind), hear (leaves rustling, chipmunk chatter), and feel (laying on a cushion of moss, warm breeze).

Many Christians are threatened by imagery because it is sometimes associated with new-age practices. This is unfortunate because it is a great tool that has a rich biblical and Christian history (Boyd, 2004). For example, Saint Teresa regularly practiced it to commune with God in the sacred place that she termed the "interior castle." Saint Ignatius recommended that individuals imagine themselves with Christ through a variety of imagery exercises that he termed "application of the senses." Cataphatic spirituality is a Christian tradition that uses visualization to enhance the spiritual disciplines. Individuals who practice this tradition visualize the scriptures when they read them and picture God responding when they pray. Unfortunately, many religious individuals shy away from these experiential practices and instead pursue spiritual growth by consuming theological information. Nothing is wrong with being an informed believer, but this is only one half of spiritual transformation. Information in and of itself does not translate to spiritual growth. Boyd (2004) states,

> I submit that one of the most fundamental problems is that many of us Western Christians have forgotten to use our imagination in spiritual matters. We have come to equate imagination with fantasy and make-believe . . . [we] identify imagination as

something that takes us away from truth rather than something that can be useful, and indeed necessary, to enable us to experience truth . . . God gave us each a brain with its remarkably fast, automatic, image-making capacity so we could interact with him, ourselves, others, and the world as personal beings . . . when our re-presentations of spiritual matters are vivid and correspond with reality, we are able to experience the things of God as real and are transformed by this experience. (pp. 72, 76)

Some Christians have concerns about using imagery to change a person's God image. Perhaps their greatest fear is that it reduces God to a technique. That is, if I use visualization to increase a client's ability to experience forgiveness, then I am reducing God to that particular intervention. In response, allow me to make a couple of points. One, God is clearly loving and gracious, but just because an exercise increases our ability to experience God in that manner does not mean that when we use that exercise we are actually experiencing the real and living God. It means that we are simply opening up, or practicing, so that we can learn to experience God's love and grace. Therefore, these exercises do not reduce God to a technique; they just use the person's psychological faculties to help them open to experiencing the healing aspects of God's love.

Another concern involves healing of memories (Seamands, 1985). This occurs when the therapist leads the client through an imagery exercise in which he or she recalls a painful memory and then imagines God intervening in that memory. In detailing this exercise, I am not positing that I somehow know how God would respond to people in past, painful events. For example, a great many people experience emotional, physical, and sexual abuse at the hands of their parents. This is clearly not God's will, but this, as with many other difficult areas, is something that is hard to explain. Yes, God could have intervened, but for some reason(s) God did not. As Isaiah wisely observed, "His ways are higher than our ways" (55:9). These painful events have a tremendously negative affect on a person's God image (Johnson & Eastburg, 1992). Using exercises that heal these events through imagery that is based on scriptural and traditional understandings of God can help restore the person's God image. As a result, he or she will have a greater capacity to experience God's grace and love.

This is clearly a controversial topic. Some people will think these exercises are great and that I am just being sensitive, whereas others will think much less of them and think I am not being sensitive enough. Ultimately, whether to use the exercises or not is up to you. You have to decide how comfortable you are with the underlying psychological and theological assumptions. That being said, what follows is a list of multiple imagery techniques that can be used to change the God image.

One intervention uses visualization to identify and change the current God image. Another technique utilizes imagery to help clients develop a new, healthier God image that is based on their understanding of the faith. A third tool involves helping clients imagine God comforting and protecting them in the presence of their old God image. A fourth intervention uses visualization to imagine God healing past, painful experiences. Another exercise discusses ways to create a relaxing script to help clients experience forgiveness. A final technique uses inner-child work to correct painful childhood experiences and hurtful God images.

Each of the following techniques requires that the therapist ready clients by describing the rationale behind imagery. Next, help clients relax and get comfortable. Then choose an imagery technique and use it as specified. Once the intervention is completed, ask clients about their experience. Pay particular attention to the way they saw and heard. Focus on the differences between their God image and the real God. Ask them what they found to be helpful and what they did not find helpful. After clients feel comfortable with the technique, you can assign it for homework and have them practice it throughout the week. The continual practice of these techniques will help them experience God in a healthier manner.

Imagery is an exercise that can be used with most clients, but it is contraindicated for those who are psychologically fragile or psychotic. These techniques often evoke strong emotion that can be overwhelming for individuals who are not stable. Imagery can also sometimes be a poor choice for those who have been physically or sexually abused. Tan (1996) warns against imposing a script or scene on clients who have been abused, because images that suggest that God touches or hugs them can be retraumatizing. In addition, therapists should be careful not to refer to God as "Father" with individuals who have been harmed by their father. In these circumstances, it is best to use language that is vague and nondescriptive to allow the client to imagine God interacting with them in a manner that feels safe and comforting, or to not use imagery at all.

Distancing and Neurolinguistic Programming

The first exercise involves identifying and changing the old God image through distancing and neurolinguistic programming (NLP) (Bandler, 1985; DeRubeis et al., 2002). *Distancing* occurs when clients recognize that they have mistaken their God image with the real God. They can then gain emotional space from it by viewing it as an inaccurate perception of a changing construct rather than an accurate perception of an unchanging deity. *NLP* is a form of therapy that utilizes the different sensory modalities and submodalities to bring about change. The primary sensory modalities are visual and auditory. Some of the main submodalities for vision are color, size, and distance. Some of the submodalities for hearing are volume, tone, and intensity.

The first step in this exercise is to have clients identify their God image. Have them imagine their God image and color in as many details as possible. The more specific they can be and the more senses they can use in creating the image, the better. Asking the following questions can help. What does your God image look like? What is its size, shape, and color(s)? What does it sound like? What is the tone, volume, and intensity of its voice? What are some of the more common things it says to you? How close or distant from you is it? How do you feel in its presence? What emotions are evoked? What do you want to do when you enter the presence of your God image?

After the God image is identified, clients can then begin modifying it. At this point, it is helpful to remind clients that this image is largely based on their caregivers and is not congruent with the real God. Clients often feel enslaved to their God image, so I encourage them to take some liberties when changing their God image. Through the visual modality, they can change the overwhelming size by making it small. They can also change the clothes so that the image looks less authoritarian. Instead of wearing flowing robes they can imagine it dressed in a Hawaiian shirt with a goofy yellow hat on. Through the auditory modality, they can change the condescending voice into an encouraging voice by altering the tone. They can adjust the volume so that instead of being loud it only whispers. They can also change the credibility of the voice. If it is authoritative, they can make it hiccup every couple of words or they can make it sound squeaky. The goal of this exercise is to show clients that their God image is not God and that they can actually control the way they experience their God image through altering their visual and auditory modalities.

Developing a New Understanding of God

The second set of exercises focuses on developing a new, healthier emotional understanding of God. This new understanding can be based on scripture, creeds, or other aspects of church history, but it has to come alive and be real to the person. Imagery can make this information emotionally meaningful and tangible by evoking language that is sensory based.

The first exercise involves helping clients identify and experience God in a new way. This begins by helping clients list a number of God's healing characteristics (e.g., compassionate, loving, gentle). Then have them visualize God behaving in each of these ways toward them. For each characteristic, have them describe how God looks and sounds and how they feel. Next, have them integrate all these perceptions into one overall mental picture of God. After this, have them compare the differences between their old God image and their new understanding of God. Asking the following questions can be helpful. How is your new understanding of God different from your old God image? In what ways do they look different? What are the different things they say? How do you feel in the presence of each one? This is just a sample of questions, so feel free to ask as many relevant questions as you can to help them visualize the differences.

Having clients draw their old God image on one piece of paper and their new understanding of God on another piece of paper can sometimes better facilitate this exercise. If they can successfully identify the differences they will be better able to discern whether a feeling or message they are getting is from their false god or the true God. They can then choose to ignore the harmful messages they get from their God image and embrace the healing messages they get from their new understanding of God.

A second exercise helps clients visualize psalms, parables, or other portions of scripture that are healing and restorative (Boyd, 2004). This practice involves helping clients develop a panoramic understanding of a scene, their role in it, and God's role. Some common areas of focus include: Luke 15 (the lost sheep, the lost coin, and the prodigal son), Psalm 139:1-18, and Psalm 23. Many people have portions of scripture that they find very meaningful, but have never made personally relevant. Visualizing these scriptures helps them open to God by encouraging them to emotionally experience feeling loved, cherished, sought out, and cared for.

Pairing Positive Emotions with Experiences of God

A third imagery intervention helps clients pair positive emotions with their experience of God. Clients unconsciously project negative experiences onto God. In order to reverse this process, they have to transfer positive experiences onto God. Have clients think of times in their lives when they felt safe and loved. Help them soak in these memories and the accompanying feelings. Then, have them begin to pray and become aware of God. Instruct them to call these images and feelings to mind each time that they pray. This continual pairing of positive healing emotions with God will eventually result in them being able to feel this way when they pray or think about God.

A colleague once told me about a client he was seeing who was abused as a child. One of the only memories she had of feeling safe was when she was curled up next to her big labrador retriever. This dog was one of the only safe objects she had. Steve used this memory to help her learn how to feel safe in God's presence. Some people feel safe and grounded at the beach, in the forest, or with a loving person. All of these images and experiences can be used to help them better understand God's love.

Helping Clients Experience God's Forgiveness

A fourth technique uses imagery to help clients experience God's forgiveness. Many clients ask for forgiveness, but do not *feel* forgiven. Instead, they feel they have to do a number of tasks to earn God's acceptance. The first step in this exercise is to talk with clients about an area they struggle with. Next, have them describe how they experience their God image and what, if anything, they do to earn its acceptance and approval. Then, have them draw on their knowledge of scripture and theology to describe how they think the real God would respond. Encourage them to fully describe a scene in which they discuss their shortcomings with God and then ask for and receive forgiveness. Focus on helping them articulate and emphasize what God would say and the way God would act toward them. After they do this, have clients write down the scene, close their eyes, and imagine the scene. Have them go through each of the steps: failing, asking for forgiveness, and receiving forgiveness. The more they repeat this exercise the more they will be able to feel forgiven.

Constructing a Relaxing Script

A fifth technique involves constructing a relaxing script that uses healing words and scenes to help clients learn to have a healthier experience of God. The therapist readies clients for this intervention by (1) insuring that they are in a quiet environment, (2) having clients sit in a comfortable position with their feet on the floor and their arms either comfortably on their lap or on the arms of the chair, and (3) asking clients to adopt a passive attitude. Clients must have a relaxed attitude and allow themselves to be led in the relaxation exercise. After these instructions, the therapist begins by reading the following script in a slow, soothing voice. The client can also record this exercise and play it back to themselves to better experience God's forgiveness.

> Get comfortable and begin to relax . . . take a deep breath . . . slowly breathe in through your nose and slowly let the air out through your mouth . . . deep breaths . . . deep and relaxing breaths . . . slowly fill your stomach with air . . . slowly let the air out through your mouth . . . deep breaths . . . deep and relaxing breaths . . . find yourself becoming more and more relaxed . . . deeply relaxed . . . feel the tension leave your body . . . feel your whole body begin to relax . . . feel your forehead loosen . . . sense your face relaxing . . . feel the stress leaving your face and body . . . feel your eyes becoming heavy . . . let your eyes close . . . become more and more relaxed . . . deeper and deeper . . . more and more relaxed . . . sense the tension leaving your shoulders . . . they are becoming heavy and relaxed . . . feel the stress leaving your body . . . sense your arms becoming heavier and heavier . . . deep and relaxed . . . your shoulders, chest, and arms are loose and heavy . . . loose and heavy . . . deeper and deeper . . . more and more relaxed . . . feel your legs growing

heavy . . . heavy and relaxed . . . your feet growing heavy . . . legs and feet heavy and heavier . . . more and more relaxed . . . deeper and deeper . . . more and more relaxed . . . your shoulders becoming heavy . . . your body feeling deep and relaxed . . . feel your eyes closing.

Now its time to go to a safe and comfortable place . . . a place where you feel deeply at peace . . . very relaxed . . . deep and relaxed . . . free of tension . . . very peaceful . . . take steps toward this special place . . . this safe place . . . feel safe and secure . . . very peaceful . . . deep and relaxed . . . as you walk toward your special place find yourself becoming more and more relaxed . . . with each step toward your special place you can count down from ten to zero . . . feeling more and more relaxed . . . more and more peaceful . . . in ten steps you will be there . . . 9 . . . 8 . . . 7 . . . feeling more and more relaxed . . . deeper and deeper . . . 6 . . . 5 . . . 4 . . . heavier and heavier . . . more and more relaxed . . . 3 . . . 2 . . . 1.

Now fully experience your safe and special place . . . become fully aware of your peaceful place . . . see . . . feel . . . smell . . . fully aware of your special place . . . feeling deeply relaxed . . . very peaceful . . . so relaxed . . . calm . . . so relaxed and calm. (Davis, Eshelman, & McKay, 1995)

Now see God approach you in your special place . . . look into His kind eyes and see His warm smile . . . feel the warmth that radiates from him. . . He is glad to see you. . . hear him say kind things . . . feel yourself becoming more and more relaxed . . . comfortable and open.

As you continue to breathe, with each breath you will become more and more relaxed. Thoughts may run through your mind, but you do not have to think, or reply, or try to do anything at all. It isn't even necessary to listen to what I'm saying, because your unconscious mind will inevitably hear everything that I'm saying without any effort on your part at all. Even now, your unconscious mind is working to help you experience God in a healthier manner. The curious occurrence is that your conscious mind may or may not really know or understand what's going on. In fact, as you hear my words and become more and more relaxed, you may choose not to remember, or you may choose to forget, but choosing to forget is your choice in the same way as choosing not to remember that which you've chosen to forget. It is interesting that as you begin to understand and become more and more relaxed, you are both aware and unaware of the change that is occurring within you. (Hammond, 1990)

Learning to fully experience God's love . . . and grace . . . and forgiveness . . . is very similar to learning to walk. As a child, your unconscious mind taught you how to walk. It wasn't an easy process and I'm sure you fell down quite a bit, but each time you got back up and you tried again. Until, eventually, you were walking without even realizing it. In a similar manner, your unconscious mind is continuing to work to help you feel God's love and forgiveness. Eventually, without even realizing it, you will have grown to experience God's love and forgiveness. It may happen gradually or it may happen quickly. The important fact to remember is that your unconscious mind will continue working on that problem after you leave, and the really curious fact is that your conscious mind may or may not really know or understand what's going on, depending on the preference of your unconscious mind. As your unconscious mind is busy sorting through alternatives, your conscious mind will remain free to carry on your daily activities.

It is time to come back . . . time to leave your special place . . . begin to feel awake, awake and alert . . . refreshed . . . and awake. . . . Time to come up now . . . feeling refreshed and awake . . . 1 . . . 2 . . . 3 . . . more alert . . . more awake . . . 4 . . . 5 . . . 6 . . . awake and alert . . . opening your eyes . . . feeling refreshed . . . 7 . . . 8 . . . 9 . . . fully alert . . . 10 . . . awake and alert. (Davis et al., 1995)

The previous script is pretty standard and general. Most people feel very relaxed and refreshed upon awakening. This exercise can be modified to more specifically help clients learn to *feel* forgiven by substituting the following script with the latter half of the previous script.

To do this you would read up to the line break before "as you continued to breathe . . ." and then transition to the following script:

See yourself talking to God . . . see His warm, loving face. . . feel him fully connecting with you and understanding how you feel . . . see each of your sins that you have asked forgiveness for, but have not felt forgiven for, represented by black boxes. Each of these boxes is next to you on the ground and each box is a different size. The larger the box, the more of a concern it is for you. . . . Each box has its own label that specifies your concern. . . . God is aware of the boxes and He is aware of you . . . continue to sense His love and warmth . . . know that He cares deeply for you and knows that you have a hard time feeling forgiven.

Now, take the first black box, pick it up, look at it, see the label, hold it out in front of you, and pass it to God. He looks at you with a warm expression and gently takes the box from your hands. . . . Feel the warmth radiating off of Him . . . allow yourself to gaze into His accepting eyes. He says, "I forgive you and love you." As He is holding the box it changes from black to white and he places the box down next to Him. . . . Feel His forgiveness move through you. Experience yourself feeling surrounded by a warm sense of grace. Reach down, grab another box, and hand it to Him. . . . Feel His forgiveness as you pass the box over to him . . . see each box you give him change from black to white . . . find yourself becoming more and more aware of his forgiveness . . . become more and more relaxed . . . peaceful and relaxed . . . deep and relaxed . . . aware of His love and presence . . . grace and forgiveness. . . . Feel the warmth of His love enwrap and clothe you. . . . Feel yourself bathed and surrounded in His grace.

After each box has been given over to Him, He says, "You are fully forgiven." As He says this, the last bit of feeling unforgiven leaves you . . . your clothes brighten and become fully white. He smiles and says that He loves you.

It is time to come back . . . time to leave your special place . . . begin to feel awake, awake and alert . . . refreshed . . . and awake. . . . Time to come up now . . . feeling refreshed and awake . . . 1 . . . 2 . . . 3 . . . more alert . . . more awake . . . 4 . . . 5 . . . 6 . . . awake and alert . . . opening your eyes . . . feeling refreshed . . . 7 . . . 8 . . . 9 . . . fully alert . . . 10 . . . awake and alert. (Davis et al., 1995)

Imagining God Healing Painful Memories

A sixth imagery technique involves having the client recollect a painful memory and then imagining God playing a healing role to correct the situation. This is sometimes popularly referred to as inner-child work or healing of memories (Bradshaw, 1988; Seamands, 1985). Healing of memories uses prayer, whereas inner-child work does not. Proponents of healing of memories suggest that when a client prays and "sees" God acting in a restorative way, he or she is actually seeing the real God. I am hesitant to say that a person's visualization of God is the same as the real, living God. God is omnipresent and in constant communion with us, but I am not 100 percent sure that our conceptualization of God is ever completely accurate. I think we can do our best to use our understanding of the Scriptures and our tradition to discover an image that is true, but I also believe that we could be "off" a little, or a lot, in our perceptions. That being said, you have to make up your own mind as to where you stand on this issue so that you can communicate it to clients when using this technique.

This exercise is comprised of several practical steps. First, have the client recall a painful memory. Nine out of ten times these memories occur in childhood. Have the client fully visualize the memory and visualize God there with them. Some people use the picture of God they developed in the earlier exercise, whereas others imagine Jesus. Next, have the person and God observe the painful experience. Then have the person imagine God stepping in and making the situation right. For example, many people imagine God confronting the harmful caregiver and comforting the child. When the client is done, have him or her describe what occurred and how he or she feels.

After this, have the client recollect the same, original scene, but experience the scene as himself or herself. That is, have the client embody the child and subjectively reexperience the memory. Then have the client watch from his or her childhood perspective as God intervenes and confronts the parent. Have the client also experience God comforting him or her as his or her childhood self. Many people imagine God holding them and telling them that they do not deserve to be treated this way, that they did not do anything wrong, and that God loves them and cares deeply for them. This subjective, corrective, emotional experience allows the client to gain healing from his or her painful memories and experience God as a healthy figure.

L. Rebecca Propst (1988) slightly modifies this exercise by having the client first imagine a scene from Scripture, and then imagine God's presence in the past, painful experience. The following caption captures her unique style as well as the healing effects that this technique can have. In this session, she is working with a woman named Ann who experienced regular physical abuse as a child. Pay particular attention to the way that she leads the client but also provides space for the client to fill in the details.

Before allowing Ann to become completely involved with her images of abuse, I helped her develop an image of the healing Christ. We started by reading one of the stories of Jesus' trial and crucifixion.

"Ann, try to imagine an image of Jesus standing in front of you right now. What is he wearing?"

"He is wearing a white robe and has brown sandals on his feet."

"Good! And as you see his white robe and his brown sandals, what color are his hair and eyes?"

"His eyes are brown and his hair is brown."

"Imagine that this is after his crucifixion. As you see his brown eyes and hair, can you see his wounds? What do they look like?"

"He has deep cuts in his hands and feet and scars on his back and legs."

"What kind of facial expression does he have?"

"He is in pain."

"Is there any other expression?"

"His eyes still look warm."

"What lets you know he is in pain?"

"His eyes have some tears in them, and his mouth is tense."

"Now, Ann, I want you to switch to the image of you with your mother. Tell me what you see."

"I see myself sitting on the floor as a young child crying."

"As you are crying, what else is happening?"

"I continued crying, so my mother tied my shoestrings together and took me to the kitchen."

"What happened then?"

"She turned on the kitchen stove and held me down on the stove." (She started sobbing at this point.)

"Ann, imagine now that Christ, whom you saw earlier, comes into the kitchen now. What would he do?"

"He walks over to the stove and takes me off the stove."

"Then what happened?"

"He is telling me that he understands what I feel, he has lots of scars too."

"Ann, imagine what Jesus' eyes look like as he tells you that he understands."

"He has tears in his eyes, and they are very warm."

"Ann, just allow yourself to look at Jesus' eyes."

This is an abbreviated version of an exchange that took about one hour, and was repeated several times. I gained a new insight into the healing Christ through this event. There is no human hell that is so deep that Jesus has not already been there. (Propst, 1988, pp. 137-138)

Connie Miller (2000) has observed that individuals who struggle with mental health issues, particularly those who are codependent, have a hard time emotionally understanding that God dwells within them. They often visualize God outside of themselves and feel distant from Him. They cognitively understand the scriptures that we are the temple of the Holy Spirit and that Christ dwells within us, but they do not emotionally grasp that idea. Propst (1988) has designed an exercise entitled "Christ dwells within us" (p. 138). She instructs clients to imagine where Christ dwells within them. Clients often report feeling warm and secure when they do this. She then has them imagine the parts of themselves that they are ashamed of while at the same time holding in mind that Christ is still with them. She describes:

After we have experienced Christ dwelling within us through imagery, we may then focus on our more loathsome aspects. I often ask individuals to show these characteristics to God in their mind's eye. I often ask them to notice that Christ has promised that he will not leave, and indeed that he does not. For some individuals, such an experience provides the first glimmer that God indeed does accept them. Often the self-esteem of those in mental anguish needs such assurance. Making that assurance more understandable and concrete via imagery completes the picture. (Miller, 2000, p. 139)

Experiential Techniques

Experiential techniques focus on the here and now and encourage clients to emotionally engage in acting out and resolving issues. For example, an empty chair is a technique that is used to help people work through issues with caregivers (Perls & Wysong, 1992). I used this intervention with Bob to help him work through issues he had with his father. I positioned an empty chair in front of him and had him imagine that his father was sitting in it. I then instructed him to begin to talk to his father about what father did that hurt him. At first he felt awkward, but soon began to tell his father how he felt. He told him how angry and heartbroken he felt by his father's constant rejection. Shortly thereafter he became livid and then began sobbing. He was able to unburden himself and say all that he wanted to but never had the opportunity to. He then had a sense of resolution and peace with his father.

As you can see, these interventions are experiential because they focus on the experience. The feeling or emotion is primary and the cognitive understanding is secondary. What follows are a number of experimental exercises that have been modified to address and change the God image.

The first is the empty chair, which occurs as described previously, but clients imagine their God image in the chair rather than their mother or father. The therapist positions the chair and has clients "see" their God image. Clients are encouraged to voice small concerns regarding what bothers them about their God image. Then, gradually, have the client share more and more painful and difficult issues—things that they have wanted to say, but have been afraid to. For example, Bob started by telling his God image that he did not like the constant judgments he felt. He stated, "You know you constantly expect more from me than I can give. That is not fair." Then he took more of a risk and stated, "You expect me to be perfect. I try my hardest to please you, but all you do is condemn and demean me. You tell me I am worthless. How do you think that makes me feel? It hurts and cuts me. I wish you would just back off and leave me alone. I wish I didn't constantly feel you hovering over me and evaluating me!" Bob was really working and eventually began to sob as he raised his voice and said, "I don't need you. All you do is cause me anguish! Just leave me alone and let me be my own person. I am man enough to stand up to your criticisms and harsh judgments. I don't need you anymore. I'm done!" This was what he had always wanted to say to his father, but could not. As a result, they were carried over to his God image. Bob worked through these issues and overcame them with his God image. He had an emotional catharsis and was then able to see how he had projected his issues with his father onto his God image. After this exercise, the issues were not as intense. As a result, he could then experience God in a more objective and healthier manner.

This technique can be slightly altered to further identify and differentiate how clients experience their God image. In this exercise, clients alternate between their self and their God image. They first state how they feel to their God image, then switch chairs and answer as their God image. Then they once again assume themselves and answer the God image. Through alternating between self and God image, clients are able to see the dynamics that occur within themselves. Clients are encouraged to continue the conversation until an agreement or consensual understanding is met. Through discussion and the releasing of emotions, clients can then integrate the self and God image.

An experiential technique that emphasizes thoughts over feelings is to role-play. Initially, clients play themselves and the therapist plays God (Beck et al., 1979). Clients verbalize what they usually say to their God image and the therapist responds in a way that is consistent with the client's understanding of Scriptures and faith. For example, clients may say, "I try so hard, but I can't be perfect." The therapist, playing God, then says back to the client, "What are you talking about 'you can't be perfect'? I never expected you to be perfect. I expect you to fail and make mistakes."

Further insight can be gained by altering this technique slightly. Clients are asked to play God while the therapist plays the client. The therapist repeats what the client usually says to their God image. Clients, in attempting to be a good representative of God, will counter the therapist's distortions and try to convince the therapist of their, God's, love. At this point, the therapist can note that they are doing well playing God, and that God sees them much as they currently see the therapist. This helps clients realize that God is much more merciful than they sometimes think. It also teaches clients that the techniques they used to attempt to change the therapist's mind can be helpful in changing their own minds.

Bibliotherapy

The last cognitive technique is bibliotherapy. Here the therapist assigns a variety of readings to help clients grow. For Christian clients, both self-help and religious books are helpful. Some self-help books that are particularly beneficial are *The Road Less Traveled* by M. Scott Peck (1978), *The Search for Significance* by Robert McGee (1998), and *Why Am I Afraid to Tell You Who I Am?* by John Powell (1969). Any respected book that attempts to integrate spirituality and psychology will be helpful. The therapist will have to judge the cognitive capacity of the clients before prescribing a certain book. It is usually beneficial to start with an easy read and then gradually move into more complicated works.

Reading Christian fantasy can also be helpful in changing the God image. Christian fantasy brings clients into a realm of childlike thought and leaves behind adult-rational thought. Reading books such as *The Chronicles of Narnia* by C. S. Lewis (1994) leads clients through an emotional experience. This process can alter the God image by enabling clients to identify with characters that relate to Aslan (i.e., God). Through this passive identification, they vicariously experience God's forgiveness, grace, and love. These healing images can be very powerful and serve as excellent reminders of God's true nature when their God image is particularly harsh and judgmental.

Individuals with depression usually have a vague understanding of theology. They generally cannot define what they believe and are often unable to disprove their faulty thinking. Reading popular works such as *Mere Christianity* by C. S. Lewis (1967), *Basic Christianity* by John Stott (1958), and *Your God is Too Small* by J. B. Phillips (1953) can help them begin to understand more about the Christian faith. As clients gain more understanding, theology can be further demystified by recommending a simple systematic theology. Through reading these books, clients will clarify their beliefs and be better equipped to dispute their irrational thoughts.

CONCLUSION

In conclusion, cognitive techniques can be quite useful in changing the God image. They are more direct and practical than the psychodynamic techniques. For this reason they can be easily taught to clients, and they make excellent homework assignments. Cognitive God image techniques begin with teaching awareness and modification of irrational automatic thoughts and end with changing the underlying depressive schemas. Through a variety of cognitive techniques, the therapist can explore and change the structure of the client's God image.

Chapter 8

Treatment Planning

Yogi Berra said, "If you do not know where you are going, you will end up somewhere else" (quoted in Levenson, 1995). The same holds true for the process of therapy. It is necessary to begin with the end in mind so that each step along the way takes you closer to achieving the overall goal. This chapter details case conceptualization and treatment planning, but first reviews key ethical issues that are central to God image work. It is necessary to have a firm understanding of these ethical standards *before* beginning the treatment planning process.

WHAT ETHICAL ISSUES ARE RELEVANT TO GOD IMAGE WORK?

God image techniques blur the boundaries between psychotherapy and religion. It is therefore necessary to be mindful of potential dangers that can harm clients' religious and psychological experience. Awareness of these issues is the first step in making sure that they do not occur. Tan (1994) has outlined a number of key ethical areas. This section reviews a few of his main points that are particularly relevant to God image work.

Imposing One's Beliefs on to the Client

One main ethical issue to be aware of is the tendency of therapists to impose their own beliefs on the client (Tan, 1994). A power differential exists in the therapist-client relationship, so therapists need to take extra steps to identify, respect, and appreciate clients' religious worldviews. Clients feel safe and willing to explore their God image when they do not sense that they are going to be judged. For this reason, it is important to avoid theological arguments and debates. These discussions are usually not helpful and often serve to obscure the underlying psychological issues.

Informed Consent

Another important ethical standard to be aware of is informed consent. A therapist should use language that is easily understood by the client to describe what the services entail (Canter, Bennett, Jones, & Nagy, 1999). Once the client is *informed,* he or she can then make a rational decision and *consent* to or not to engage in the services. Before clients seek to change their God image, they should be forewarned of a number of points. First, having a negative God image is not recognized as a psychological disorder, so insurance companies will not pay for therapy that focuses solely on this issue. Now, if the client is depressed and their relationship with God is indicated in their depression, then insurance will likely pay for these services as long as the main focus is on the alleviation of depression and not on changing the God image. Second, research supports that the God image can change through various psychological techniques and treatment programs, but a significant amount of research has not yet been conducted in this area. Plenty of narrative and theoretical support is available, but the amount of focused research available in this area is less than the amount of research available in other areas (e.g., interpersonal and cognitive treatment of depression). Third, psychotherapy is not a panacea. It is not a 100 percent cure-all. Therapy usually progresses in a similar way as the stock market: it goes up and down, but for the most part continues to go up. Therapy will certainly consist of healing experiences, but it will also evoke painful emotions that will feel uncomfortable and influence the way people experience others and God.

Competence

A third ethical area to be mindful of is competence (Tan, 1994). This is generally seen as practicing only in areas in which you have had course work and/or supervision. God image work falls under the larger category of the integration of psychology and spirituality, so courses or workshops in this area may be sufficient. The God Image Institute (www.godimage.com) offers a number of individual and group trainings in God image theory and technique.

Supervision is also an essential part of practicing competently. When a therapist is being supervised, it means that he or she sees clients under someone else's oversight and license. The supervisor assumes vicarious liability for supervised therapist's work with clients. Usually, the therapist meets with his or her supervisor on a weekly basis to discuss clients. Before starting therapy, the therapist must let clients know that he or she is in supervision.

Medication

A fourth area that Tan (1994) discusses is "applying only religious interventions to problems which may require medication or other medical and/or psychological treatments" (p. 390). Individuals with certain disorders need medication to help them stabilize. It would be unethical, harmful, and risky to rely solely on psychosocial interventions when it is clear that medication is indicated. Similarly, focusing only on the God image with someone who is chronically depressed would also be unethical. In this situation, therapists should first help clients develop coping skills and then later address God image issues.

Helping Clients Distinguish Between the God Image and the True God

Humans are trapped in their subjectivity. The psychological faculties that color how they perceive others also color how they perceive God. One of the first steps in God image work is to help clients differentiate between what they believe are God's true characteristics and their God image. The interventions aim to adjust the God image so that it more closely resembles the true God. The techniques should not be used in a manner that suggests God is simply an idea to be used for therapeutic gains. Rather, a clear distinction should be made that highlights that the interventions are designed to change the person's unhealthy *perceptions* of God.

Now, times will occur when the client cognitively holds harmful concepts of God. This could be a result of bad theology or a hurtful church background. Therapists have several approaches to choose from to address this issue. The first is to explore the harmful beliefs with the client. Therapists can use Richards & Bergin's (1997) level two approach to gain more understanding. Another option is to refer the client to a clergyperson to help him or her clarify and potentially change what he or she believes. A third option is to challenge the beliefs. However, as mentioned before, these types of interventions usually result in little therapeutic effect. If a therapist challenges the client's beliefs, then the therapist should be competent to do so as evidenced by a solid theological background. A fourth option is to refer the client to another therapist if the current therapist feels as if he or she cannot help the client in an effective and ethical manner.

A number of other ethical issues exist that therapists should be aware of. A number of these issues have been discussed in other chapters, and more directly in this chapter, but these are only a start. Clergy and clinicians need to be intimately familiar with the ethical guidelines that govern their profession.

WHAT ARE CASE CONCEPTUALIZATION AND TREATMENT PLANNING?

Case Conceptualization

Therapists use case conceptualization to identify how clients' problems developed, are maintained, and can be solved. Eells (1997) defines,

> Case formulation is a hypothesis about the causes, precipitants, and maintaining influences of a person's psychological, interpersonal, and behavioral problems. . . . It should serve as a blueprint guiding treatment, as a marker for change, and as a structure enabling the therapist to understand the patient better. (p. 2)

She views case conceptualization as comprised of two parts: "descriptive" and "prescriptive" (p. 2). The *descriptive* part is comprised of the different components we discussed in Chapter 5. It includes the person's presenting problem, psychospiritual history, and test results. It seeks to describe these factors, rather than explain them. The *prescriptive* part interprets the descriptive information by looking at it through a theoretical lens such as psychodynamic theory or cognitive theory. This frames the client's problems and prescribes steps that can be taken to solve the problems.

To better understand these case conceptualization distinctions, consider Bob again. I first focused on the descriptive aspects of his case conceptualization by cataloging his presenting problem, history, and test results. After this, I moved into the second, prescriptive part of the case conceptualization process by interpreting this information through the different theoretical orientations. A cognitive prescription suggested that he developed a depressive schema in childhood and maintained this schema through negative self-talk. It further indicated that he could decrease his depression and change his emotional experience of God by changing his negative thinking patterns. A psychodynamic prescription suggested that he developed a people-pleasing pattern in his childhood relationship with his father and maintained it through establishing relationships with domineering others. This approach further suggested that this harmful interpersonal pattern and corresponding negative experience of God could change by experiencing a new, more assertive, relationship with the therapist.

Each conceptualization caused me to look at Bob in a different manner. In this way, the orientation is similar to a pair of glasses you wear. When wearing the cognitive glasses, you will focus on the way the client thinks. When wearing the psychodynamic glasses, you will focus on the way the client relates. It is possible to take a lens from each of these sets of glasses so you can see the client from both cognitive and relational approaches. This is referred to as being eclectic, and occurs when you integrate different theories and treatments to help the client.

Choosing an orientation is based on several factors. One factor is the fit between the orientation and your personality style. For example, active and directive people usually prefer to practice cognitive therapy, whereas those who emphasize relationships and emotions tend to practice psychodynamic therapy. This book only discusses a couple of orientations, but many more are available that are also effective. It is important to find an orientation that naturally fits who you are. A second factor in choosing an orientation is the nature of the client's problem. If a form of therapy works better for a particular problem, then it is wise to use that orientation over another. For example, panic disorder responds better to cognitive therapy than it does to psychodynamic approaches. Therefore, the therapist should choose to use cognitive treatment. A third factor is the client's characteristics. Generally, psychodynamic approaches work better with more sophisticated people than they do with those who are less complex. Cognitive therapy, on the other hand, works well for individuals with both high and low intelligence.

Once you have chosen an orientation, it takes time to immerse yourself in it. Allow it to saturate the way you think about the client. In particular, focus on what it posits about how the problem is caused, how the problem is maintained, and how the problem can be solved. Once you have a thorough grasp of the orientation, you can then transition to treatment planning.

Treatment Planning

What is a treatment plan? A treatment plan is a psychological road map that you and the client create to get from point A to point B. It charts a course from where clients are now to where they ultimately want to arrive. In a sense, you as a therapist are a travel guide. Clients will come to you because they are lost, stuck, or going in circles. Your job is to give them direction by creating a map and walking with them toward their destination.

A couple of preliminary steps must be taken before starting the treatment planning process. The first preliminary step involves completing the God image interview and any God image assessment instruments. The second step is to decide which orientation you are going to use. The treatment plan flows out of the orientation, so it is necessary to decide whether you are going to use an eclectic approach or focus solely on cognitive or psychodynamic techniques.

The treatment plans outlined in this chapter are representative of eclectic, cognitive, and solution-focused approaches. These styles of therapy often focus on concrete goals and measurable objectives. Psychodynamic treatment planning, on the other hand, emphasizes intrapsychic and interpersonal changes that tend to be more abstract and less quantifiable. This style of treatment planning is *not* represented in the following discussion or the examples that are provided in this chapter. Nonetheless, in Chapter 6 I attempted to provide you with concrete psychodynamic interventions that can be measured. I have integrated these techniques into the following treatment plans so you can see how they work.

The treatment plan typically consists of five steps. The first step is to help clients identify and prioritize their presenting problems. The second step is to transform those problems into goals. The third step is to help clients identify techniques that they can practice to reach those goals. The fourth step is to determine what interventions you will use to help clients meet their goals. The fifth step is to assign a review date to see if the goal has been accomplished. We will now discuss each of these steps in greater detail.

Prioritize Presenting Problems

The first step is to help clients specify their exact problems. Some clients will enter therapy to change their God image, whereas others will see this as a secondary goal or not be interested in changing their God image at all. Presenting problems influence the treatment plan, so you will only use God image techniques for individuals who are interested in changing their emotional experience of God. Once you have labeled the problems, the aim is to help clients make them as specific as possible. The clearer and more detailed the problem, the easier it will be to address it.

Clients sometimes struggle with identifying their presenting problem. To help them, you can ask the miracle question: "Suppose one night, while you were asleep, there was a miracle and your problem was solved. How would you know?" (de Shazer, 1988, p. 5). A variant of this question can be asked to clarify difficulties with their God image, "Suppose one night, while you were asleep, there was a miracle and your perception of God was healed, how would you know?" For example, when I asked Lilith this question she responded, "I'd be able to experience Him as He really is. I wouldn't feel Him as distant and demanding. Instead, I'd be acutely aware that He accepts me as I am and does not require me to earn His love and approval."

These questions clarify problems by helping clients articulate how their life would be different. After the problems are spelled out, prioritize them by listing them in the order of significance. In general, painful and overwhelming issues should be at the top of the list and less pressing issues should be at the bottom of the list.

Transform Problems into Goals

The second step of treatment planning is to transform client problems into goals. Goals, defined and undefined, are extremely powerful because they bring order to life and focus attention and energy. When I first started running cross-country, my coach indicated that by week eight I would be running between fifty to sixty miles a week. At that point I was lucky if I could run two to three miles in a day. However, with daily practice, by week eight, I was clocking fifty to sixty miles a week. If I had not set my mind on this goal, I would have never achieved it. Therapy works in a similar manner. In order for therapeutic progress to occur, you and the client have to deliberately focus attention and effort on achieving the client's goals.

How do you change problems into goals? Usually you can help clients identify goals by looking at the opposite of their problems. For example, one of Bob's main problems was that he experienced God as rejecting when he did not perform his church duties flawlessly, had sexual thoughts, and missed devotions. To transform this problem into a goal we looked at the opposite. If Bob was feeling *rejected,* then we wanted him to feel *accepted.* More specifically, the goal was for Bob to experience God as accepting when he did not perform church duties flawlessly, had sexual thoughts, and missed devotions. We often make the mistake of thinking that God is less accepting and loving of us when we sin. God does not distance Himself from us when we sin; God is not surprised by our sin but has accounted for it and wants to help us grow through it.

For a goal to be meaningful, it has to be achievable, specific, and measurable. *Achievable* means it cannot be out of reach. *Specific* means that it is clear and detailed. *Measurable* means that progress, or lack of progress, can be assessed. Bob's goal was achievable because he had the capacity to experience God as accepting. It was specific because we had detailed the exact times when he did not experience God as accepting. It was measurable because we could assess his experience of God's acceptance by having him rate it on a scale of 1 to 10 or by using the God image instruments.

Identify Which Techniques to Use

The third step in the treatment planning process is to specify steps clients can take to reach their goal. When choosing these steps it is important to keep a few points in mind. One, you do not want to have clients agree to do exercises that are too difficult for them. When Bob started therapy, he was moderately to severely depressed and very busy. It would have been counterproductive for me to ask him to complete the GIATR seven nights a week. He was simply too depressed and too busy for this to be a realistic goal. If he would have agreed and failed, then he would have demeaned himself for not completing the task. A second point to keep in mind is to make sure that clients understand the exercise or intervention. Clients sometimes smile and nod when they do not actually get it. For this reason it is important to use easy-to-understand language and have them explain it back to you in their own words to insure that they understand the technique. A third point is to make the steps measurable.

Ensure Clients Understand How and Why the Chosen Technique Works

The fourth step of the treatment planning process consists of what you will do to help clients achieve their goals. If one of Bob's steps is that he will use the GIATR four days a week, then it is my responsibility to teach him how to use this exercise by reviewing it with him and making sure that he understands the underlying cognitive principles. The therapist's step will be intimately related to the client's step. For example, if a client's step is to use the empty chair technique in session, then a related therapist's step would be to facilitate this process by explaining how it works.

Assign a Review Date

The fifth and final step is to write down a due date for each goal. The date should leave enough time for both you and the client to take the necessary steps, but not too much time. Tying exercises and interventions to specified dates grounds them in reality. It is a way of holding both you and the client accountable by keeping the treatment focused. It is all too easy to get off track. Having a review date is a gentle reminder to keep you and the client on task.

Now that you understand the different parts of the process, introducing the treatment plan to the client will be discussed. The first step is to give the client a blank copy of a treatment plan (see Appendix) and explain the rationale behind it by discussing each of the five steps. Next, enlist the client to help you fill in each of the different components. Start by writing the number one problem, transform it into a goal, discuss specific steps you and the client can take, and then agree on a review date. Follow this same procedure for each of the client's problems. Once the plan is completed, you can make a copy of it so that clients can take it with them. Encourage clients to regularly review it so they can stay focused on achieving their goals. Some clients carry it in their day planner, hang in on their refrigerator, or tape it to their computer to help them remember to practice the exercises.

WHAT DO GOD IMAGE TREATMENT PLANS LOOK LIKE?

What follows are two separate treatment plans. These are included for illustration purposes so that you can see how each of the five steps look when used with clients. The first treatment plan is for Bob (Exhibit 8.1) and the second treatment plan is for Lilith (Exhibit 8.2).

Before constructing Bob's treatment plan, I had to first conduct the God image interview and God image assessment. Then I had to choose an orientation. I decided to use an eclectic approach, because I felt that both cognitive and psychodynamic interventions would be effective in solving his problems. After these preliminary steps, we started the treatment plan by identifying and prioritizing this list. Then we translated these problems into goals and decided upon interventions that we could use to reach these objectives. Finally, we assigned a review date for each goal to keep ourselves accountable and focused on the treatment plan.

The steps in formulating the treatment plan do not change, so I followed the same steps with Lilith. Similar to Bob's treatment plan, I decided to use an eclectic approach. She was sophisticated and self-aware, so I planned to use psychodynamic interventions and capitalize on these strengths. In addition, she was a very active and structured person, so I knew she would respond well to cognitive exercises.

To sum up, God image work is an ethical and deliberate process. Therapists need to be mindful of several ethical issues when working with a client's emotional experience of God. Knowing and acting on these principles is essential to good client care. In addition to ethics, solid clinical work is built upon strong case conceptualization and

EXHIBIT 8.1. Treatment Plan (Bob)

Problem	Goal	Client will	Therapist will	Review date
Bob experiences God as rejecting when he does not perform his church duties flawlessly, has sexual thoughts, and misses devotions.	Bob will experience God as accepting when he does not perform his church duties flawlessly, has sexual thoughts, and misses devotions.	Use the God image automatic thought record (GIATR) four days a week to counter his rejecting God image automatic thoughts.	Teach Bob how to use the GIATR, explain the cognitive principles underlying the GIATR, and review his GIATR on a weekly basis.	10/21/04
Bob has difficulty feeling God's forgiveness, even though he has asked for it and believes he is forgiven.	Bob will learn to experience God's forgiveness.	Use two different forgiveness imagery techniques, three days a week, to increase his ability to emotionally experience God's forgiveness.	Teach Bob how imagery works, walk him through these two exercises, and follow up on a weekly basis.	11/1/04
		Examine how his cognitive errors affect his ability to experience God's forgiveness.	Identify his cognitive errors and explain how they influence his God image.	11/1/04
Bob feels that he has to be overly people pleasing to others (to the point of burnout) so that they will not reject him.	Bob will experience himself as confident and assertive in his relationships with others.	Explore past and present relationships in which this self-debasing and people-pleasing pattern developed and is maintained.	Provide him with a new relationship in which he can experience himself as confident and assertive and the therapist as accepting of him and these qualities.	11/15/04
		Explore his people pleasing defense and gradually increase the amount of confidence experienced in relationships with others and God.	Teach him about defenses through the triangle of conflict diagram and help him gradually become more assertive in the therapeutic relationship.	11/15/04

EXHIBIT 8.1 *(continued)*

Problem	Goal	Client will	Therapist will	Review date
		Identify the unhealthy "shoulds" his God image uses to condemn him and then disobey those "shoulds" by doing what he should not do (e.g., He "should" always happily do what others request of him. Have him disobey this should by assertively saying no.)	Help him uncover his God image "shoulds" and then support him when he disobeys them.	11/21/04
Bob unrealistically expects himself to be a perfect husband and minister.	Bob will develop realistic expectations for himself as a husband and minister.	Identify the underlying contracts, or depressive schemas, that are vague and unrealistic. Renegotiate these contracts so that they are specific and reflect what can be realistically expected of a husband and minister.	Teach the client about depressive schemas. Help the client renegotiate these contracts with his wife and church. Support him as he takes risks by breaking old contracts and following the new contracts.	11/21/04
Bob's experience of God hounds him by telling him that he "should" always be happy and never feel upset or angry.	Bob's experience of God will allow him to feel upset and angry without condemning him.	Identify the physiological sensations that accompany anger and practice stating to others and God when he feels upset and angry about something.	Give Bob a copy of the feeling word list and help him identify past and present experiences in which he felt angry, but had difficulty recognizing it.	11/28/04

_____   _____   _____   _____

Client's Name   Date   Therapist's name   Date

212

EXHIBIT 8.2. Treatment Plan (Lilith)

Problem	Goal	Client will	Therapist will	Review date
Lilith feels that she always has to be strong and put together with God. She does not feel that God accepts her if she is weak and vulnerable.	Lilith will allow herself to be weak and vulnerable with God.	Explore her past and present relationships to see how this interpersonal pattern developed with her mother and is maintained through her God image.	Teach Lilith about the square of persons so she can gain insight into how she repeats and maintains this relational pattern.	10/15/04
		Use imagery during her daily devotions to envision scenarios in which she is vulnerable with God and visualizes Him accepting and caring for her.	Help Lilith write and visualize a scene in which she can be weak and still be accepted by God.	10/15/04
		Find stories in the Scriptures in which a vulnerable person experienced God's love and grace.	Lead Lilith in a visual exercise in which she imagines herself watching this scene play out. Then have her embody the character to subjectively experience God's love and grace.	10/21/04
Lilith drives herself to the point of exhaustion to please her God image.	Lilith will emotionally understand that God accepts her as she is and that she does not have to be a workaholic to win His love.	Identify automatic thoughts and underlying schemas that cause her to feel driven to compulsively accomplish things to please God by using the GIATR five days a week.	Teach Lilith how to use the GIATR and identify underlying schemas by looking for reoccurring themes.	11/1/04

EXHIBIT 8.2 *(continued)*

Problem	Goal	Client will	Therapist will	Review date
		Recognize differences between her God image and the real God through a drawing technique and an imagery exercise. Then, express unresolved feelings toward her God image through the empty chair technique.	Lead Lilith through these exercises by explaining the rationale and detailing each step in the process.	11/15/04
		Find and meditate on scriptures that are personally relevant and communicate God's grace, love, and acceptance.	Teach Lilith the relationship between thoughts and feelings and help her identify scriptures that are appropriate and relevant.	11/21/04
Lilith no longer finds pleasure in activities that she used to enjoy.	Lilith will find pleasure in activities that she used to enjoy.	Use a day planner to schedule activities that she used to enjoy, then follow through with the activities and rate the degree of pleasure she experiences.	Teach Lilith how to use this exercise and explain how behavior influences thoughts and feelings.	11/1/04

Client's Name _____ Date _____

Therapist's name _____ Date _____

purposeful treatment planning. Therapists should have a solid understanding of how the client's problems developed, are maintained, and can be solved. Once this formulation is established, relevant goals can be set and specific exercises and techniques can be used to reach those goals.

Epilogue

It is hard to believe that I am finally writing these words. This book has taken considerable time, energy, and money (mostly on Starbucks coffee). However, it will be more than worth it if it has provided you with the ability to help others change their God image.

I encouraged you to take the tests and work through the exercises so that the material would be personally meaningful to you. Reading about the theory and technique is helpful, but experiencing the theory and technique gives you a much more in-depth, holistic understanding. My goal was for you to gain both head and heart knowledge.

You can read all the books you want and consume vast amounts of information, but if that material does not emotionally impact you it will not affect how you relate to others. People who are depressed need a real, live example of God's love. They need to be able to recognize God's healing power in you and sense that you are connected and open to God.

In psychodynamic supervision, a concept called parallel process is used (Beres, 1957). This occurs when therapists treat their clients in the same manner that their supervisors treat them. I supervise five psychology students at Regent University. If I treat my students with grace and compassion, then they will in turn treat their clients with grace and compassion. If I am overly critical and judgmental, then they will go on to criticize and judge their clients. In a very real way, people "catch" how you treat them and then go on to treat others in this same manner.

A. W. Tozer (1961) observed that people relate to others in the same manner that they feel God relates to them. The Pharisees are frequently picked on for being overly judgmental, rigid, and harsh, but in their minds they were treating others as they felt God treated them. For good or bad, we often interact with others in the manner that we sense God interacts with us. This is one reason why exploring your God image is so important. God can be loving and compassionate toward you, but if you are not open to it, you will not receive it. As a result, you will not be able to "catch" God's love and pass it on to others.

I hope that these concepts and exercises have helped you open to the real and living God. Please know that these techniques are not meant to be a substitute for an authentic, mysterious, challenging, and dynamic relationship with God, nor are they meant to be a full representation of all of God's characteristics. They specifically focus on God's love, grace, and forgiveness because these are the very areas that many individuals (clergy and mental health professionals included) have a difficult time experiencing.

That being said, no matter how open we are to God's love, we will never fully experience it. We can immerse ourselves in Scripture, spiritual disciplines, and therapy, and still have a flawed understanding of God. We simply do not have the capacity to fully comprehend God's mercy.

When my wife and I were in graduate school, we had an adopted grandmother named Agnes (a beautiful, earthy, and hardworking woman who managed to keep a good-sized garden well into her nineties). She was a very practical person who had a great way of explaining things. Her grandson was mildly mentally retarded. In explaining his limitations to us, she said, "He has a little brain that can't hold much." Agnes saw the brain as similar to a cup: some people have little Dixie cups that hold a couple of sips and others have giant mugs that hold several gulps. Regardless of our brain "size," I think it is safe to say that we all have Dixie cup brains when it comes to understanding God.

This inherent limitation causes us to ask many questions. Some can be answered and some cannot. The questions we can answer provide us with a sense of security and increased understanding. One question I have attempted to answer through this book is "Why is God always mad at me?" This is a question that many religious and depressed individuals ask. I hope that this book has provided you with the cognitive and emotional understanding that is required to answer this question. In addition, I pray that hurting people can find God's love, compassion, and grace through a healing relationship with you.

In closing, I want to thank you for reading this book. Even though the idea of the God image has been around since the early 1900s, it is just now starting to catch on. Consequently, much more research is needed to see what kind of implications it has for work in churches (e.g., sermon delivery, worship, small group studies, spiritual formation) and religiously oriented counseling centers (e.g., how different disorders influence the God image). My colleagues and I are doing some of this research and hope to collaborate with others who are personally and professionally interested in the God image. If you would like to partner with us, then log onto www.godimage.com and drop me a note. I would love to hear from you.

Appendix

Blank Therapy Forms

The following forms are blank versions of the GIATR and Treatment Plan used by Bob and Lilith in Chapters 7 and 8.

God Image Automatic Thought Record

Situation	Feelings	Automatic thought(s)	Real God response	Outcome
Actual event leading to feeling God's disappointment	Specify sad, anxious, angry, etc. Rate 0 to 100	Write irrational God image automatic thought(s) that preceeded emotion(s). Rate belief in irrational God image thought(s), 0 to 100 percent.	(Drawing on your own experience of prayer and Scripture) Write real God response to irrational God image automatic thought(s). Rate belief in real God response, 0 to 100 percent.	Rerate belief in irrational God image automatic thought(s), 0 to 100 percent. Specify and rate subsequent feelings, 0 to 100.

Treatment Plan

Problem	Goal	Client will	Therapist will	Review date

Client's Name _____ Date _____

Therapist's name _____ Date _____

223

References

Ainsworth, M.D.S. (1978). *Patterns of attachment: A psychological study of the strange situation*. Hillsdale, NJ: Lawrence Erlbaum Associates.

Alexander, F. (1956). *Psychoanalysis and psychotherapy: Developments in theory, technique, and training*. New York: W.W. Norton & Company.

American Psychiatric Association (APA). (2000). *Diagnostic and statistical manual of mental disorders* (4th ed., text rev.). Washington, DC: Author.

Baker, M.W. (1998). The loss of the selfobject tie and religious fundamentalism. *Journal of Psychology and Theology, 26*(3), 223-231.

Bandler, R. (1985). *Using your brain for a change*. Utah: Real People Press.

Baumeister, R.F. (1995). Self and identity: An introduction. In A. Tesser (Ed.), *Advanced social psychology* (pp. 51-98). Boston, MA: McGraw-Hill.

Beck, A.T. (1976). *Cognitive therapy and the emotional disorders*. New York: Penguin.

Beck, A.T., Emery, G., Rush, A.J., & Shaw, B.F. (1979). *Cognitive therapy of depression*. New York: The Guilford Press.

Beit-Hallahmi, B., & Argyle, M. (1975). God as a father-projection: The theory and the evidence. *British Journal of Medical Psychology, 48*, 71-75.

Benson, P.L., & Spilka, B.P. (1973). God-image as a function of self-esteem and locus of control. *Journal for the Scientific Study of Religion, 13*, 297-310.

Beres, D. (1957). Communication in psychoanalysis and creative process. *Journal of the American Psychoanalytic Association, 5*, 408-432.

Blatt, S., & Behrends, B. (1987). Internalization, separation-individuation, and the nature of the therapeutic action. *International Journal of Psychoanalysis, 68*(2), 279-297.

Blatt, S.J., Quinlan, D.M., Pilkonis, P.A., & Shea, M.T. (1995). Impact of perfectionism and need for approval on the brief treatment of depression: The national institute of mental health treatment of depression collaborative research program revisited. *Journal of Consulting and Clinical Psychology, 63*(1), 125-132.

Bly, R. (1988). *A little book on the human shadow*. San Francisco: Harper.

Boivin, M.J. (2003) Finding God in Prozac or finding Prozac in God: Preserving a Christian view of the person midst a biopsychosocial revolution. *Christian Scholars Review, 32*, 159-176.

Bowlby, J. (1969). *Attachment and loss*. New York: Basic Books.

Boyd, G.A. (2004). *Seeing is believing: Experience Jesus through imaginative prayer*. Grand Rapids, MI: Baker Books.

Bradshaw, J. (1988). *Healing the shame that binds you*. Ft. Lauderdale, FL: Health Communications.

Brenner, C. (1973). *An elementary textbook of psychoanalysis*. New York: Anchor.

Buri, J.R., & Mueller, R.A. (1993). Psychoanalytic theory and loving God concepts: Parent referencing versus self-referencing. *The Journal of Psychology, 127*(1), 17-27.

Canter, M.B., Bennett, B.E., Jones, S.E., & Nagy, T.F. (1999). *Ethics for psychologists: A commentary on the APA ethics code*. Washington, DC: American Psychological Association.

Carter, J.D., & Narramore, B.S. (1979). *The integration of psychology and theology*. Grand Rapids, MI: Zondervan.

Cheston, S.E., Piedmont, R.L., Eanes, B., & Lavin, L.P. (2003). Changes in clients' image of God over the course of outpatient therapy. *Counseling and Values, 47*, 96-108.

Covey, S. (1990). *The seven habits of highly effective people*. New York: The Free Press.

Danvanloo, H. (1995). *Unlocking the unconscious: Selected papers of Habib Davanloo*. New York: Wiley & Sons.

Davis, M., Eshelman, E.R., & McKay, M. (1995). *The relaxation & stress reduction workbook* (4th ed.). Oakland, CA: New Harbinger Publications.

DeRubeis, R.J., Tang, T.Z., & Beck, A.T. (2002). Cognitive therapy. In K.S. Dobson (Ed.), *Handbook of cognitive behavioral therapies* (pp. 349-392). New York: The Guilford Press.

de Shazer, S. (1988). *Clues: Investigating solutions in brief therapy*. New York: W.W. Norton & Company.

Eells, T.D. (1997). *Handbook of psychotherapy case formulation*. New York: The Guilford Press.

Egan, G. (2002). *The skilled helper: A problem management and opportunity-development approach to helping*. Pacific Grove, CA: Wadsworth.

Ellenberger, H.F. (1970). *The discovery of the unconscious: The history and evolution of dynamic psychiatry*. New York: Basic Books.

Emmons, R.A. (1999). *The psychology of ultimate concerns*. New York: The Guilford Press.

Fairbairn, W.R.D. (1954). *An object relations theory of the personality*. New York: Basic Books.

Feist, J., & Feist, G. (1998). *Theories of personality*. Boston, MA: McGraw-Hill.

Freud, S. (1915). *The unconscious* (Standard ed., vol. 14, pp. 166-204). London: Hogarth Press.

Freud, S. (1923). *The ego and the id* (Standard ed., vol. 19, pp. 12-66). London: Hogarth Press.

Freud, S. (1927). *The future of an illusion* (Standard ed., vol. 21, pp. 5-56). London: Hogarth Press.

Fromm, E. (1956). *The art of loving* (1st ed.). New York: Harper.

Gaultierre, B., & Gaultierre, K. (1989). *Mistaken identity*. Grand Rapids, MI: Baker Press.

Gay, P. (1989). *The Freud reader*. New York: W.W. Norton & Company.

Gilligan, C. (1983). *In a different voice: Psychological theory and women's development*. Boston: Harvard University Press.

Goleman, D. (1997). *Emotional intelligence*. New York: Bantam Books.

Greenburg, J.R., & Mitchell, S.A. (1983). *Object relations in psychoanalytic theory*. Cambridge, MA: Harvard University Press.

Halcrow, W., Hall, T.W., & Hill, P.C. (2003). A multidimensional approach to correspondent and compensatory attachment to God. Paper presented at Regent University's colloquium series, November, Virginia Beach, Virginia.

Hall, T.W., & Edwards, K.J. (1996). The initial development and factor analysis of the Spiritual Assessment Inventory. *Journal of Psychology and Theology, 24*(3), 233-246.

Hall, T.W., & Edwards, K.J. (2002). The Spiritual Assessment Inventory: A theistic model and measure for assessing spiritual development. *Journal for the Scientific Study of Religion, 41*(2), 341-357.

Hammond, D.C. (1990). *Handbook of hypnotic suggestions and metaphors*. New York: W.W. Norton & Company.

Harley, W.F. (2001). *His needs, her needs: Building an affair-proof marriage*. Grand Rapids, MI: Baker Books.

Hartmann, H. (1958). *Ego psychology and the problem of adaptation*. New York: International University Press.

Harvey, J., & Katz, C. (1985). *If I'm so successful, why do I feel like a fake? The imposter phenomenon*. New York: St. Martin's.

Hazan, C., & Shaver, P. (1987). Romantic love conceptualization as an attachment process. *Journal of Personality and Social Psychology, 52,* 511-524.

Hill, C.E., & O'Brien, K.M. (2002). *Helping skills: Facilitating exploration, insight, and action* (1st ed.). Washington, DC: American Psychological Association.

Horner, A.J. (1984). *Object relations and the developing ego in therapy*. Northvale, NJ: Jason Aronson.

Howard, K.I., Kopta, S.M., Krause, M.S., & Orlinsky, D.E. (1986). The dose-effect relationship in psychotherapy. *American Psychologist, 41,* 159-164.

Johnson, W.B., & Eastburg, M. (1992). God, parent and self concepts in abused and nonabused children. *Journal of Psychology and Christianity, 11,* 235-243.

Jones, J.W. (1991). *Contemporary psychoanalysis and religion*. New Haven, CT: Yale.

Jones, J.W. (1997). Looking forward: Future directions for the encounter of relational psychoanalysis and religion. *Journal of Psychology and Theology, 25,* 136-142.

Jordan, M.R. (1986). *Taking on the gods: The task of the pastoral counselor*. Nashville, TN: Abingdon.

Kaplan, H.I., & Sadock, B.J. (1998). *Synopsis of psychiatry.* Baltimore, MD: Williams and Wilkins.

Kirkpatrick, L.A., & Shaver, P.R. (1990). Attachment theory and religion: Childhood attachments, religious beliefs, and conversion. *Journal for the Scientific Study of Religion, 29*(3), 315-334.

Kopta, S.M., Howard, K.I., Lowry, J.L., & Beutler, L.E. (1994). Patterns of symptomatic recovery in psychotherapy. *Journal of Clinical and Consulting Psychology, 62,* 1009-1016.

Koss, M., & Shiang, J. (1993). Research on brief psychotherapy. In A. Bergin & S. Garfield (Eds.), *Handbook of psychotherapy and behavior change* (pp. 664-700). New York: Wiley & Sons.

Lawrence, R.T. (1991). The God Image Inventory: The development, validation and standardization of a research psychometric instrument for research, pastoral and clinical use in measuring the image of God. Unpublished doctoral dissertation, Catholic University of America.

Lawrence, R.T. (1997). Measuring the image of God: The God Image Inventory and the God Image Scales. *Journal of Psychology and Theology, 25,* 214-226.

Levenson, H. (1995). *Time-limited dynamic psychotherapy: A guide to clinical practice.* New York: Basic Books.

Lewis, C.S. (1967). *Mere Christianity.* London, UK: Fontana Books.

Lewis, C.S. (1994). *The chronicles of Narnia.* New York: HarperCollins.

Mahler, M., Pine, F., & Bergman, A. (1975). *The psychological birth of the human infant: Symbiosis and individuation.* New York: Basic Books.

Malan, D.M. (1979). *Individual psychotherapy and the science of psychodynamics.* London: Butterworth.

Martin, D.G. (1995). Basic skills. In D.G. Martin & A.D. Moore (Eds.), *Basics of clinical practice* (pp. 2-18). Prospect Heights, IL: Waveland Press.

Martin, D.G., & Moore, A.D. (1995). *Basics of clinical practice: A guidebook for trainees in the helping professions.* Prospect Heights, IL: Waveland Press.

Maxmen, J.S., & Ward, N.G. (1995) *Essential psychopathology and its treatment.* New York: W.W. Norton & Company.

McCullough-Vaillant, L.M. (1997). *Changing character: Short-term anxiety-regulating psychotherapy for restructuring defenses, affects and attachments.* New York: Basic Books.

McDargh, J. (1983). *Psychoanalytic object relations theory and the study of religion: On faith and the imaging of God.* Lanham, MD: University Press of America.

McGee, R.S. (1998). *Search for significance.* Nashville, TN: Thomas Nelson.

McGee, R.S., Springle, P., & Joiner, S. (1990). *Rapha's twelve-step program for overcoming chemical dependency: With support materials from the search for significance* (2nd ed.). Houston, TX: Rapha Publications.

McKay, M., Davis, M., & Fanning, P. (1998). *Thoughts & feelings: The art of cognitive stress intervention.* Richmond, CA: New Harbinger Publications.

McWilliams, N. (1994). *Psychoanalytic diagnosis: Understanding personality structure in the clinical process.* New York: The Guilford Press.

Meissner, W.W. (1984). *Psychoanalysis and religious experience.* New Haven, CT: Yale.

Meissner, W.W. (1991). The phenomenology of religious psychopathology. *Bulletin of the Menninger Clinic, 55,* 281-298.

Menninger, K. (1958). *Theory of psychoanalytic technique.* London: Imago.

Miller, C. (2000). The technique of Souldrama and its applications. *International Journal of Action Methods, 52*(Winter), 173-186.

Moon, G.W. (1997). *Homesick for Eden: A soul's journey to joy.* Ann Arbor, MI: Vine.

Neimeyer, R.A., & Raskin, J.D. (2002). Varieties of constructivism in psychotherapy. In K.S. Dobson (Ed.), *Handbook of cognitive behavioral therapies* (pp. 393-430). New York: The Guilford Press.

Nichols, M.P. (1995). *The lost art of listening.* New York: The Guilford Press.

Pargament, K.I., Kennell, J., Hathaway, W., Grevengoed, N., Newman, J., & Jones, W. (1988). Religion and the problem-solving process: Three styles of coping. *Journal for the Scientific Study of Religion, 27*(1), 90-104.

Peck, M.S. (1978). *The road less traveled: A new psychology of love, traditional values, and spiritual growth.* New York: Simon & Schuster.

Perls, F., & Wysong, J. (1992). *Gestalt therapy verbatim.* Highlands, NY: Gestalt Journal Press.

Phillips, J.B. (1953). *Your God is too small.* New York: Macmillan.

Powell, J.J. (1969). *Why am I afraid to tell you who I am? Insights on self-awareness, personal growth and interpersonal communication.* Chicago: Argus Communications.

Propst, L.R. (1980). The comparative efficacy of religious and nonreligious imagery for the treatment of mild depression in religious individuals. *Cognitive Therapy and Research, 4*(2), 167-178.

Propst, L.R. (1988). *Psychotherapy in a religious framework: Spirituality in the emotional healing process.* New York: Human Sciences Press.

Propst, L.R., Ostrom, R., Watkins, P., Dean, T., & Mashburn, D. (1992). Comparative efficacy of religious and nonreligious cognitive-behavioral therapy for the treatment of clinical depression in religious individuals. *Journal of Consulting and Clinical Psychology, 60*(1), 94-103.

Richards, P.S., & Bergin, A.E. (1997). *A spiritual strategy for counseling and psychotherapy* (1st ed.). Washington, DC: American Psychological Association.

Rizzuto, A.M. (1979). *The birth of the living God.* Chicago: University of Chicago Press.

Rogers, C. (1961). *On becoming a person: A therapist's view of psychotherapy.* Boston: Houghton Mifflin.

Satir, V. (1972). *Peoplemaking*. Palo Alto, CA: Science and Behavior Books.

Seamands, D.A. (1985). *Healing of memories*. Wheaton, IL: Victor Books.

Spero, M.H. (1990). Parallel dimensions of experience in psychoanalytic psycho-therapy of the religious patient. *Psychotherapy, 27*, 53-71.

Sperry, L. (1999). Biopsychosocial therapy. *Journal of Individual Psychology, 55(2)*, 233-247.

Stolorow, R., & Atwood, G. (1992). *Context of being: The intersubjective foundations of psychological life*. Hillsdale, NJ: Analytic Press

Stott, J.R.W. (1958). *Basic Christianity* (1st ed., rep. ed.). Grand Rapids, MI: Eerdmans.

Strength, J.M. (1998). Expanding Davanloo's interpretive triangles to explicate the client's introjected image of God. *Journal of Psychology and Theology, 26(2)*, 172-187.

Strupp, H.H., & Binder, J.L. (1984). *Psychotherapy in a new key*. New York: Basic Books.

Sullivan, H.S. (1953). *The interpersonal theory of psychiatry*. New York: W.W. Norton & Company.

Superko, H. R., & Tucker, L. (2003). *Before the heart attacks: A revolutionary approach to detecting, preventing, and even reversing heart disease*. Emmaus, PA: Rodale.

Tan, S.Y. (1994). Ethical considerations in religious psychotherapy: Potential pitfalls and unique resources. *Journal of Psychology and Theology, 22*, 389-394.

Tan, S.Y. (1996). Religion in clinical practice: Implicit and explicit integration. In E.P. Shafranske (Ed.), *Religion and clinical practice of psychology* (pp. 365-386). Washington, DC: American Psychological Association.

Teyber, E. (1997). *Interpersonal process in psychotherapy: A relational approach* (3rd ed.). Pacific Grove, CA: Brooks/Cole.

Tillich, P. (1958). *Dynamics of faith*. New York: Harper & Row.

Tisdale, T.T., Key, T.L., Edwards, K.J, Brokaw, B.F., Kemperman, S.R., Cloud, H., Townsend, J., & Okamato, T. (1997). Impact of treatment on God image and personal adjustment, and correlations of God image to personal adjustment and object relations development. *Journal of Psychology and Theology, 25*, 227-239.

Tozer, A.W. (1961). *The knowledge of the holy*. New York: Harper & Row.

Van Leeuwen, M.S. (1985). *The person in psychology: A contemporary Christian appraisal*. Leicester, England: InterVarsity Press

Weiner, I.B. (1998). *Principles of psychotherapy*. New York: Wiley & Sons.

White, S.A. (1984). Imago Dei and object relations theory: Implications for a model of human development. *Journal of Psychology and Theology, 12(4)*, 286-293.

Winnicott, D.W. (1971). *Playing and reality*. New York: Tavistock.

Wolpe, J. (1958). *Psychotherapy by reciprocal inhibition*. Stanford, CA: Stanford University Press.

Wright, H.N. (1986). *Self-talk, imagery, and prayer in counseling.* Waco, TX: Word Books.

Yalom, I.D. (1995). *The theory and practice of group psychotherapy* (4th ed.). New York: Basic Books.

Zuckerman, E.L. (1995). *Clinician's thesaurus.* New York: The Guilford Press.

Zweig, C., & Abrams, J. (1991). *Meeting the shadow: The hidden power of the dark side of human nature.* New York: Penguin.

Index

Page numbers followed by the letter "f" indicate figures.

Order a copy of this book with this form or online at:
http://www.haworthpress.com/store/product.asp?sku=5138

PASTORAL CARE OF DEPRESSION
Helping Clients Heal Their Relationship with God

_____in hardbound at $34.95 (ISBN-13: 978-0-7890-2382-7; ISBN-10: 0-7890-2382-2)

_____in softbound at $22.95 (ISBN-13: 978-0-7890-2383-4; ISBN-10: 0-7890-2383-0)

Or order online and use special offer code HEC25 in the shopping cart.

COST OF BOOKS_____

POSTAGE & HANDLING_____
(US: $4.00 for first book & $1.50
for each additional book)
(Outside US: $5.00 for first book
& $2.00 for each additional book)

SUBTOTAL_____

IN CANADA: ADD 7% GST_____

STATE TAX_____
(NJ, NY, OH, MN, CA, IL, IN, PA, & SD
residents, *add appropriate local sales tax)*

FINAL TOTAL_____
(If paying in Canadian funds,
convert using the current
exchange rate, UNESCO
coupons welcome)

Prices in US dollars and subject to change without notice.

☐ **BILL ME LATER:** (Bill-me option is good on
US/Canada/Mexico orders only; not good to
jobbers, wholesalers, or subscription agencies.)
☐ Check here if billing address is different from
shipping address and attach purchase order and
billing address information.

Signature_____

☐ **PAYMENT ENCLOSED: $_____**

☐ **PLEASE CHARGE TO MY CREDIT CARD.**

☐ Visa ☐ MasterCard ☐ AmEx ☐ Discover
☐ Diner's Club ☐ Eurocard ☐ JCB

Account # _____

Exp. Date_____

Signature_____

NAME_____

INSTITUTION_____

ADDRESS_____

CITY_____

STATE/ZIP_____

COUNTRY_____ COUNTY (NY residents only)_____

TEL_____ FAX_____

E-MAIL_____

May we use your e-mail address for confirmations and other types of information? ☐ Yes ☐ No
We appreciate receiving your e-mail address and fax number. Haworth would like to e-mail or fax special
discount offers to you, as a preferred customer. **We will never share, rent, or exchange your e-mail address
or fax number.** We regard such actions as an invasion of your privacy.

Order From Your Local Bookstore or Directly From
The Haworth Press, Inc.
10 Alice Street, Binghamton, New York 13904-1580 • USA
TELEPHONE: 1-800-HAWORTH (1-800-429-6784) / Outside US/Canada: (607) 722-5857
FAX: 1-800-895-0582 / Outside US/Canada: (607) 771-0012
E-mail to: orders@haworthpress.com

For orders outside US and Canada, you may wish to order through your local
sales representative, distributor, or bookseller.
For information, see http://haworthpress.com/distributors

(Discounts are available for individual orders in US and Canada only, not booksellers/distributors.)

PLEASE PHOTOCOPY THIS FORM FOR YOUR PERSONAL USE.
http://www.HaworthPress.com   BOF06